The MEDIEVAL UNIVERSITIES:
their development and organization

The Medieval Universities:

their development and organization

A. B. COBBAN

Methuen & Co Ltd

First published 1975 by Methuen & Co Ltd
11 New Fetter Lane London EC4P 4EE
© 1975 A. B. Cobban
Printed in Great Britain
by W & J Mackay Limited, Chatham

ISBN 0 416 81250 3

DISTRIBUTED IN THE USA BY
HARPER & ROW PUBLISHERS INC
BARNES & NOBLE IMPORT DIVISION

Contents

Preface

In some respects, the history of the medieval universities is conterminous with that of Europe from the twelfth to the sixteenth centuries. It would therefore be impossible to reduce this historical vastness, in all its complexities and ramifications, to the compass of a single volume. This study endeavours to take cognizance of the enormous amount of research completed since the appearance in 1895 of Rashdall's monumental three-volume work on the medieval universities; and it attempts to emphasize aspects of university history, such as social and economic data, the European collegiate movement, and medieval student power, which have not had their deserved prominence in the general interpretative scheme. The purely intellectual achievements of the universities, which embrace so much of Europe's fabric of thought, are not the primary concern of this volume.

I am indebted to the editor of *Past and Present* for permission to use in chapter seven material adapted from my article, 'Medieval Student Power', *Past and Present*, no. 53 (1971), pp. 28 ff. In a more general sense, I am deeply grateful to Professor Walter Ullmann for his encouragement, counsel and assistance over the years, although he is not responsible for any of the opinions expressed in this book.

University of Liverpool
September, 1973

ALAN B. COBBAN

Abbreviations

A.H.R.	*American Historical Review*
Archiv	*Archiv für Literatur- und Kirchengeschichte*
B.J.R.L.	*Bulletin of the John Rylands Library*
Camb. Docs.	*Documents relating to the University and Colleges of Cambridge,* 3 vols., ed. by the Queen's Commissioners (London, 1852)
Chartularium	*Chartularium Universitatis Parisiensis,* 4 vols., ed. H. Denifle and E. Chatelain (Paris, 1889–97)
E.H.R.	*English Historical Review*
J. Eccles. Hist.	*Journal of Ecclesiastical History*
J.T.S.	*Journal of Theological Studies*
Kristeller	'The School of Salerno: its Development and its Contribution to the History of Learning', *Bulletin of the History of Medicine,* xvii (1945), pp. 138 ff.
Statuta Antiqua	*Statuta Antiqua Universitatis Oxoniensis,* ed. S. Gibson (Oxford, 1931)
Statutes	*Statutes of the Colleges of Oxford,* 3 vols., ed. by the Queen's Commissioners (Oxford and London, 1853)
Statuti	*Statuti delle Università e dei Collegi dello Studio Bolognese,* ed. C. Malagola (Bologna, 1888)

Statuts	(*Les*) *Statuts et Privilèges des Universités françaises depuis leur fondation jusqu'en 1789*, 3 vols., ed. M. Fournier (Paris, 1890–2)
Studi e memorie	*Studi e memorie per la storia dell'università di Bologna*
T.R.H.S.	*Transactions of the Royal Historical Society*
Universities	H. Rashdall, *The Universities of Europe in the Middle Ages*, 3 vols., 2nd ed., F. M. Powicke and A. B. Emden (Oxford, 1936)
V.C.H.	*Victoria County History*

All other abbreviations are considered self-explanatory.

PART I

I

University proem

The Roman educational achievement lay, not so much in any indigenous contribution, but in the act of transmission of Hellenistic civilization to Christian Europe.[1] Graeco–Roman culture and its techniques of instruction formed the framework into which was woven the texture of Christian education of the middle ages. As the educational process must be continually adapted to meet the requirements of change so the material values of a pagan culture had to be recast to fill the spiritual wants of a Christian community. Accordingly, the perennial and, in an absolute sense, insoluble problem facing medieval educationalists was how to adapt to the service of Christian society a system of education firmly rooted in pagan soil. The process of adaptation and the partial reconciliation between the polarized ingredients of classical and Christian thought furnished one of the main areas of intellectual activity in western Europe in the pre-Reformation era. Insofar as the medieval universities from *c.* 1200 became the focal points of this activity, they may be regarded as the institutional heirs of that same type of educational dilemma which so dramatically confronted the early Christian teachers.

The transition from Greek to Graeco–Roman and early medieval education was characterized by an increasing emphasis on educational utility. In its earliest phase, Greek education was designed, not to equip for a professional career or to cultivate a particular art, but rather to develop the

[1] See e.g. the conclusions of H. I. Marrou, *Histoire de l'éducation dans l'antiquité* (Paris, 1948), pp. 390–1.

student's personality and his ethical being.[1] Greek literature, athletics and music provided the institutional means, and practical imitation played a decisive part. This somewhat amorphous and rarefied form of education, confined to the sons of wealthy aristocratic families, was given a more utilitarian complexion towards the end of the fifth century B.C. by the class of teachers known collectively as the Sophists. The Sophists, of whom Isocrates was perhaps the leading exponent, conceived of education as a training for an active participation in civic affairs, and their advocacy of rhetoric and dialectic as necessary subjects for advanced study focused attention upon the useful and socially applicable features of intellectual life. Although Plato and Aristotle gave a more sublime and profound purpose to higher education it was the less exalted ideology of Isocrates that was implanted in the cities of the Hellenistic and Graeco–Roman world.[2] In the early Roman Republic education was largely a private business centred on the *paterfamilias*.[3] The son was reared in the ways of his father; he followed paternal precepts and absorbed the current conventions. Intellectual attainments were subordinated to a type of unimaginative instruction based on the *mos maiorum* and directed towards the production of a man of affairs conditioned to subordinate his person and talents to the ends of the corporate good, the service of the state. But Rome could not escape the gradual infusion of Hellenistic culture, a movement well advanced by the middle of the second century B.C. The differential between early and later Roman education is the contrast between a domestic training founded on the family unit and custom and a formal teaching deriving its strength from the study of literature, rhetoric and ingredients of philosophy.[4] Following the impact of Greek culture there was an initial period when everything Greek was in vogue including the recreational arts of music and dancing. But a reaction rapidly set in against these latter characteristics of Greek life, and the practical seriousness in the Roman outlook pronounced these subjects unsuitable for the sons of the aristocracy: they were fast reduced to an insignificant part of education whose

---

[1] For the characteristics of Greek education see Marrou, op. cit., passim; R. R. Bolgar, *The Classical Heritage and its Beneficiaries from the Carolingian Age to the end of the Renaissance* (New York, 1964), esp. pp. 26 ff.; D. Knowles, *The Evolution of Medieval Thought* (London, 1962), esp. pp. 59–63; M. L. Clarke, *Higher Education in the Ancient World* (London, 1971), passim.
[2] On the aims of Isocrates and the Sophists see conveniently Knowles, op. cit., pp. 60–2.
[3] A. Gwynn, *Roman Education from Cicero to Quintilian* (Oxford, 1926), pp. 12 ff.; Knowles, op. cit., pp. 63–4.
[4] Gwynn, op. cit., pp. 40–1.

centre of gravity now lay in the arts of grammar and rhetoric.

The Greek science of rhetoric became the subject *par excellence* of Roman higher education and was adapted to serve a social situation where public speaking and the art of persuasion were essential tools of civil and military life. To educationalists of the calibre of Cicero and later Quintilian the danger arising from the primacy of rhetoric was the tendency to regard training in this one discipline as, in itself, a satisfactory form of advanced education. They consequently stood out against the excessive attention given to the arid technicalities of rhetoric which could only lead to a pedantic narrowing in educational life. Cicero's broadly-based ideal, expressed in his *De Oratore*, was that of the *doctus orator*, the man who combines in his person an extensive knowledge of all the sciences with a wide experience of the problems of everyday living. It was a form of education designed not only to make a man learned but humane and just, and eminently fitted to lead in society.[1] Although Quintilian in his *Institutio Oratoria* accorded a more central place to rhetoric in higher education than Cicero would have endorsed, he is equally concerned that education should be a blueprint for life, an enlargement of the spirit, producing intellectual and moral excellence.[2] But reformative treatises of this nature which advocated scarcely realizable programmes could not arrest the engulfing cult of rhetoric and, under the Empire, it retained its position as the core of higher learning. The utilitarian stamp of Roman education was further reinforced when the organs of secondary and advanced instruction were brought under the direct supervision of the imperial government. The establishment of chairs of Greek and Latin rhetoric in Rome by the Emperor Vespasian *c.* A.D. 70[3] was probably the first official recognition of the state's responsibility for education, inaugurating a system of public control which progressively expanded and endured until the fifth century. There seems little doubt that the aims of successive emperors were to transform the schools into recruiting grounds for potential imperial officials whether in the central or provincial administration. This development did not materially affect the existing priorities of the educational syllabus, and rhetoric was still regarded as the

---

[1] For Cicero's educational philosophy see ibid., pp. 57–8, 100–1, 118–22; also W. M. Smail, *Quintilian on Education* (Oxford, 1938), pp. xii–xiii.

[2] Quintilian's educational programme is discussed by Smail, op. cit., esp. pp. xx–xxii, xxvii, xxxiv–v, xl–xliv; also, Bolgar, *The Classical Heritage* . . ., cit., pp. 30–1, 35.

[3] Smail, op. cit., p. vi; Clarke, *Higher Education in the Ancient World*, cit., pp. 8, 32; S. d'Irsay, *Histoire des universités françaises et étrangères des origines à nos jours*, i (Paris, 1933), p. 31.

soundest of all preparations for state service.[1] The harnessing of Graeco–
Roman education for state purposes had a lasting impact which pervaded
the centuries following the collapse of the Roman Empire in the west.
Although the imperial schools fell victims to the disruptive effects of the
Germanic invasions of the fifth century and, except in Italy and parts of
France,[2] largely disappeared, they nevertheless furnished the principal
model for the Christian schools which arose in the converted barbarian
kingdoms of western Europe. As a result, not only was there a physical
continuity in the form of the educational syllabus and methods of instruction between the schools of the late Roman Empire and those of the early
middle ages but the Christian schools were *ab initio* conditioned by that
utilitarian outlook which had so permeated the Graeco–Roman system. By
definition, the objective had changed: instead of service to the *respublica* there
was substituted service to the Church, the eventual ordering of educational
resources to ensure the maintenance of a literate priesthood. Education
was reduced to its bare bones to meet the basic wants of an ecclesiastically
orientated society, and the divorce between worldly practice and the ideology
of study as an humane and universal pursuit was rendered complete.

Apart from the glittering achievements of the Anglo-Saxon and Irish
schools and those of the Iberian peninsula, the west European educational
effort between the sixth and early eighth centuries was conducted on a low
and desultory level, with no sustained programme for the education of the
clergy or for the preservation of minimal standards of clerical literacy.[3]
With Charlemagne's government, however, there emerged a delineated
educational policy promoted by the king as one aspect of a wider social and
religious transformation of the Frankish people.[4] In this overall ideological
rebirth in government and society, grounded on Christian principles, the
revival of letters and learning had a necessary revitalizing purpose: but it
was an instrument in the process of reformation and not an end in itself.[5]

---

[1] Marrou, *Histoire de l'éducation . . .*, cit., pp. 412–14. There is evidence, however, that
rhetorical teaching under the Empire tended to become more theoretical and pedantic,
divorced from practical realities: see Clarke, op. cit., pp. 40–5; Knowles, *The Evolution
of Medieval Thought*, cit., p. 64.

[2] See e.g. S. d'Irsay, op. cit., pp. 32–3.

[3] M. L. W. Laistner, *Thought and Letters in Western Europe A.D. 500–900* (2nd ed.,
London, 1957), part ii, pp. 85 ff., passim.

[4] See W. Ullmann, *The Carolingian Renaissance and the Idea of Kingship* (London, 1969),
Lecture I (The Renaissance of Society), pp. 1 ff.

[5] 'In short, the social Renaissance entailed a literary Renaissance which was scholarship
devoted to the rebirth of Frankish society, a rebirth in the Christian sense as understood
at the time. The literary Renaissance was a means to an end': Ullmann, op. cit., p. 14.

As in any age there were individual or group cultural attainments which far transcended the norm. These scholarly achievements on the margins of literate society, however, should not mask the essentially utilitarian core of Carolingian education.

By contrast, the broad humanistic revival which formed a major element in the intensification of the intellectual life of western Europe in the late eleventh and twelfth centuries marked a partial return to the kind of values embodied in Cicero's educational programme. Against the background of greater political and social stability, of economic and urban revival, of a quickening in communications, scholars set out to achieve a more systematic absorption of the classical heritage. Apart from the study of classical data relating to the specialized subjects of logic, rhetoric, law and medicine, their investigations embraced, under the umbrella heading of grammar, a diversity of as yet undefined topics such as history, literary criticism and political theory.[1] The strength and momentum of this humanistic upsurge, both in its literary and deeper senses, its emphasis on a leisured, wide ranging approach to education, its advocacy of a thorough, painstaking mastery of classical culture, all gave rise to the hope that it might prevail against the cult of utility and endow the educational activity of western Europe with a higher purpose. Between 1000 and 1150, scholars in the west became aware of a vast corpus of classical material which had hitherto been but dimly glimpsed. The concomitant growth of facilities for the copying of manuscripts and for the interpretation and teaching of the material, especially in the cathedral and urban schools, seemed to ensure the longevity of the movement. But its very success, the appearance of a profusion of material in excess of its rate of absorption caused opposition groups to question the efficacy of saturating society with data whose value in terms of Christian ethics had yet to be assessed.[2] Apart from the distrust aroused by the alleged excesses of individual scholars in the fields of rhetoric or logic and the disquiet caused by the prevalence of erotic poetry, there was a general sense of unease that Christian civilization was being infiltrated by disruptive and distorting pagan morality.[3] A broad humanistic culture could not freely develop in this climate of gathering hostility: the pattern of advance and reactionary challenge led to unsatisfactory scholarly compromise and a reassertion of utilitarian criteria in the educa-

[1] Bolgar, *The Classical Heritage*, p. 200. One of the best recent studies on medieval humanism is R. W. Southern, 'Medieval Humanism' in *Medieval Humanism and other Studies* (Oxford, 1970), pp. 29 ff.
[2] Bolgar, op. cit., loc. cit.
[3] Bolgar, p. 201.

tional process, reminiscent of the *via media* of St Augustine with respect to pagan and Christian thought.[1] A more cautious and selective attitude towards the classical revival replaced the earlier euphoric zeal in the second half of the twelfth century.[2] Ingredients of classical learning might be serviceably used to broaden and elucidate Christian intellectual life but any movement towards the swamping of the established order with an alternative pagan culture must be resisted. The humanistic tide was arrested and fragmented, and the utilitarian pressures and counter-attractions of late twelfth-century society, of which more will be said below,[3] prevented literary humanism *per se* from becoming entrenched as the basis of higher education which, on the eve of the birth of the universities, was firmly deflected into concrete and definable areas.

The universities were not to be the direct outgrowth of a movement which echoed the Ciceronian ideal of the *doctus orator*; their roots were inextricably bound up with utilitarian values. They evolved as institutional responses to the pressures to harness educational forces to the professional, ecclesiastical and governmental requirements of society. Their immediate precursors, the cathedral and urban schools, may sporadically have served to promote educational ideals which went beyond the practical wants of society.[4] But their essential purpose was to increase educational opportunities for students of ability destined for professional employment within the ecclesiastical hierarchy or civil government, or in some legal or medical capacity. In this sense, the cathedral and urban schools were secular in intent, catering for the needs of an increasingly urbanized society with a steadily growing population. The clerical status of the students of the cathedral schools should not disguise the fundamentally secular direction of their interests. Many of these schools acquired a specialist nature, becoming recognized centres for such disciplines as theology, law, rhetoric or the *quadrivium* subjects. Sometimes the character of a school changed with the mobility of teaching personnel: but several retained their academic concentrations.[5] The cathedral and municipal schools marked a

---

[1] On Augustine's educational ideas see Bolgar, pp. 52–4; Laistner, op. cit., ed. cit., pp. 51–3.

[2] Bolgar, p. 201.

[3] See below, pp. 15 ff.

[4] For the cathedral schools see G. Paré, A. Brunet and P. Tremblay, *La renaissance du xiie siècle: les écoles et l'enseignement* (Paris and Ottawa, 1933); E. Lesne, 'Les écoles de la fin du viiie siècle à la fin du xiie' in *Histoire de la propriété ecclésiastique en France* (Lille, 1940), vol. v; S. d'Irsay, *Histoire des universités . . .*, cit., vol. i.

[5] See Bolgar, op. cit., p. 195.

decisive phase in the transition from a monastically-dominated culture to one in which professional concern was an overriding feature. Nevertheless, the fast-expanding demand for education in the second half of the twelfth century could not be satisfactorily met by the rather limited facilities of the cathedral schools,[1] and when these volatile centres gave way to the collectivized university system the scope for free-ranging study was, at the average level, even more circumscribed by the need to channel education along more precise curricular lines.

The theoretical basis of medieval education was the concept of the seven liberal arts. The idea of an organized body of learning suitable for public instruction was incorporated by Plato in Book VII of the *Republic*.[2] It is perhaps this Platonic system of planned education that provides the most distant antecedent for the curricula of the universities. The Greek notion of liberal studies was that of an educational régime designed for the free citizen:[3] there were deep divisions between those who, with Plato, promoted a philosophical and metaphysical view of education aimed at inculcating moral and intellectual excellence and those such as Isocrates who advocated that liberal studies be more directly geared to practical involvement in community affairs.[4] It was this Greek vision of education, based on a wide erudition and partitioned into organized branches of knowledge, which acquired theoretical fixation and progressively sharper definition in Roman and medieval society. Cicero had used the terms *artes liberales* and *liberalis disciplina* but did not provide, in any one place, a detailed programme of liberal studies.[5] In the first century B.C., however, the Roman Varro compiled his *De Novem Disciplinis*, a pioneer treatise on nine disciplines, namely, grammar, logic, rhetoric, geometry, arithmetic, astronomy, music, medicine and architecture.[6] In the late fourth century St

[1] See e.g. L. Boehm, 'Libertas Scholastica und Negotium Scholare: Entstehung und Sozialprestige des Akademischen Standes im Mittelalter' in *Universität und Gelehrtenstand 1400–1800* (Limburg ander Lahn, 1970), pp. 24–5.

[2] S. d'Irsay, op. cit., p. 29.

[3] H. Parker, 'The Seven Liberal Arts', *E.H.R.*, v (1890), pp. 417 ff. at p. 417; Clarke, *Higher Education in the Ancient World*, cit., p. 2. But see John of Salisbury's equivocal discussion of the meaning of the *artes liberales* in the *Metalogicon*, ed. C. C. J. Webb (Oxford, 1929), bk. 1, ch. 12, pp. 30–1 and trans. D. D. McGarry, *The Metalogicon of John of Salisbury* (Berkeley and Los Angeles, 1955), pp. 36–7. John conjectures that the arts are called 'liberal' either because 'quod antiqui liberos suos his procurabant institui' or 'quod querunt hominis libertatem, ut curis liber sapientie vacet . . .' (Webb, p. 31; McGarry, p. 37).

[4] See e.g. Knowles, *The Evolution of Medieval Thought*, cit., pp. 60–2.

[5] Laistner, *Thought and Letters in Western Europe*, cit., pp. 40–1.

[6] Ibid., p. 40; Knowles, op. cit., p. 73; Parker, art. cit., pp. 432–5.

Augustine had planned a treatise on the liberal arts but this was never completed and survived only in fragmentary form:[1] his main educational contribution is contained in the *De Doctrina Christiana* which embodied his search for a measure of compatibility between classical and Christian thought and set out a course of study for the Christian priest and teacher. Although St Augustine devotes sections to the liberal arts in this treatise, he does not present a comprehensive analysis of this subject. Of seminal importance was the appearance, in the early fifth century, of the *De Nuptiis Mercurii et Philogiae* of Martianus Capella which is, in essence, an exposition of seven liberal arts, comprising those listed by Varro less medicine and architecture which were perhaps becoming more professionally organized although not in any fully-fledged technical sense.[2] Capella's classification acquired a marmoreal permanence and, augmented by later treatises such as the sixth-century *Institutiones* of Cassiodorus and the *Etymologiae* of Isidore of Seville, the Graeco–Roman concept of organized liberal studies was transmitted to medieval Europe.

With the passage of time, it became customary to divide the seven liberal arts into the *trivium* subjects of grammar, logic and rhetoric, and the *quadrivium* grouping of arithmetic, geometry, astronomy and music. It is unlikely that this formalized division is to be found much before the seventh century, and may have been established only in the Carolingian age.[3] Education in the *trivium* and *quadrivium* was generally pronounced a necessary preparation for the study of Christian theology.[4] But in the conditions of Europe in the centuries following the break up of the Roman Empire in the west this proved a vainglorious aspiration. The chronic dearth of educational facilities, the desperate shortage of money for study purposes, the immense ethical and technical difficulties experienced in adapting a largely pagan corpus of learning to Christian require-

---

[1] On St Augustine and the liberal arts see Laistner, op. cit., pp. 50–2; Parker, art. cit., pp. 427–9, 435–6.

[2] For Martianus Capella see Laistner, op. cit., p. 40; Bolgar, op. cit., pp. 35–7; Parker, art. cit., pp. 437 ff. V. L. Bullough, *The Development of Medicine as a Profession* (Basel and New York, 1966) traces the gradual professionalization of medicine from the classical period to the sixteenth century and establishes the key rôle of the universities in that development. The formation of medicine as a profession must not therefore be facilely antedated. For a time in the classical period it seemed that medicine might evolve as a profession, but the lack of institutionalized medical knowledge arrested this growth (Bullough, p. 31). On architecture in the classical world see Clarke, op. cit., pp. 113–14.

[3] Laistner, op. cit., p. 41.

[4] See e.g. Knowles, *The Evolution of Medieval Thought*, p. 74: also C. H. Haskins, *Studies in Medieval Culture* (Cambridge, 1929), p. 46.

ments, all these combined to render sterile the loftiest aims of contemporary educational theorists. Before 1000, *quadrivium* subjects were given a minimal emphasis as they were deemed inessential for the training of a body of literate clergy. Sometimes they were wholly omitted from the syllabus or at best treated in a rudimentary factual way. The need to master enough arithmetical skill to calculate the dates of movable church festivals was often the sum total of *quadrivium* expertise absorbed by the average student priest. Of the *trivium* subjects, grammar held primacy of place as the fundamental discipline in a society struggling to achieve a modest level of literacy. Rhetoric remained an option for those who had the aptitude for more advanced studies but was insufficiently related to a community which had few of the outlets for oratorical expression of the Graeco–Roman world. Education was, for most, an almost purely literary experience which did not fully extend the analytical faculty: and this literary character was reflected in the grammatical, historical and even theological works of the period.[1] Dialectic was accorded a subordinate niche in the curriculum and its potentialities as a method of rational inquiry lay dormant. From the twin arts of grammar and rhetoric was generated the groundwork for the literary humanism of the eleventh and twelfth centuries; and from the dialectical revival of the late tenth and eleventh centuries, promoted among others by Gerbert of Aurillac and Berengar of Tours,[2] there emerged that intellectual whirlpool which buttressed and partially moulded the exciting new developments in philosophy and speculative theology that were sustained and vastly augmented by the rediscovered corpus of Aristotelian logical, philosophical and scientific texts with their Arabic and Jewish commentaries. This dialectical focus led to a dwarfing of the literary aspects of the classical heritage and had the most profound repercussions for European education. For the transition from grammar and rhetoric to logic as the central curricular magnet is indicative of an intellectual metamorphosis which marked a decisive departure from an educational system based upon the cumulative knowledge and thought patterns of the past to one deriving its strength from a forward-looking spirit of creative inquiry.

It is apparent that the treatises on the liberal arts embraced an encyclopaedic ideal, and are wholly misleading as to the *de facto* basis of education in the early medieval period. In the monastic, cathedral and urban schools, and later in the universities, the educational realities, at the ordinary level, were seldom in accordance with the breadth of view outlined in these

[1] Knowles, op. cit., p. 75.
[2] On the revival of dialectic see ibid., ch. viii, pp. 93 ff.

theoretical constructions. At centres such as the cathedral schools of
Chartres and Hereford, for at least some years in the twelfth century,
efforts were seemingly made to ascribe an equal emphasis to all of the seven
liberal arts as the ideal foundation for the educated man;[1] and in the universities the well-placed scholar with the necessary leisure and financial
security might go some way towards realizing the broadly based ideal of
liberal studies. But for the majority of students, both of the pre-university
and university age, the main priority was the speedy absorption of a selected area of learning in preparation for a chosen career. The principle of
utility rather than the considerations that went to shape Cicero's *doctus
orator* or the educated élite of John of Salisbury's *Metalogicon*[2] is a more
accurate commentary upon the operation of medieval education in terms
of mass experience.

The seven liberal arts remained a theoretical statement of educational
intent throughout the medieval period. That the mastery of the liberal arts
was generally regarded as a prelude to higher studies, and especially to
theology, may seem surprising as several of the arts had only a tenuous
bearing on theology, and astronomy – not yet purged of its astrological
admixtures – was often deemed a suspect weapon in the theologian's armoury. But with the Greek legacy of liberal studies there was also imbibed
the belief that the exercise and enlargement of the mind over a range of
disparate disciplines was a necessary preparation for more permanent engagement in study at the highest level. Theology assumed in the hierarchy
of medieval education the crowning position which philosophy had occupied in the Greek world. And the early Christian schoolmen, lacking an
alternative complex of categorized studies, acknowledged the liberal arts
as the only feasible propaedeutic training for Christian theology. This
rationalization was projected into the university age finding stereotyped
expression in the doctrine that the universities inculcated an extensive
education in the liberal arts as the pathway to study of more intrinsic

---

[1] See the poem of Simon du Fresne, canon of Hereford, *c.* 1195–7, inviting Gerald of
Wales to come to Hereford in which it is said that all the seven liberal arts, along with
geomancy and legal subjects, were taught: the poem is edited by R. W. Hunt, 'English
Learning in the late Twelfth Century', *T.R.H.S.*, 4th ser., xix (1936), pp. 36–7. On
Chartres, generally regarded as the epitome of a broad literary culture, see the fundamental essay of R. W. Southern, 'Humanism and the School of Chartres' in *Medieval
Humanism and other Studies*, cit., pp. 61 ff. which has left Chartrian studies in a state of
interesting suspension.
[2] For John of Salisbury's educational ideas see D. D. McGarry, 'Educational Theory
in the *Metalogicon* of John of Salisbury', *Speculum*, xxiii (1948), pp. 659 ff.

worth.[1] But the reality was very different, as the groundwork in arts was often eclectically superficial and far removed from the encyclopaedic ideal.

The inclusion of logic as one of the arts was a recognition that clarity of analytical thought rather than public eloquence would better serve a society which had lost its appetite for oratorical expertise. Likewise, the mathematical and scientific subjects of the *quadrivium* conceived, not as specialist disciplines but as basic to the arts curriculum helped to provide a more realistic alternative to the rarefied schemes of Cicero or Quintilian. Writers such as Capella, Augustine and Cassiodorus may not have had much contemporary educational impact, but their works on education forged a theoretical framework within which the Graeco–Roman heritage could be transformed into terms which had some meaning for medieval society. They also helped to preserve the encyclopaedic view of learning which was so important to keep alive in a society which could little afford the luxury of educational breadth. It may be that these authors owed their inspiration to Varro's *De Novem Disciplinis* several centuries before, but whereas Varro had been content to classify knowledge, Capella and his successors had gone beyond this point by attempting to arrange their material in the form of model curricula. By so doing they brought the classification of knowledge out of an academic vacuum and into the realm of teaching experience.[2]

One might suppose that the process of discovery and assimilation of the classical heritage, which reached an apogee in western Europe between 1000 and 1150, would have furnished a cultural base for the nascent universities. If this humanistic activity is seen from its widest angle, there is substance in the idea; but if humanism is taken in a literary sense to mean principally a cultivation of classical literature and the stylistic imitation of ancient authors, then the continuity is tenuous. In its broadest and deepest terms, however, the humanistic movement of the eleventh and twelfth centuries bequeathed a set of values which were firmly implanted in the universities. Of fundamental importance were the belief in the dignity of man who, even in his fallen state, was capable of the fullest intellectual and spiritual enlargement, the belief in an ordered universe accessible to rational inquiry, and the possibility of man's mastery of his environment through

---

[1] See the comments of Parker, art. cit., pp. 420–2. On the evolution of the seven liberal arts and for a detailed discussion of each as university subjects, with accompanying teaching methods, see P. Glorieux, *La faculté des arts et ses maîtres au xiiie siècle* (Paris, 1971), pp. 13–46.

[2] Bolgar, *The Classical Heritage*, p. 43.

his intellect, cumulative knowledge and experience.[1] These combined assumptions underlay the educationally expansionist programmes of the cathedral and urban schools in the pre-university era between c. 1050–1200, although the extent to which they were developed varied enormously from centre to centre and, even within the same school, there might be alternating periods of high intellectual activity followed by relative quiescence.[2] Secular and of the world, these non-monastic schools supplied modest institutional means for the extension of rational inquiry to every area of systematized learning. This liberating force was cradled in the conviction that, outside the realm of revealed truth, man's capacity for knowledge and understanding was almost unlimited. The buoyant optimism of the schoolmen of the twelfth century, their sense of a profound regeneration in the human condition, and their new found confidence in man's reason and innermost powers amounted to a soaring reorientation in the thinking of western Europe. Amid the early enthusiasms some naiveté and disproportion were inescapable, and some of the freshness faded with the passage of time; but the central principles endured and were creatively implemented in Europe's earliest universities. It is in this sense that one may speak of a continuous humanistic tradition linking the outlook, aspirations and values of scholars of the eleventh and twelfth centuries with those of their university successors. The momentum of inquiry into natural phenomena was sustained and accelerated by an intellectual élite in the universities, and the frontiers of the supernatural were progressively moved back. Man was accorded a central place in the scheme of things and criteria, both pagan and Christian, were adduced to render intelligible the Creator, mankind and the whole natural order. The thirteenth century may have evinced a close regard for controlled, co-operative investigation and systematic analysis and shown less concern with the self-exploratory psychology and individualistic emphasis of twelfth-century schoolmen: but behind the transition from an individual to a more corporate intellectual enterprise the deeper levels of humanistic thought and approach remained firmly enshrined.

While these fundamental humanistic values were built into the fabric of the university world, the more superficial level of literary humanism was

[1] R. W. Southern analyses the central features of the medieval humanistic movement in 'Medieval Humanism' in *Medieval Humanism and other Studies,* cit., pp. 29–33 and passim. See also C. Morris, *The Discovery of the Individual 1050–1200* (Church History Outlines 5, London, 1972).
[2] See Southern's cautionary remarks in 'Humanism and the School of Chartres' in ibid., pp. 74–5.

quickly reduced to secondary importance. From the outset, the study of the classical authors was largely squeezed out of Europe's first university curricula, finding only a pale reflection in the elementary subject of grammar which, at Paris and the English universities, was relegated to the position of a necessary but preliminary study of the arts course proper, a study which might well be completed by the student before he came up to the university.[1]

The persistent clerical distrust of pagan literature was a constant force militating against the permanent entrenchment of the study of the classical authors as a major preoccupation of Christian education, especially when an alternative Christian literature had reached significant proportions. The strength of the opposition in the second half of the twelfth century may be gauged from contemporary testimony. For example, Peter Comestor, chancellor of Notre Dame of Paris from 1164, preached that the arts might be a useful aid to the study of scripture but that the outpourings of the classical authors were to be avoided.[2] Alexander of Villedieu, author of the verse grammar, the *Doctrinale*, launched *c.* 1200 a powerful attack upon the cathedral school of Orléans, one of the principal centres of humanist studies before the mid-thirteenth century, describing it as a 'pestiferous chair of learning . . . spreading contagion among the multitude' and adding that 'nothing should be read which is contrary to the scriptures'.[3] The sermons of Jacques de Vitry (*d.* 1240) to the students of Paris, although they are couched in more moderate tones, echo similar caveats against the study of the classical authors.[4] The intensification of the attacks on literary humanism was probably geared to some extent to the availability of a contemporary Latin literature suitable for teaching purposes. Much of this didactic Christian literature was in verse form and some of it such as the Latin epic poems, the *Alexandreis* of Gautier of Lille (written 1176-9) and the *Tobias* of Matthew of Vendôme (*d. c.* 1200) was widely utilized as text books in the schools and universities.[5] Part of the enormous appeal of works of this kind lay in their close stylistic affinity to contemporary spoken Latin and they were still being prescribed in some of the universi-

---

[1] The phasing out of classical literature from the arts course does not preclude an unofficial sponsoring of classical learning by university teachers in the thirteenth and fourteenth centuries: see Bolgar, op. cit., p. 222.
[2] L. J. Paetow, *The Arts Course at Medieval Universities*, Illinois University Studies, vol. iii, no. 7 (Urbana-Champaign, 1910), p. 20.
[3] Ibid., p. 21.
[4] Ibid., pp. 21–2.
[5] Ibid., p. 24.

ties of southern France in the fourteenth century.[1] The appearance of contemporary Latin grammars as a counter-attraction to the time-honoured grammar texts of Donatus and Priscian was an important feature in the growth of the alternative culture. Many of these grammars were written in verse form as it was believed that rhyme and metre were aids to memory. But the most vital development in grammar was the application of logical inquiry to grammatical problems thereby transforming grammar into a speculative study. This movement brought grammar into the orbit of the main dialectical trends of late twelfth- and early thirteenth-century intellectual life, and rendered classical grammatical forms outmoded and remote. The two most influential grammars of the new style, both in hexameter verse, were the *Doctrinale* of Alexander of Villedieu, written *c.* 1199, and the *Graecismus* of Eberhard of Béthune, which appeared in 1212.[2] The *Doctrinale* became rapidly entrenched in the schools in the thirteenth century and, in the fourteenth and fifteenth centuries, achieved a grammatical primacy in the universities. The *Graecismus* was a more advanced work than the *Doctrinale*, having a section on Greek etymology, but it too became widely rooted in the universities, and together these works tended to overshadow and, in some respects, to supersede the classical models of Donatus and Priscian.

Among the reasons for the diminishing importance of the classical authors must be reckoned the counter-attraction of scientific and mathematical interests and the magnetic pull of the lucrative studies of law and medicine. Exciting new vistas were opened up from the mid-twelfth century by a deepening awareness of the potentialities of science and mathematics stimulated and supported by the infiltration into western Europe of substantial areas of Greek, Arabic and Jewish thought. The key philosophical and scientific system was that of Aristotle derived directly from Greek translation or from Arabic and Hebraic sources; and the new consciousness of this material resulted from the increasing contacts of the peoples of northern Europe with southern Italy, Sicily, the Byzantine Empire and, above all, Spain. The business of absorption by the west of Aristotle's logical, philosophical, scientific, ethical, political and literary treatises was one that was phased over the hundred years or so between 1150 and 1250.[3] The lure of Greek and Arabic science attracted a con-

[1] Ibid., pp. 24–5.
[2] Ibid., pp. 36–9; also, Bolgar, op. cit., pp. 208–10.
[3] On the rediscovery of Aristotle see conveniently Knowles, *The Evolution of Medieval Thought*, ch. xv, pp. 185 ff.

course of itinerant Englishmen in the twelfth century who travelled extensively in the quest for scientific data. For example, a high proportion of the scholars who journeyed to Spain in the twelfth century for scientific motives were Englishmen, including Roger of Hereford, Daniel of Morley, Alfred of Sareshel, Roger of Chester, and the ubiquitous Adelard of Bath who also went to Sicily and the eastern Mediterranean.[1] The pioneer achievements of English scholars in the realm of mathematics and the natural sciences found a temporary institutional home in centres such as the cathedral school of Hereford[2] and a later permanence in the university of Oxford. The twelfth-century English scientific tradition, embodied at Oxford and unhampered by the papal ban on the teaching of the New Aristotle imposed at Paris in the first half of the thirteenth century, graduated from a random study of scientific data to a more fully integrated mathematical investigation into physical phenomena, underpinned by a method of scientific inquiry comprising observation, hypothesis and experimental verification.[3] This Aristotelian-inspired scientific advance led scholars far from the static world of the classical authors to a belief that a new perception and understanding of natural phenomena, and therefore of God's creation, were for the first time, within man's grasp. The intellectual dynamics of the age lay with this thrusting, forward movement, and classical literary culture seemed the very antithesis of discovery and progress.

The professionally-geared studies of law and medicine exercised an almost mesmeric influence over Europe's earliest generations of university students, although the appeal of medicine was markedly more pronounced in southern Europe than in the north. The prospect of monetary gain and an established position within the social order were powerful incentives to the student of ability, and there was strong temptation to hasten over an arts training to embark upon more lucrative study. This short-circuiting of the arts course and the neglect of the classical authors was a criticism

1 For the activities of Englishmen in the twelfth-century scientific movement see Hunt, 'English Learning in the late Twelfth Century', cit., pp. 19 ff: also, C. H. Haskins, *Studies in the History of Medieval Science* (Cambridge, 1927), esp. chs. ii, vi.

2 According to the poem of Simon du Fresne (see above, p. 12, n. 1), the *quadrivium* subjects at Hereford were given an equal emphasis with those of the *trivium*: on Hereford as a scientific and mathematical centre see e.g. B. Lawn, *The Salernitan Questions* (Oxford, 1963), pp. 35–6, 64–5.

3 For these scientific developments and Robert Grosseteste's personal contribution see A. C. Crombie, *Robert Grosseteste and the Origins of Experimental Science* (Oxford, 1953), passim, and Crombie, 'Grosseteste's Position in the History of Science' in *Robert Grosseteste: Scholar and Bishop*, ed. D. A. Callus (Oxford, 1955), pp. 98 ff.

levelled especially at those students of law who, by advancing directly from only a rudimentary experience in arts to the superior faculty of law, were deemed educationally superficial and motivated by pecuniary reward.[1] The poetic treatise of John of Garland, the *Morale Scolarium*, although compiled in 1241, highlights sentiments about the worldliness of the student body which are reminiscent of the complaints voiced by schoolmen, such as John of Salisbury, in the second half of the twelfth century: 'If you are a real scholar you are thrust out in the cold. Unless you are a money-maker, I say, you will be considered a fool, a pauper. The lucrative arts, such as law and medicine, are now in vogue, and only those things are pursued which have a cash value.'[2] In the early thirteenth century there was deep concern that subjects like law and medicine would obliterate the study of letters altogether. The *ars dictaminis* or *dictamen*, the art of composing letters and formal documents, was a specialized offshoot of law and rhetoric which developed as a thriving, lucrative competitor to traditional classical learning.[3] Established firmly in the universities of Italy and provincial France in the thirteenth century, *dictamen* appealed as a rapid passport to worldly success. Itinerant teachers of the art, such as Ponce de Provence, enticed students to throw over their classical studies to engage in the more worthwhile enterprise of the *ars dictaminis*.

The applied subjects of law, medicine and *dictamen* were the natural enemies of literary humanism since they propelled the emergent universities towards integration in community professional life and away from a stilled contemplation of the finite inheritance of classical antiquity. As the earliest universities were not planned, but developed spontaneously over a period of time, they did not at first consciously choose one educational programme in preference to another. The vocational function was imposed upon them from outside because they were the product of vocational needs. They were not directly the outcome of a fine educational ideal but came into being when west European society had reached that point in its corporate growth which dictated the establishment of permanent centres of higher education capable of concentrating its available talent for socially useful employment. The excessive fragmentation of teaching facilities which characterized the pre-university era was superseded by a more rational

[1] See e.g. Paetow, *The Arts Course at Medieval Universities*, cit., p. 27.
[2] John of Garland, *Morale Scolarium*, ed. L. J. Paetow in *Two Mediaeval Satires on the University of Paris* (Berkeley, 1927), p. 189 (trans. p. 155).
[3] See e.g. Paetow, *The Arts Course at Medieval Universities*, pp. 28–9. Much information on *dictamen* and *dictatores* will be found in Haskins, *Studies in Medieval Culture*, cit., chs. i, vi, ix.

marshalling of man and resources to produce Europe's first collectivized educational endeavours. As the universities were from the start service institutions, it is intelligible that literary humanism found but slight expression in their early curricular arrangements. Orléans, the last bastion of humanistic studies among the thirteenth-century universities, had become by the beginning of the fourteenth century largely a centre of law, a victim of the prevailing utilitarianism in advanced education.[1]

Perhaps the most recognizable immediate reason for the ousting of classical studies from the curricula of the new universities was the position of dominance attained by logic in the arts course. Initially, there had been no necessary antagonism between logic and the classical authors. Just as dialectical analysis could be used in the elucidation of matters of faith, so logic could be applied to the content of Graeco–Roman learning. But the dialectical revival, which had its tentative stirrings in the tenth century, advanced with meteoric pace in the twelfth and began to absorb a disproportionate amount of intellectual energy at the expense of established classical norms of education. Critics such as John of Salisbury were loud in their denunciation of the shallow logicians who spurned to equip themselves with a broad foundation in the liberal arts and the classical authors.[2] John of Salisbury was not antithetical to logic, only to its excesses. Logic had a useful and vitalizing function within the framework of a broad educational programme.[3] The pursuit of logic *per se* as the hallmark of the educated man must be avoided; logic was an instrument, not an education, and must be effectively grouped and controlled.[4] There is here a parallel with the attitude of Cicero and Quintilian to the all-engulfing fascination of rhetoric for their own society, and the tendency to equate it with the entirety of higher education. But the intellectual currents of the period ran counter to the arguments of the humanists, and logic more than anything else sounded the knell of humane learning in the universities. In the first flush of optimism, logic seemed to provide the means whereby man could introduce order and system into the apparently chaotic world which enveloped him. Methods of logical arrangement and analysis made it seemingly possible to penetrate into the heart of nature, to see hitherto unrelated facts in their essential interrelationships. With this flexible, infinitely subtle in-

[1] Paetow, op. cit., pp. 19, 28.
[2] See John of Salisbury, *Metalogicon*, ed. cit., bk. 1, ch. 3, pp. 9–12 (trans. by McGarry), cit., pp. 13–16.
[3] E.g. *Metalogicon*, bk. 2, ch. 9, pp. 76–7 (trans. pp. 93–5) n. 54; ch. 11, p. 83 (trans. pp. 100–1); bk. 4, ch. 28, p. 194 (trans. pp. 244–5).
[4] 'Fere enim inutilis est logica, si sit sola': bk. 4, ch. 28, p. 194 (trans. p. 244).

strument of logic it seemed that the bounds of knowledge could be almost indefinitely extended and, by adopting the kind of procedures outlined in Abelard's *Sic et Non*, the area of intellectual conflict minimized. Logic came to be regarded as the intellectual panacea, the *sine qua non* for deep understanding in every field of human study whether theology, law, medicine, grammar, or the natural sciences. For its exponents, dialectic was a force of electric change, the quintessence of all that was new and exciting in the academic sphere at the birth of the universities. By contrast, humane learning seemed essentially conservative and static, wedded to the restoration and perpetuation of a dead culture. The contest between classical studies and logic was represented graphically *c.* 1250 in the French allegorical poem by the *trouvère* Henri d'Andeli, *Battle of the Seven Arts*,[1] in which grammar, championed by Orléans and supported by the humanists and the classical authors, goes forth to do battle with logic of Paris and is utterly defeated. The poet's expressed hope for a revival in the fortunes of the classics in the next generation was not to be realized, and even at Orléans humane studies surrendered to law.

The universities were conceived at a time of European urban and economic revival, of radical communal activity and of more accessible communications arising from commercial and Crusading enterprise. A purely humanistic culture was inadequate to sustain an educational system in a vibrant, expanding environment which had unleashed vigorous new forces of intellectual energy. Although the universities were, in some sense, the cumulative outcome of the humanistic tradition inherited from Graeco–Roman civilization and indeed embodied fundamental humanistic values, they were alien to the leisured world of literary humanism, and their intellectual roots were inseparably bound up with the European-wide ascendancy of logic, speculative theology and law to their primatial positions in the academic hierarchy.

[1] Paetow, op. cit., p. 19.

II

1. Concept of a university

The medieval university was essentially an indigenous product of western Europe. Classical civilization did not produce the equivalent of these privileged corporate associations of masters and students with their statutes, seals and administrative machinery, their fixed curricula and degree procedures.[1] Centres of higher education such as the philosophical schools of Athens, dating from the fourth century B.C.,[2] the law school of Beirut which flourished between the early third and mid-sixth century,[3] or the imperial university of Constantinople, founded in 425 and functioning intermittently until 1453,[4] may have anticipated the medieval universities in some respects, for example in terms of embryonic organization and the emergence of regular courses of study.[5] But collectively the distinguishing features of the medieval university seem to have been nowhere reproduced

---

[1] See the comments of S. Stelling-Michaud, 'L'histoire des universités au moyen âge et à la renaissance au cours des vingt-cinq dernières années', XIᵉ Congrès International des Sciences Historiques, Rapports, i (Stockholm, 1960), p. 98; also C. H. Haskins, The Rise of Universities (New York, 1923), pp. 3–4.

[2] On the philosophical schools of Athens see Clarke, Higher Education in the Ancient World, cit., ch. 3, pp. 55 ff.

[3] Ibid., pp. 116–17, 136.

[4] Ibid., pp. 130 ff.

[5] E.g. the Beirut law school had a regular academic course of five years with definite curricular arrangements (ibid., pp. 116–17). The University of Constantinople combined, in one centre, teachers of grammar, rhetoric, philosophy and law (ibid., p. 130); also S. S. Laurie, Lectures on the Rise and Early Constitution of Universities (London, 1886), pp. 15–16.

in previous institutional form; and there does not appear to be any organic continuity between the universities which evolved towards the end of the twelfth century and Greek, Graeco–Roman, Byzantine or Arabic schools. However much the universities may have owed to the impulse of Greek, Roman or Arabic intellectual life their institutional crystallization was a new departure born of the need to enlarge the scope of professional education in an increasingly urbanized society.

Although there may have been no real physical continuity between the universities and the schools of the ancient world, a fictional link was generated in the form of the *translatio studii* whereby the centre of learning was deemed to have passed from Athens to Rome, from Rome to Byzantium and hence to Paris.[1] This notion of the *translatio studii*, which appeared in the Carolingian age, acquired a popular currency with the emergence of the universities which were then seen as the embodiment of the *studium* and, as such, ranking alongside the other two great powers by which Christian society was directed, the spiritual (*Sacerdotium*) and the temporal (*Imperium*).[2] The ideological thesis that the universities were the lineal successors to the Greek, Graeco–Roman and Byzantine schools with respect to the *translatio studii* may be historically unsound, but it probably helped provide propagandist support for the universities in their struggle to establish themselves, in their first period of life, as a quasi-independent order in the community free from undue ecclesiastical or secular control.[3]

The terminology relating to medieval universities and the problems of contemporary definition are still among the more intractable matters surrounding the origins of the universities. The word 'university' has nothing to do with the universality of learning, and it is only by accident that the Latin term *universitas* has given rise to the established nomenclature.[4] For

[1] Stelling-Michaud, art. cit., pp. 98–9; H. Rashdall, *The Universities of Europe in the Middle Ages*, 3 vols., ed. F. M. Powicke and A. B. Emden (Oxford, 1936), i, pp. 2, 23. See also C. Morris, *The Discovery of the Individual 1050–1200*, cit., p. 50 and note.

[2] E.g. the statement of Alexander of Roes *c.* 1281: 'Hiis siquidem tribus, scilicet sacerdotio imperio et studio, tamquam tribus virtutibus, videlicet vitali naturali et animali, sancta ecclesia catholica spiritualiter vivificatur augmentatur et regitur' quoted in Rashdall, op. cit., ed. cit., i, pp. 2, n. 1, 23; trans. in G. Leff, *Paris and Oxford Universities in the Thirteenth and Fourteenth Centuries* (New York, 1968), p. 3. See also H. Grundmann, 'Sacerdotium, Regnum, Studium,' *Archiv für Kulturgeschichte*, 34 (1952), pp. 5 ff.

[3] As late as the fifteenth century Paris University still claimed to be the inheritor of the *studium* as transmitted from ancient Egypt to Paris via Athens and Rome: see *Chartularium Universitatis Parisiensis*, 4 vols., ed. H. Denifle and E. Chatelain (Paris, 1889–97), v, no. 2120.

[4] On *universitas* see H. Denifle, *Die Entstehung der Universitäten des Mittelalters bis 1400* (Berlin, 1885), pp. 29 ff.; Rashdall, op. cit., i, pp. 4 ff., 15; Leff, op. cit., pp. 16–17.

universitas was a general word of wide application in the twelfth, thirteenth and fourteenth centuries and was used to denote any kind of aggregate or body of persons with common interests and independent legal status: it indicated a defined group whether a craft guild or a municipal corporation.[1] When employed in an academic context the term referred not to the university as an abstraction, as a complete entity in itself, but to the body of masters and students or of masters and students combined depending upon the organizational type of the particular university. It was not, it seems, until the late fourteenth and fifteenth centuries that *universitas* came into use as a convenient shorthand label applied especially to academic corporations,[2] just as terms like *collegium, congregatio* or *corpus* came to acquire similar association with specific groupings in society.

The medieval term which most closely corresponds to our concept of a university is *studium generale*.[3] For most of the thirteenth century this designation appears to have had no precise technical or legal signification. Initially, *studium generale* may have been an entirely descriptive phrase, the *studium* part indicating a school where there were organized facilities for study and *generale* referring neither to the general or universal nature of the subjects taught nor to the number of students involved, but to the ability of the school to attract students from beyond the local region. The extent of the range of attraction which a thirteenth-century school had to exhibit before it would be classified as 'general' is, however, a vexed question to which there is no easy solution. Was it necessary for the school with claims to be 'general' to draw students from another country, or simply from different parts of the same country, or even from a more limited area? Moreover, the term *studium generale* is not much found in the first half of the thirteenth century. The earliest documentary evidence for the use of the term appears to be with reference to the University of Vercelli in 1237.[4] And the first papal enactment which employs *studium generale*

---

[1] See e.g. the detailed exposition by P. Michaud-Quantin, *Universitas: expressions du mouvement communautaire dans le moyen âge latin* (L'Eglise et l'Etat au Moyen Age, 13, Paris, 1970), passim and Michaud-Quantin, 'Collectivités médiévales et institutions antiques' in *Miscellanea Mediaevalia*, i, ed. P. Wilpert (Berlin, 1962), pp. 239 ff.

[2] Denifle, op. cit., esp. pp. 34 ff.; Rashdall, op. cit., i, pp. 16–17.

[3] On the concept of *studium generale* see Denifle, op. cit., ch. 1, pp. 1 ff., and Rashdall, op. cit., i, pp. 6 ff.; ii, pp. 2–3. See also Stelling-Michaud, 'L'histoire des universités . . .', art. cit., pp. 99–100 and G. Ermini, 'Concetto di "Studium Generale" ', *Archivio Giuridico*, cxxvii (1942), where the divergent views of H. Denifle, C. Meiners, F. C. von Savigny, A. Pertile, F. Schupfer and G. Kaufmann on the essential features of *studia generalia* are conveniently summarized.

[4] Denifle, op. cit., p. 2 and n. 2.

seems to be that of Innocent IV of 1244 or 1245 establishing the University of the Court of Rome.[1] In the second half of the thirteenth century the usage is more common, but it is not until the fourteenth century that it acquired a precise juristic meaning and became the normal term to express the abstraction of a fully-fledged university. Throughout the thirteenth century several terms were used with apparently much the same connotation as the currently imprecise *studium generale*, for example *studium universale*,[2] *studium commune*[3] and *studium solempne* (or *solemne, solenne*).[4] But perhaps the alternative term to *studium generale* which was most frequently employed in the thirteenth century was simply *studium*. It was used in the first half of the thirteenth century in both papal and non-papal sources in relation to such centres as Bologna, Paris, Oxford, Palencia, Vercelli, Padua, Naples, Valencia and Toulouse.[5] And *studium* continued to be common throughout the remainder of the century and even beyond.[6] In view of the alternating nature of the terminology it is improbable that there is much distinction to be drawn between *studium* and *studium generale* as used in the thirteenth century, that is to say, before the latter assumed a strict legal meaning.

The *Siete Partidas* (1256–63), the legislative code of Alfonso X of Castile, provides one of the earliest commentaries on the nature of the *studium generale*. Title XXXI,[7] given over to the universities, deals with such matters as the payment of teachers and teaching methods, university discipline, the organization of student life, examinations and the granting of the licence, and jurisdictional affairs. Two basic requirements are here stipulated for *studium generale* status: the school must have masters for each of the seven arts and also for canon and civil law; and a *studium generale* could only be erected by authority of the pope, the emperor, or the king.[8] This attempted definition lacks reference to theology and medicine as superior faculty studies; and the right of a king to confer *studium generale* status in

---

[1] Ibid., p. 3 and n. 11.
[2] One of the earliest occurrences of *studium universale* is to be found in documentation for 1229–30 relating to the University of Toulouse (ibid., p. 2).
[3] An early instance of the expression is in connection with the nascent University of Oxford in *c.* 1190 (Rashdall, *Universities*, i, p. 6, n. 2; iii, p. 31 and n. 2.)
[4] Used e.g. by Pope Alexander IV in 1256 with reference to Montpellier (Denifle, op. cit., p. 3 and n. 10; see also Rashdall, op. cit., i, p. 6, n. 2).
[5] Denifle, op. cit., pp. 5–6.
[6] Ibid., pp. 6–7.
[7] *Las Siete Partidas des rey don Alfonso el Sabio*, 3 vols., ed. por la real academia de la historia (Madrid, 1807), ii, titulo xxxi, pp. 339–46.
[8] Titulo xxxi, ley 1 (p. 340).

the full ecumenical sense was not to be generally accepted, and was doubt-less prompted by the actions of Spanish rulers in founding *studia generalia* without papal or imperial assistance.[1] Later juristic thought classified such foundations as *studia generalia respectu regni* on the grounds that privileges granted to a *studium* by a local ruler had no validity beyond the confines of the kingdom.[2] Although the section on *studium generale* in the *Siete Partidas* is historically important because it is a *rara avis* at this juncture in the thirteenth century and is an early example of secular legislative activity for universities, it furnishes only a partial and presumably Spanish view of *studia generalia* which is not in any way definitive. As one of the few contemporary accounts of the *studium generale* before the late thirteenth and fourteenth centuries the *Siete Partidas* is somewhat disappointing.

Clearly, the conception of *studium generale* was a vague one for most of the thirteenth century, and only towards the end of it was it beginning to achieve a precise legality. Originally, the expression meant no more than a celebrated school which attracted students from a wide area and which could provide teaching, not only in arts, but in at least one of what became the superior faculties in the universities, law (civil and canon), theology or medicine. Facilities of this nature presuppose that the school was capable of maintaining an adequate teaching staff from year to year. In *c.* 1200 only centres such as Bologna, Paris, Oxford and Salerno could sustain teaching in the higher disciplines and, consequently, only these few would have been customarily regarded as 'general'. But with the multiplication of *studia* in Italy and France, moulded on the archetypal universities of Bologna and Paris, it was natural that some of these centres should claim for themselves the status of *studium generale*. It seems that any school could assume 'general' standing, but whether it came to be accepted as such would, in all proba-bility, be decided by the force of custom. Before legal precision was evolved, the final arbiter of whether a school was *generale* as opposed to *particulare* was informed educated opinion.

A wholly new dimension came into being when papal and imperial authority arrogated the right to establish *studia generalia* by specific enact-ment. The first imperial university, and indeed the first university of all to be erected by a definite act, was founded at Naples in 1224 by the Emperor Frederick II: the earliest papal university was that of Toulouse

---

[1] The main features of the Spanish universities are summarized by Rashdall, op. cit., ii, pp. 64–5; also H. Wieruszowski, *The Medieval University: Masters, Students, Learning* (New York, 1966), pp. 91–4.
[2] Rashdall, op. cit., i, p. 11; ii, p. 79.

created by Gregory IX in 1229; and in 1244 or 1245 Innocent IV established a *studium generale* in the papal curia at Rome.[1] These foundations seem to have given birth to the idea that the power to erect *studia generalia* was vested in papal or imperial prerogative.[2] This notion gathered momentum and was accepted doctrine by the fourteenth century. The consequence of this was that the *generale* constituent of the expression *studium generale* was radically transformed. Whereas *generale* had formerly been no more than a descriptive adjunct pointing to the drawing capacity of the school, it had now acquired an ecumenical character conferred by papal or imperial endowment, and especially by the former. If *studia generalia* were to be created artificially and were to derive a universal nature from papal or imperial authority, it became necessary to define more closely the privileges which stemmed from this enhanced but delimited academic situation. And here there was little that was innovatory. As part of their organic growth the earliest universities had evolved a number of *de facto* special privileges, and the most important of these were incorporated as essential ingredients of the status of *studium generale* as defined by fourteenth-century Italian juristic thought from which much of the medieval commentary on university terminology is derived.

In the course of the thirteenth century there were two privileged concepts which, above all, came to be associated with the expression *studium generale*. The more concrete of the two was the right of beneficed clergy to receive the fruits of their benefices while non-resident at a *studium generale* for the purposes of study. Dispensation of ecclesiastics from residence for study in the schools had been granted by the papacy and individual bishops from the twelfth century. In 1207 Innocent III had attempted to limit this privilege to schools of a reputable standard, but did not specify these as *studia generalia*.[3] The bull of Honorius III of 1219, *Super Speculam*, granted non-residence with revenues for five years to holders of prebends and benefices engaged as teachers or students of theology in theological schools.[4] This privilege was not confined to Paris or any other *studium generale*, and presumably applied to all *studia* or *scholae* where theology was taught at a satisfactory level. But in the mid-thirteenth century the canonist Hostiensis (Cardinal Henry of Susa), in his *Summa* on the Decretals, interpreted the non-residence provisions of *Super Speculam* to

[1] For these three foundations see ibid., i, p. 8.
[2] Ibid., i, pp. 8–9; Leff, *Paris and Oxford Universities . . .*, cit., p. 18.
[3] Rashdall, op. cit., i, p. 9, n. 2.
[4] The bull is printed in *Chartularium Universitatis Parisiensis*, cit., i, no. 32.

apply exclusively to a *studium generale* and not to a *studium specialis*,[1] which seems to be synonymous with *studium particulare*. Doubtless the opinion of Hostiensis was coming to reflect a general canonistic view that non-residence with revenues ought to be confined to *studia generalia* as the best safeguard both for the maintenance of theological standards and for the prevention of misuse of ecclesiastical incomes.[2] Cases from the middle years of the thirteenth century indicate that dispensation from residence was, in practice, being closely related to the status of *studium generale*. Innocent IV, in his foundation bull for the university of the papal curia at Rome (1244–5), specifically granted the privilege of non-residence to beneficed clerks.[3] And in 1246 Innocent IV issued a bull granting regents non-residence in the *studium* which the king of Aragon proposed to found at Valencia;[4] while in 1260 Alexander IV recognized as a *studium generale* the school founded at Seville by Alfonso the Wise for the study of Latin and Arabic, and conferred the privilege of non-residence on the students.[5] The schools of Narbonne provide an interesting commentary on this matter of non-residence. In 1247 Innocent IV, petitioned by the archbishop of Narbonne, granted to the teachers and students at Narbonne the same privilege of non-residence enjoyed by 'scolares in studiis generalibus commorantes'.[6] Narbonne was not then a *studium generale*; consequently, the award illustrates both that dispensation from residence was a recognized prerogative of a *studium generale* and that this privilege might be exceptionally conferred on a reputable *studium* even if it were not 'general'. By the fourteenth century the privilege of dispensation from residence for beneficed clergy had become a salient feature of the privileged nature of a *studium generale*.

The second and more theoretical privilege which came to be exclusively associated with the status of *studium generale* was that of the *ius ubique docendi*:[7] that is to say, the right of the holder of a degree from a *studium generale* to teach in any other university without undergoing further examination. This power claimed by a *studium generale* to endow its masters with

---

[1] See the quote from Hostiensis in Denifle, *Die Entstehung* . . ., cit., p. 19, n. 94.
[2] The financing of clergy to study in sub-standard schools was considered tantamount to fraudulent misuse of ecclesiastical revenues.
[3] Extracts from the papal award are given by Denifle, op. cit., p. 302, n. 326, and by Rashdall, op. cit., ii, p. 28, n. 3.
[4] Rashdall, op. cit., ii, p. 107.
[5] Ibid., ii, p. 91. Little is known about the school in the thirteenth century.
[6] *Les régistres d'Innocent IV* (ed. E. Berger), i (Paris, 1884), no. 2717.
[7] On the *ius ubique docendi* see Rashdall, op. cit., i, pp. 9–15; also Stelling-Michaud, 'L'histoire des universités . . .', art. cit., p. 100.

a teaching licence of universal validity would have established the untrammelled mobility of university teachers, would have made possible a European-wide academic commonwealth which transcended race and provincialism in the collective pursuit and dissemination of learning. Although the concept of the *ius ubique docendi* was perhaps the most important legal attribute of a *studium generale* from the late thirteenth century, and was normally included in the foundation charters of new fourteenth-century universities,[1] the reality was very different, and it is doubtful if it acted as much of a binding force on Europe's medieval universities.

The origin of the *ius ubique docendi* is to be sought ultimately in the monopoly power to grant the teaching licence (*licentia docendi*) which the heads of cathedral schools had exercised within their defined jurisdictional areas from the twelfth century.[2] But the emergence of the universities with their degree-awarding procedures helped to advance the idea that the possessor of a master's or doctor's degree from a *studium generale* carried with it a teaching licence of general application. In the case of the earliest universities this evolved as a prescriptive right: it was a *de facto* privilege which centres such as Bologna and Paris enjoyed because graduates of these celebrated schools were deemed to have a natural superiority over products of lesser *studia*. But when, in 1233, Pope Gregory IX conferred the *ius ubique docendi* on the graduates of the papally-founded University of Toulouse with all the privileges exercised by the Parisian masters,[3] two grades of *ius ubique docendi* were thereby thrown into relief: the customary type of Paris and Bologna and this newly-born artificially-endowed licence of ecumenical validity. In the course of time, a third category appeared, namely the officially conferred *ius ubique docendi* whose application was general but with the exception of named universities; for example, in 1255 Alexander IV awarded the graduates of the *studium generale* at Salamanca the right to teach in all *studia generalia* except Bologna and Paris;[4] and in 1332 John XXII excepted Paris from the terms of the *ius ubique*

---

[1] See Rashdall, op. cit., i, pp. 9–10; Leff, op. cit., p. 18.
[2] On this subject see P. Delhaye, 'L'organisation scolaire au xiie siècle', *Traditio*, v (1947), pp. 211 ff., esp. pp. 253 ff. (Ecoles des maîtres agrégés).
[3] The bull is printed in M. Fournier, *Les Statuts et Privilèges des Universités françaises depuis leur fondation jusqu'en 1789* (Paris, 1890–2), i, no. 506. The *ius ubique docendi* provision is thus expressed: 'Et ut quicumque magister ibi examinatus et approbatus fuerit in qualibet facultate, ubique sine alia examinacione regendi liberam habeat potestatem'.
[4] See the bull of Alexander IV in *Archiv für Literatur- und Kirchengeschichte*, v (ed. H. Denifle and F. Ehrle, Freiburg im Breisgau, 1889), pp. 170–2. The restrictions with respect to Bologna and Paris were removed in 1333: Rashdall, op. cit., ii, p. 78.

docendi conferred upon the University of Cahors.[1] From such instances it is clear that the status of *studium generale* was considered to be compatible with a limited right of *ius ubique docendi*.

When the university system came within the orbit of papal and imperial authority there was pressure to place the status of *studium generale* and the *ius ubique docendi* on a more rational basis. This affected the position of *studia generalia* with only customary (*ex consuetudine*) as opposed to documentary claims to 'general' recognition and to the universal teaching licence. In 1289 Pope Nicholas IV formally recognized as a *studium generale* the University of Montpellier which had long been treated as 'general' by custom, and conferred upon its doctors the *ius ubique docendi*.[2] And in 1291–2 two bulls were issued by Nicholas IV which officially bestowed the *ius ubique docendi* upon the old-established universities of Paris and Bologna.[3] In 1306, by a bull of Clement V, Orléans, which had been recognized as a *studium generale* before the mid-thirteenth century (i.e. *ex consuetudine*), was granted all the privileges of the *studium generale* of Toulouse which included the *ius ubique docendi*.[4] In the case of Padua, a confirmation of all its privileges as a *studium generale* was obtained by a bull of Clement VI in 1346.[5] However, this process of rationalization was not entirely complete and not without its anomalies. For example, Oxford seems never to have procured officially the *ius ubique docendi*, although both Edward I and Edward II unsuccessfully petitioned the papacy to have the privilege granted.[6] Likewise, the University of Angers appears to have had no express papal recognition of the *ius ubique docendi* even when, in the fourteenth century, it was widely acknowledged to be a *studium generale*.[7] While these cases point to the inconsistencies in the more centralized university system that was emerging under distant papal and imperial tutelage, it is nevertheless true that by the fourteenth century the

[1] See the bull of John XXII in Fournier, op. cit., ii, no. 1425.
[2] See ibid., ii, no. 903.
[3] The bull for Paris is printed in C. E. Bulaeus, *Historia Universitatis Parisiensis*, iii (Paris, 1666), pp. 449–50 and in *Chartularium Universitatis Parisiensis*, cit., ii, no. 578; and for Bologna in M. Sarti, *De Claris Archigymnasii Bononiensis Professoribus a saeculo xi usque ad saeculum xiv* (Bologna, 1769–72) I, i, p. 59.
[4] See Fournier, op. cit., i, no. 19.
[5] For this bull see A. Riccobonus, *De Gymnasio Patavino* (Padua, 1722), fos. 4, 5.
[6] See e.g. Leff, *Paris and Oxford Universities* . . ., cit., pp. 94–5. Edward II's letter of 26 December 1317 to the pope requesting that the *ius ubique docendi* be formally conferred on the University of Oxford is printed in *Chartularium Universitatis Parisiensis*, ii, no. 756. See also G. L. Haskins, 'The University of Oxford and the "ius ubique docendi" ', *E.H.R.*, lvi (1941), pp. 281 ff.
[7] Rashdall, *Universities*, ii, pp. 154–5.

ius ubique docendi had become one of the cardinal legal hallmarks of the status of *studium generale*, and a school lacking this capacity to confer degrees carrying a teaching licence of wide application was distinguished as a *studium particulare*.[1] It is probable that there were such 'particular' schools in France and Italy employing university graduates to teach beyond an elementary arts level. Some may even have tried to institute graduation machinery, but unless they could base a claim to 'general' standing either upon established custom or on a papally or imperially awarded teaching licence these *studia* would have been classified as 'particular' by fourteenth-century juristic opinion.

It would be misleading to imagine that the *ius ubique docendi* provides a realistic model for the operation of the medieval university system. The ideal of a university commonwealth of teachers moving freely from one position to another among Europe's *studia generalia* is one that was scarcely realized. Although much needs to be discovered about the professional careers of university teachers, there is sufficient evidence to indicate that university particularism tended to prevail against the supranational implications of the *ius ubique docendi*. Here one must remember that the *ius ubique docendi* was an artificially forced concept imposed upon the university world by papal or imperial decree. As such, it was an attempt to circumvent the natural inequalities of *studia generalia* with respect to institutional maturity and degree of community recognition. It was a mechanical contrivance designed to reduce the *studia generalia* to a fictive common denominator. Not surprisingly, the old-established universities were unwilling to implement a system which detracted from their achieved position in the van of higher education. After granting the privileges of Paris, including the *ius ubique docendi*, upon the University of Toulouse in 1233, Gregory IX had to mollify the Parisian masters with the assurance that no interference with their own privileges was intended.[2] The sensitivity of the Paris masters was not misplaced as the Toulouse settlement prefigured the progressive dilution of the monopolistic powers of the earliest universities which inevitably ensued from the multiplication of *studia generalia* invested with the teaching licence of ecumenical validity. Although the old-established universities were pressurized into theoretical conformity by seeking confirmation of the status of *studium generale* and the acquisition of the *ius ubique*

[1] On *studium particulare* see below, pp. 34 ff.

[2] *Chartularium Universitatis Parisiensis*, i, no. 101. Examining of Toulouse graduates was to continue at Paris in spite of the award of the *ius ubique docendi* to the University of Toulouse. See also C. E. S. Smith, *The University of Toulouse in the Middle Ages* (Wisconsin, 1958), p. 58.

docendi, they gave only limited effective support to the projected international academic order.

The principle of the mutual recognition of degrees and the teaching licence broke down even in the case of major universities like Paris and Oxford. In the early fourteenth century something akin to an academic tarriff war raged between these *studia generalia*, each refusing to accept and licence the graduates of the other without fresh examination.[1] And the conflict between Paris and Oxford is only a striking instance of what appears to have been a fairly common phenomenon. Many universities continued to impose examination on graduates from elsewhere before allowing them to teach their own students; for example, Montpellier, Angers and Orléans insisted in the most explicit terms that all potential regent masters from other universities should be subject to examination.[2] As there was no written system of examination at medieval universities, degrees being normally awarded on the twin bases of physical completion of course requirements and a series of private and public oral examinations and exercises of presumably varying severity, there existed few stable criteria by which one university could evaluate the standard attained by a graduate of another without carrying out its own investigation. The *ius ubique docendi* might theoretically impose a uniformity of standard, but this was unreal and appears to have been treated as such. Moreover, as was stressed at the University of Orléans in 1321, the unrestricted immigration of 'foreign' doctors into a university might lead to vitriolic disputes among the teaching masters for the custom of the available students and to the situation whereby some teachers had only a handful of students or none at all.[3] More specifically, financial considerations militated against the implementation of the universal teaching licence on any scale. The growth of salaried lectureships, which date from the thirteenth century in the universities of southern Europe and later spread to those of the north,[4] had two main effects for the operation of the *ius ubique docendi*. Academic

[1] See *Statuta Antiqua Universitatis Oxoniensis*, ed. S. Gibson (Oxford, 1931), *De resumentibus* (before 1313: revised dating of G. Pollard) pp. 53–4: '. . . quia ex mutua vicissitudine obligamur ad antidota, eos qui Oxonienses receperunt ad determinandum et ipsi Oxonie ad determinandum admitti poterunt, et qui Parisius vel alibi ubi Oxonienses a resumpcione maliciose excluduntur, nec ipsi Oxonie admittantur'.
[2] See the statutes of the Montpellier university of medicine, 1220, in Fournier, *Statuts*, ii, no. 1194; for Angers see Rashdall, op. cit., i, p. 14, n. 3; and for Orléans see the statute of 20 June 1321 in Fournier, i, no. 78.
[3] Fournier, i, no. 78.
[4] On the growth of salaried lectureships see A. B. Cobban 'Medieval Student Power', *Past and Present*, no. 53 (1971), pp. 28 ff. at pp. 47–8 (with notes).

mobility tended to be curbed as there was increased financial inducement for teachers to remain for several years in one position: and secondly, when the salaried system became more entrenched, teaching posts were inevitably limited to a minority of graduates. Consequently, the *ius ubique docendi* implications of the mastership or doctorate came for many to be no more than a titular honour. Generally speaking, it may be said that the way in which the universities developed did not set up the conditions for the realization of the *ius ubique docendi*. The university system did not encourage a wandering scholar population *per se*; individuals moved from centre to centre for a definite purpose and not as part of an army in restless quest for knowledge. Indeed, the concept of *ius ubique docendi* is something of a red herring for university history.[1] Although a crucial legal attribute of the rank of *studium generale* from the late thirteenth century, it received only a minimal observance. For circumstances dictated a pattern of academic protectionism rather than free intercourse, and this was the path trodden by the university system of medieval Europe. The relative failure of papal and imperial authority to make the universities prisoners of ecumenical conformity is eloquent testimony of the boisterous individuality that is so marked a feature of university growth in the middle ages.

There was probably no final contemporary agreement as to what exactly constituted a *studium generale*. It was no easy matter to formulate a legal definition which would encompass all the possible permutations involved in this thorny problem. The terminology had emerged piecemeal in the first half of the thirteenth century, had crystallized by 1300, and was given more rigorous legal form in the fourteenth century. Although it would not be possible to present a definitive view of a *studium generale*, even in the fourteenth century, one can underline features which seem to be common to most. In essence, a *studium generale* was a guild organization of masters or students or of masters and students combined, having a high degree of juridical autonomy, the right to elect its own officers, statutory making powers, and a communal seal. It had the drawing strength to attract students from a wide area and, in addition to arts, offered instruction in at least one of the superior faculties of law, theology, or medicine, maintaining a nucleus of regent masters to meet diverse teaching requirements. From the late thirteenth century it seems to have been necessary for a *studium* to have papal or imperial endorsement of its 'general' standing.

[1] P. Delhaye in his otherwise excellent and scholarly article does not question the universal validity of the teaching licence; see 'L'organisation scolaire . . .', *Traditio*, v (1947), p. 268.

It may be that occasionally a municipality or ruler purported to found a *studium generale ab initio*, without reference to pope or emperor;[1] but unless, in the fourteenth century, papal or imperial recognition were subsequently obtained, the *studium* would not be received as 'general'. Associated with the status of *studium generale* were a number of privileges, the two most important of which were that of dispensation from residence for beneficed clerks studying or teaching at a *studium generale*, and the theoretical concept of the *ius ubique docendi*, which endowed the university with a prestigious aura but not with much in the way of practical benefit. A *studium generale* might exhibit further privileges, but a clear distinction has to be drawn between those rights which were common to *studia generalia* and those which were additional privileges not vested in the status of *studium generale* itself. Rights common to *studia generalia* cannot by definition embrace their particular relationships with external authorities. The relationships of European *studia* with external bodies, whether episcopal, archiepiscopal, civic, regal or imperial were clearly so diverse that they could not be reduced to a simple formula, and could not be deduced from the general title of *studium generale*. For example, freedom from episcopal or archiepiscopal authority was not a right inherent in the fourteenth-century concept of a *studium generale*; for this, a university required an express papal award.[2]

The documentation arising from the process of rationalization which overtook Europe's universities in the late thirteenth and fourteenth centuries gives an insight into the variety of situations with which the papal and imperial powers had to grapple. If one examines the matter through papal legislation, it is found that papal letters or formal bulls for the erection of *studia generalia* fall into one of at least four categories.[3] They may erect a new *studium generale* where none has existed before;[4] they may found a *studium* on the basis of an older one which has since declined or even disappeared;[5] they may seem to erect a new *studium* without reference

---

[1] See Rashdall's discussion in op. cit., i, p. 11, n. 1 (cont. on p. 12).

[2] On particular and common privileges of *studia generalia* see the comments of A. B. Cobban, *The King's Hall within the University of Cambridge in the later Middle Ages*, Cambridge Studies in Medieval Life and Thought, 3rd. series, vol. 1 (Cambridge, 1969), p. 107.

[3] See Cobban, 'Edward II, Pope John XXII and the University of Cambridge', *B.J.R.L.*, xlvii (1964), pp. 49 ff. at p. 70, and the same author's *The King's Hall*, cit., pp. 35–6.

[4] E.g. see the foundation-bull for Prague (1347–8) printed in *Monumenta Historica Universitatis Praguensis*, ii (ed. Dittrich and Spirk, Prague, 1834), pp. 219–22; also Rashdall, op. cit., ii, p. 215.

[5] See e.g. the foundation-bull for Perpignan (1379) printed in Fournier, *Statuts*, ii, no.

to a former one, though it is known that an existing *studium* was flourishing at the time of the papal letter;[1] or lastly, the existence of a *studium generale* is admitted in the preamble of the document which then, on request of the ruler to strengthen it, proceeds to confirm the institution.[2] It is possible that several schools, which had some claim to be regarded as *studia generalia ex consuetudine* in the thirteenth century found themselves victims of selective rationalization and were denied the legal standing of *studium generale*. The schools at Lyons and Rheims may have come within this category.[3] It is difficult to explain their arrested development, but it is well to consider that a number of small schools in France and Italy had been thought of as *studia generalia* either implicitly or explicitly but which, through decline or some other cause, were not regarded later as proper candidates for fully-fledged university status. The existence of such schools must make one wary of thinking of the *studia generalia* of the thirteenth century as embracing only those which ultimately received official standing.

The concept of *studium particulare* was essentially a negative one used normally in contradistinction to *studium generale*. It seems therefore not to be found before the expression *studium generale* gained currency in the third and fourth decades of the thirteenth century: and even in the remainder of the century it is not used with any frequency. The *Siete Partidas* of Alfonso X of Castile (1256–63) stated that an *estudio particular* could be established by any municipal council or bishop whereas an *estudio general* must be founded by a pope, emperor, or king.[4] Beyond this, it is not further defined, although the commentary on the *estudio general* suggests by contrast that an *estudio particular* would not have a guild organization of masters and students and would provide far fewer teaching facilities than a 'general' school: indeed, if very small, it may have only a single teaching master.[5] It does not appear that the term *studium particulare* refers to any one kind of school, but to a variety of types ranging from an elementary school to one of relatively advanced educational form. By definition, the drawing

---

1438, in conjunction with the earlier history of the *studium* given by Rashdall, op. cit., ii, pp. 96–7.

[1] E.g. see the bull of Nicholas IV for Montpellier (1289) in Fournier, op. cit., ii, no. 903, together with the past history of the university outlined in Rashdall, op. cit., ii, pp. 119 ff., esp. at p. 130.

[2] See e.g. the bull of Alexander IV for Salamanca (1255) in *Archiv für Literatur- und Kirchengeschichte*, cit., v, pp. 168–9; also the remarks of Rashdall, op. cit., ii, p. 77.

[3] Rashdall, op. cit., i, pp. 8, n. 1, 13 and n. 1; ii, pp. 4, 331 ff.

[4] *Las Siete Partidas . . .*, ed. cit., ii, titulo xxxi, ley 1 (p. 340).

[5] Loc. cit.

power of the *studium particulare* would not be extensive and most 'particular' schools served the needs of a town or a limited region. Many of them appear to have been engaged in the education of the clergy locally as an end in itself, but some were probably geared to the university system. For example, in the Italian universities it was common for students to enrol for a law degree without undergoing the arts course, having already acquired a good proficiency in arts prior to entering the university.[1] A competent arts training, with perhaps elements of legal instruction, could certainly be obtained in some of the town or municipal *studia particularia* of the more advanced type; and it is likely that several of them came to be regarded as feeder schools for the universities. But the view that *studia particularia* had their being only as subordinate institutions dependent on the universities would do violence to the numerous schools which were rooted in local education and fulfilled a self-contained purpose.

The term *studium particulare* was not much favoured by the founders of thirteenth-century *studia*. It is not easy to discover instances in which the title is expressly used when establishing a school: instead, founders, whether municipal authorities or cathedral chapters, tend to use *studium* by itself or else they describe the school with reference to the specific functions for which it was founded, for example, *scolae grammaticales* or *scolae artibus*: sometimes the school is not conceptualized as a definite entity and the foundation is simply announced through the employment of teachers for required disciplines.[2] The impression gained is that the founders of lesser *studia* were disinclined to avail themselves of the title *studium particulare* either because the term had inferior connotations or because it was not naturally current outside juristic circles.

The terminology governing the medieval universities is hedged around with anomalies which presumably reflects an incomplete policy of rationalization superimposed by legal authority on a spontaneous, haphazard movement. In the earliest phase of their existence, the universities were guild organizations without permanent buildings or any of the trappings and encumbrances which are allegedly necessary for their twentieth-century successors. But stripped of all the adjuncts which have cumulated over the centuries, the inflated administrative machinery, the financial, building and

---

[1] E.g. see S. Stelling-Michaud, *L'Université de Bologne et la pénétration des droits romain et canonique en Suisse aux xiiie et xive siècles*, Travaux d'Humanism et Renaissance, xvii (Geneva, 1955), p. 81.

[2] I am indebted to my research student Miss S. Winterbottom for useful information about thirteenth-century 'particular' schools in Aragon and Valencia.

other concerns which so detract from the primary academic purpose, the modern university is, in essence, the lineal descendant of the medieval *studium generale*. For the most part, teachers and students still function in group associations, the acquisition of a degree is still the practical end product of a competitive system whose criteria and standards are those of the teaching guild, and the ceremonial and terminology are strongly evocative of the medieval past. Whatever the differences in scale and technology, there is a hard core of perennial problems which have taxed the minds and ingenuity of university legislators from the thirteenth century to the present day. Matters of organizational form and democratic procedures, the housing and disciplining of the academic population, curricular, teaching and degree arrangements, the acceptable extent of student participation in university affairs, university-community relations and the eternal struggle to preserve university independence vis-à-vis external authorities, these are just some of the issues which reveal the strands of continuity linking the medieval *studia generalia* and the universities of the modern world. Beyond the superstructural layers of the twentieth-century university one arrives ultimately at a derivative from a medieval archetypal form.

2. Salerno: proto-university

Because the school of Salerno in the twelfth century enjoyed a reputation in medicine equal to that of Bologna in law and Paris in theology, it has sometimes been reckoned among Europe's earliest universities.[1] But it would be mistaken to recognize Salerno as a *studium generale* in the fully extended sense of the term. Although the Salernitan school was one of medieval Europe's first and most celebrated centres of medieval study, with a continuous existence until 1812,[2] it did not measure up to the normally accepted view of university status. It is true that, in addition to medical facilities, Salerno had an arts school and in the twelfth and thirteenth centuries was an important reception and distribution point for Greek and Arabic science and philosophy;[3] nevertheless, Salerno did not provide superior faculty teaching in any other discipline than medicine. Moreover, even after the school acquired a measure of legal recognition

---

[1] Even P. O. Kristeller in his otherwise excellent article, 'The School of Salerno: its Development and its Contribution to the History of Learning', *Bulletin of the History of Medicine*, xvii (1945), pp. 138 ff. regards Salerno as 'the earliest university of medieval Europe': see e.g. pp. 138, 145. (cited hereafter as Kristeller).

[2] Of the extensive literature on the Salernitan school see the accounts of S. d'Irsay, *Histoire des universités*, cit., i, pp. 99–110; Rashdall, *Universities*, i, pp. 75–86; Kristeller, pp. 138 ff.; C. Singer, 'The School of Salerno and its Legends' in *From Magic to Science* (London, 1928), pp. 240 ff.; V. L. Bullough, *The Development of Medicine as a Profession*, cit., pp. 49 ff.

[3] See e.g. Kristeller, esp. pp. 151–63, 169–71 and B. Lawn, *The Salernitan Questions*, cit., passim.

as a centre of medical study from the Emperor Frederick II in 1231,[1] the degree awarding powers of the Salernitan doctors were circumscribed by royal decree, and it was not until 1359 that unfettered liberty was conceded to confer degrees and to grant medical licences valid for the whole kingdom.[2] Organizationally, Salerno was remarkably slow to achieve any kind of maturity. Before 1200, evidence of organization is sparse, and it seems clear that a medical *collegium doctorum* was not established until late in the fifteenth century.[3] Although institutional growth was piecemeal in the majority of medieval universities, in the case of the Salernitan school the process was elongated to such an extent that it was incompatible with university standing.

The weakness of Salerno was that it failed to encompass its medical and allied intellectual achievements, at their apogee in the twelfth century, with a cementing organization which would have ensured progressive development towards full university rank. The arrested nature of the Salerno school invites comparison with those distinguished twelfth-century schools which, for one reason or another, were not transformed into *studia generalia*. But it would be misleading to equate Salerno with an unfulfilled Hereford or Rheims: it was a good deal more than a frustrated cathedral school. Rather it was a hybrid society which, among universities, was an institution *sui generis*. It was a university *manqué* in that it was probably given a limited recognition by some as a *studium generale* in medicine alone[4] (which sounds rather paradoxical) but not as a *studium generale* in the comprehensive sense. The history of medieval universities reinforces that institutional response must follow quickly upon academic achievement if the intellectual moment is not to be dissipated. The absence of regular organization may initially provide a fillip for free-ranging inquiry, but perpetuation and controlled development can only be gained through an institutional framework. The late twelfth and early thirteenth centuries was the period when university organization was taking positive shape in Europe, but the school of Salerno seems to have contributed little to the movement other than the corpus of materials which formed the main ingredient of the medical curricula of the medieval universities.[5] There is

---

[1] See J. L. A. Huillard-Bréholles, *Historia Diplomatica Friderici II*, 7 vols., (Paris, 1852–61), iv, p. 150; Kristeller, pp. 171 ff.
[2] Kristeller, pp. 180–1.
[3] Ibid., pp. 186–7.
[4] The school is described as a *studium generale* in medicine in a statute of 1280 granted to Salerno by Charles I of Anjou: ibid., p. 178.
[5] See e.g. d'Irsay, op. cit., i, p. 109; Kristeller, p. 158.

no proof that Salerno pioneered medical faculty organization: indeed, it is likely that its own later organizational features were derived from the established universities.

The school of Salerno does not easily fit into the academic categories of the middle ages. Although it was one of Europe's oldest institutes of higher learning, it remained basically a specialized centre of medical study which acquired some of the attributes of a university, but which, though often grouped with Paris, Bologna, Montpellier and Oxford, could not technically be described as a *studium generale*.

The origin of the Salernitan school is wrapped in oblivion, but the view that it was founded by four masters, a Greek, a Latin Christian, a Jew and an Arab, is now discarded as legendary.[1] The legend, however, graphically points to the mixture of cultural streams which fused in southern Italy and Sicily and formed the milieu in which the Salernitan medical renaissance had its being. Some continuity in medical practice, as in other areas, had endured in this region of *Magna Graecia*, from the Graeco–Roman world. There are many notices of physicians in southern Italy in documents of the ninth and tenth centuries,[2] although these do not prove the existence of a school at Salerno. But the testimony of the chronicler, Richer of Rheims, reveals that Salerno as a celebrated centre of medical practitioners was known in northern France late in the tenth century.[3] The Salernitan school may have existed earlier, but the available fragmentary evidence consigns it to the second half of the tenth century.[4] At the time of the emergence of the medical school, Salerno was already established as a main political and ecclesiastical force in southern Italy.[5]

In the early years of its existence Salerno was noted for its practical medical skill rather than for academic learning.[6] The school was an assemblage of medical practitioners, and presumably there was some rudimentary kind of teaching given, but there is as yet no evidence of formalized instruction or guild association, or of a corpus of medical literature specifically related to Salerno. Although the Salernitan school was to acquire a definite lay character, its composition at the outset was apparently mixed. Many of the early doctors are described as *clerici*, but the number later diminished probably as a consequence of the prohibition on the study and practice of

---

[1] This legend is discussed by Singer, 'The School of Salerno and its Legends' in op. cit., pp. 241–3, and by Kristeller, p. 143.
[2] Kristeller, loc. cit.　　[3] Ibid., pp. 143–4.　　[4] Ibid., p. 145.
[5] A good summary of Salerno's position is given in ibid., p. 145, n. 27.
[6] Ibid., p. 145.

medicine which, from the twelfth century, was progressively applied to the clergy.[1] In the eleventh century the first signs of medical literature occur, although problems of dating and authorship are legion.[2] Among these early treatises is the controversial work on gynaecology known as *Trotula*. This has given birth to the thesis that the treatise was written by a woman doctor and teacher of Salerno of the eleventh century named Trotula who was the wife of Matthaeus Platearius, a Salernitan writer and teacher with whom she produced the *Regimen Sanitatis Salernitum*, an encyclopaedic work on medicine.[3] The alleged existence of one *magistra* of medicine has led to speculation about a series of women doctors and teachers at Salerno, the so-called 'Ladies of Salerne'.[4] Although the tradition of Trotula as a woman doctor can be traced back in medical literature to the thirteenth century, there is no proof from the eleventh and twelfth centuries which would establish Trotula as an historical personage,[5] or at least as a doctor and teacher as opposed to a midwife and herbalist. It is possible that 'Trotula' referred not to a person at all but to the collected works of a Salernitan doctor, Trottus.[6] There are, however, objections to this thesis, some of them quite serious, and the identification of 'Trotula' is still unresolved. There were doubtless women of Salerno who specialized as midwives or who practised simple herbal cures and folk-medicine, and their activities have been recorded in several Salernitan texts.[7] But there is nothing to prove that such women were either teachers or authors of medical treatises. On the other hand, one cannot ignore the fact that professional women were granted royal licences to practise surgery at Salerno in the early fourteenth century, and in 1422 Costanza Calenda is named as a Salernitan doctor.[8] In view of this later evidence, the possible existence of earlier women doctors cannot be lightly dismissed. But the idea that this proto-university of Salerno owed its pristine prominence to a colony of distinguished women doctors is one which belongs more to the realm of historical fiction than to historical fact.

[1] Ibid., p. 146 and n. 29.
[2] Ibid., pp. 146 ff.
[3] See the arguments of K. C. Hurd-Mead, 'Trotula', *Isis*, xiv (1930), pp. 349 ff.
[4] For a sceptical view of the 'Ladies of Salerne' see Singer, 'The School of Salerno and its Legends' in op. cit., pp. 243–4; also G. W. Corner, 'The Rise of Medicine at Salerno in the Twelfth Century', *Annals of Medical History*, new series, iii (1931), pp. 1 ff. at pp. 13–14.
[5] See the comments of Kristeller, p. 148, n. 39.
[6] See the arguments of Singer, art. cit., p. 244 and the counter arguments of Hurd-Mead, art. cit., p. 356, n. 16.
[7] See Corner, art. cit., pp. 13–14.   [8] Kristeller, p. 148, n. 39.

The earliest literature at Salerno is concerned more with medical practice than with theoretical considerations. It combines elements of surviving Greek and Graeco–Roman medicine with contemporary skills, and the frequent modifications of the texts indicate that adjustments were made in the light of developing medical experience. The growth of this literature in the eleventh century was probably accompanied by more methodical teaching arrangements; there is, however, nothing to indicate regularly appointed teachers, a fixed curriculum, or degree procedures.

A vitalizing new dimension was added to the Salernitan medical school towards the end of the eleventh century with the introduction of Latin versions of numerous treatises on Arabic science and medicine and of Greek medical works which had been translated into Arabic. This literary activity was mainly the achievement of Constantine the African,[1] the scholar of Arabic descent who settled in Salerno c. 1077 prior to moving to the monastery of Montecassino where he did much of his translating work before his death in 1087. Constantine appears to have taught medicine at Montecassino, but it is not certain that he did so at Salerno. Among his translations from the Arabic the most influential medical treatises were the *Viaticus* of Al Dschaafar, the compilations of Isaac Judaeus on diets, fevers and urines, and above all, the enormous encyclopaedia of medicine of Haly Abbas written at Baghdad a hundred and fifty years previously, containing sections on anatomy, the pulse, fevers, symptoms and crises, and surgery, and entitled by Constantine the *Pantegni*. The translations of Greek works from the Arabic were not so innovatory as a number of writings of Hippocrates, Galen and other Greek physicians had been in regular circulation before the eleventh century. Nevertheless, Constantine's translations of Hippocrates including the *Aphorisms*, the *Prognostica* and the treatise on acute diseases, along with commentaries and treatises of Galen, gave a new impetus to the study of Greek medicine at this point in time. The translations of Constantine the African provided the Salernitan doctors with a vast increase in medical data and stimulated a vigorous literary movement which manifested itself in the writing of at least fifty medical works in the following hundred years. Of profound consequence was the marriage of Greek and Arabic medicine which the translations made possible. Before the late eleventh century Salernitan medicine had been conducted in a direct practical manner which did not lend itself easily to academic exposition. But Arabic medicine was characterized by a system-

---

[1] On the work of Constantine the African see ibid., pp. 151 ff. and d'Irsay, op. cit., i, pp. 104–6; Corner, art. cit., p. 3.

atic formalism and theoretical texture which served to qualify the empiricism of the school of Salerno without destroying the commonsense basis of its medical régime.[1] Arabic influence was not, however, pronounced in Salernitan literature before the second half of the twelfth century, and even then early medical tradition was by no means swamped by the Arabic admixture;[2] rather it was integrated as a constituent element in a Graeco–Arabic synthesis which furnished a body of material suitable for academic treatment. The appearance in the twelfth century of medical commentaries by doctors of Salerno first on indigenous Salernitan treatises and then on the Greek and Arabic translations of Constantine is a sound measure of the extent to which instruction at Salerno was moving from a practical to a theoretical plane.[3] This involved the adoption of the 'scholastic' method of dialectical analysis and logical classification which was similarly infiltrating most areas of contemporary learning such as theology, law, and grammar. The group of Greek and Arabic texts made available by Constantine together with this growing body of accompanying commentary became the foundation of the medical curricula which were being established in the universities in the second half of the thirteenth century. For this reason, it appears that Salerno's primary contribution to university development lay in the formation of a medical curriculum that was subsequently exported to Paris and hence to the other universities which developed medical studies.[4]

The Salernitan contribution in the twelfth century was not confined to the field of medicine: it embraced Greek and Arabic science and philosophy. The earliest Latin translation of Ptolemy's *Almagest* was made by a student of Salerno.[5] But the most impressive addition to philosophical literature is contained in the works of the Salernitan master Urso of Calabria.[6] He appears to be one of the earliest western authors to make extensive use of Aristotle's writings on natural philosophy. A number of his medical treatises are strongly infused with Aristotelian conceptions and, with colleagues of the Salernitan school, he greatly facilitated the

[1] See e.g. Corner, art. cit., esp. pp. 5, 11.
[2] Kristeller, p. 155.
[3] On the growth of the commentary at Salerno see ibid., pp. 156–9. The earliest known Salernitan commentary (early twelfth century) is that of Matthaeus Platearius on the *Antidotarium Nicolai*.
[4] Ibid., p. 158.
[5] Lawn, *The Salernitan Questions*, p. 31; Kristeller, p. 160; C. H. Haskins, *Studies in the History of Medieval Science*, cit., pp. 159, 191.
[6] For the work of Urso of Calabria see Kristeller, pp. 161–2; Lawn, op. cit., index references.

transmission of Aristotelian doctrines in western Europe before the emergence of the universities. In purely medical terms, Urso made a powerful individual contribution towards establishing the science of medicine on a rational philosophical basis.

The Salernitan school reached its apogee in the twelfth century. Its medical literature was then at its most extensive, a regular curriculum was in the process of formation, and intellectual horizons had broadened out to embrace Greek and Arabic natural science and philosophy. The school had become a centre of distribution, an exporter of ideas and of scholars. For example, Gilles of Corbeil, who studied at Salerno, was the first known teacher of medicine at Paris *c.* 1180.[1] But despite its position as the foremost medical school in twelfth-century Europe there is still no reliable evidence of organizational growth or of a *collegium* of physicians with degree- and diploma-awarding powers. Clearly, individual teachers held classes for groups of students seemingly staged on a private *ad hoc* basis. Presumably, there evolved some unofficial co-operation among the Salernitan teachers, but nothing approaching regular guild organization.

Although little is known about teaching methods in the twelfth-century Salernitan school, something of the prevailing medical and surgical content may be gleaned. Physiology and pathology were grounded on the theory of the four humours, blood, phlegm, yellow and black bile:[2] and disease was connected with an unusual amount of one or more of these humours in the patient.[3] Diagnosis was commonly made on the basis of pain, fever, the pulse or urine.[4] Before the translations of Constantine the African the Salernitan doctors had apparently possessed rudimentary anatomical texts derived from simplified versions of Galen's treatises on anatomy.[5] These were probably supported by anatomical demonstration using animal dissection.[6] But Constantine's work opened up to Salerno a vitalizing corpus of Arabic theoretical anatomy which was compounded with Greek and Graeco–Roman anatomical survivals thus producing an integrated structure similar to that which occurred over the whole medical field. This

---

[1] D'Irsay, op. cit., p. 109 and 'The Life and Works of Gilles of Corbeil', *Annals of Medical History*, vii (1925), pp. 362 ff.; Kristeller, p. 158, n. 75.
[2] Corner, 'The Rise of Medicine at Salerno in the Twelfth Century', art. cit., p. 6.
[3] Ibid., p. 7.
[4] Loc. cit.
[5] Ibid., pp. 10–11.
[6] Loc. cit.; Kristeller, pp. 156, 162. C. Singer, however, denies that dissection took place at Salerno: *A Short History of Anatomy from the Greeks to Harvey*, 2nd ed. (New York, 1957), p. 68.

anatomical advance, however, was not sustained at Salerno throughout the medieval period, and in the thirteenth century the impetus passed to Bologna and Montpellier. For the greater part of the thirteenth century anatomical study in the universities was of an exclusively theoretical nature.[1] It is only towards the end of the century that evidence of human dissection is available, and the earliest reference is found at Bologna *c.* 1300.[2] Dissection of the human body probably began as part of the forensic investigations necessary for legal processes; and in the course of time the post-mortem examination was incorporated into the realm of anatomical study.[3] Human dissection was fairly common at Bologna by the end of the first quarter of the fourteenth century, and was later extended to Padua and Montpellier.[4] Bolognese teachers such as Thaddeus of Florence (Taddeo di Alderotto, 1223–1303) and his celebrated pupil Mondino di Luzzi (*c.* 1270–1326),[5] the author of the *Anothomia* (1316), a pioneering manual of anatomical instruction, helped to establish anatomy as a systematic discipline suitable for university study and exposition, and firmly geared to dissection as the ultimate demonstrable form of proof. The arrested development of anatomy at Salerno is symptomatic of the general decline which seems to have overtaken the medical school in the thirteenth century and led to the dispersal of specialized medical study among Europe's new universities.

From surviving manuscript material something may also be deduced about surgical practice at twelfth-century Salerno. The section on surgery in Constantine's *Pantegni* provided a textbook for Salerno, but the earliest extant indigenous product appears to be the anonymous collection now titled the *Bamberg Surgery* (*c.* 1150).[6] This is not a systematic treatise: rather it is a random assemblage of notes, memoranda, prescriptions and extracts from a variety of authors. The collection ranges over theoretical matters, diagnosis, practical prescriptions and operative technique. Among the conditions specifically treated are wounds, fractures and dislocations, surgical lesions of the eye and ear, diseases of the skin, haemorrhoids, sciatica, hernia and bloodletting. The *Bamberg Surgery* reproduces much established Greek and Arabic procedures, although often in an ambiguous or inaccurate way. There are, however, innovations: for example, pioneering

---

[1] Singer, *A Short History of Anatomy*, p. 70.
[2] Loc. cit.   [3] Ibid., pp. 70–1.   [4] Ibid., pp. 71, 87, 88.
[5] Ibid., pp. 72 ff.; Rashdall, *Universities*, i, pp. 236, 237, 245.
[6] On the *Bamberg Surgery* see G. W. Corner, 'Salernitan Surgery in the Twelfth Century', *British Journal of Surgery*, xxv (1937–8), pp. 84 ff. at pp. 85–9.

accounts are given of a truss for inguinal hernia, for the treatment of goitre with substances containing iodine, and for a form of surgical anaesthesia, that is to say, the 'soporific sponge' soaked in juice of hyoscyamus and poppy. The near contemporary *Surgery* of Roger Frugardi,[1] a compilation of the teachings of this eminent surgeon when resident at Salerno, was reduced to written form *c.* 1170 by Guido Aretino, a teacher of logic. Roger's *Surgery* was widely used at Salerno, Bologna and other universities throughout the medieval period. In part, it derives from the *Pantegni*, but for the rest it is of Greek origin allied to current surgical practice. Unlike the *Bamberg Surgery*, Roger's treatise is a systematic exercise in operative and medicative surgery and is entirely practical in character: it was particularly useful for the treatment of wounds and fractures of the skull. The most popular work on gynaecology and obstetrics was that currently known by the name of *Trotula* to which reference has already been made. It seems to be based largely on a few surviving fragments of Greek obstetrics supplemented with borrowings from Constantine: it is not a production of markedly high medical calibre.[2] The early Salernitan attention to common sense precepts and folk wisdom on health, diet, hygiene and the use of drugs was sustained as a peripheral accompaniment to the scholarly core of Graeco–Arabic medicine, and found its fullest written expression in the thirteenth-century rhyming compilation, the *Schola Salernitana* or *Regimen Sanitatis Salernitanum*.[3]

Although the thirteenth century witnessed a dilution in the monopolistic sway of Salernitan medicine and the passing of the centre of medical gravity to the emergent universities, it also provides the first definite proof of belated institutional development at Salerno. The earliest legal recognition of the Salernitan school is contained in the constitutions of Melfi issued by the Emperor Frederick II in 1231.[4] Salerno was accorded the position of chief medical centre in southern Italy and Sicily; no one was permitted to teach medicine or surgery outside Salerno, and the title of master was reserved for those who submitted to examination by a board of Salernitan masters and royal officials. While royal officials participated in the examining procedure, it seems that the master's title, the necessary prerequisite for teaching, was awarded by the school itself, although later in the century,

---

[1] On the *Surgery* of Roger Frugardi see ibid., pp. 91–7.
[2] See the comments of Corner, 'The Rise of Medicine at Salerno in the Twelfth Century', art. cit., p. 13.
[3] Ibid., p. 14. On the dating and composition of the *Regimen Sanitatis* see Kristeller, pp. 169–70.
[4] See above, p. 38, n. i. Salerno is not, however, described as a *studium generale*.

under Charles I of Anjou, this was made temporarily dependent on royal decree.[1] This was different from the regulations governing the granting of the licence. The licence to practise medicine at places other than Salerno was ultimately a matter for royal authority: the candidate was first examined before the Salernitan masters and then, armed with a certificate testifying to his loyalty and knowledge, signed by the masters and royal representatives, he presented himself to the king for the licence. These arrangements both for the mastership and the licence show a degree of royal intervention and paternalism incompatible with autonomous status which, in these matters, was not obtained until 1359.[2] And if, from at least the thirteenth century, the teaching masters at Salerno formed, with royal representatives, *de facto* examining commissions, a permanent *collegium doctorum*, legally recognized as an anticipated body in 1442,[3] was not established until late in the fifteenth century as a fully independent entity with its own statutes, privileges and sole right to award degrees and licences.[4]

In *c.* 1241 Frederick II enacted a regular curriculum of study for medicine which, although Salerno is not mentioned by name, would certainly have applied at this time to the Salernitan school.[5] A major point of interest is that three years of training in logic are prescribed prior to five years spent in medical instruction. This is the first evidence that a subject other than medicine was formally taught at Salerno, and seems to be the earliest documented example of that close curricular link between logic and medicine which became so marked a feature in the medieval universities. By 1277 teachers of arts are found at Salerno and separate degrees in arts were instituted.[6] It was quite common practice at Salerno and the Italian universities for a student in arts to qualify as a teacher of logic, embark on medical studies, and finally emerge as a teacher of medicine.[7] An analysis of Salernitan degrees reveals that between 1473 and 1811 the most common degree was a combined one in arts (philosophy) and medicine.[8] Separate degrees in arts (philosophy) or medicine at Salerno and in southern Europe generally were perhaps regarded as being less than academically complete. Arts was a preparation for either law or medicine, and law and medicine must be firmly grounded in arts. The history of the medical school at Salerno well illustrates the involvement of medicine with logic and natural philosophy which was so fundamental to the medical curricula of the universities in the middle ages.

---

[1] Kristeller, p. 176.   [2] Ibid., pp. 180–1.   [3] Ibid., p. 185.   [4] Ibid., p. 186–7.
[5] See Huillard-Bréholles, op. cit., iv, pp. 235–7; Kristeller, pp. 174–5.
[6] Kristeller, p. 176.   [7] Ibid., p. 178.   [8] Ibid., p. 187.

In a statute of 1280 conferred on the school of Salerno by Charles I of Anjou the school is for the first time specifically designated a *studium generale* in medicine.[1] Whatever this phrase precisely means, it is clear that Salerno was never to be anything more than a severely truncated form of university. Salerno did not measure up to the fully-fledged concept of a medieval university; and not until late in its development was it able to keep at bay royal interference in its teaching and medical practice. But it has its importance as an agent for the transmission of Graeco–Arabic medical and scientific data to western Europe on a considerable scale and as the institution under whose roof coalesced the main ingredients of the medical curricula of the medieval universities: its teachers and doctors restored, integrated, enlarged upon and made available for academic consumption the best of Greek, Graeco–Roman, Arabic and contemporary medical doctrine and practice. As an influence on medical faculty organization in the universities, however, its impact was minimal: indeed, the organization that was built up in the universities was fed back into the Salernitan school and provided the model for its belated institutional growth. In the context of European education Salerno commands attention as one of the earliest medical centres and professional schools in the middle ages; in several respects it was an embryonic university that failed to keep pace with the creative institutional movement so necessary to harness the intellectual forces from which the universities were sprung. External factors such as the sack of the city of Salerno by the Emperor Henry VI in 1194, the proximity of the University of Naples (founded 1224), which led to unsettling complications for Salerno, and Frederick II's struggle with the papacy, which subjected southern Italy to much disruptive warfare, may have contributed to Salerno's decline, but they are unlikely to have been crucial. The central weakness of Salerno was its failure to develop a protective and cohesive organization to sustain its intellectual advance.

[1] Ibid., p. 178.

III

Bologna: student archetype

The idea that the medieval university system was the offspring of monopolistic clerical control is rudely shattered when one considers that Bologna, the earliest university of all, was in origin a lay creation designed for the career interests of laymen studying Roman law. It was not until the 1140s that canon law, the preserve of clerical teachers and students, was entrenched at Bologna as a discipline alongside the Roman law. But before the establishment of this twin legalistic base the Bolognese *studium* was essentially lay both in terms of its personnel and in the direction of its thought.[1] This is partially to be explained by the fact that the educational framework of northern Italy, which had been sustained by the continuity in city life in the centuries following the collapse of the western Roman Empire, was of a predominantly municipal and lay character: the educational content was grammatical and rhetorical in emphasis, and was frequently turned towards the production of practical legal skills such as pleading in the courts and the compilation of official documents.[2] The revitalization of municipal life in Europe in the eleventh and twelfth centuries brought to the cities of northern Italy an expansion in the career opportunities for laymen trained in the Roman law; and this increased professional demand stimulated a heightened school activity in the area

[1] See e.g. W. Ullmann, *Principles of Government and Politics in the Middle Ages*, 1st ed. (London, 1961), p. 228.
[2] See d'Irsay, *Histoire des universités* . . ., cit., i, pp. 78–80; H. Rashdall, *Universities*, i, pp. 108–11; D. Knowles, *The Evolution of Medieval Thought*, cit., p. 158.

between Rome and the Alps, and especially in the centres of Ravenna, Pavia and Bologna.

But in addition to this professional boost to lay educational life in northern Italy, there was, from the late eleventh century, a powerful impetus to lay intellectual development arising from the polemical turmoil of the Investiture Contest. As Roman law was the best available ideological weapon with which to confront papal hierocratic doctrine, this legal system became the natural concern of laymen involved in generating an embryonic political theory to refute the claims of papal governmental thought.[1] Roman law by itself was to prove too narrow a base and was too theocratically inspired to provide an effective counter to the hierocratic system, which had reached a point of sophisticated maturity and strength after centuries of evolutionary refinement.[2] But these early attempts by lay scholars at north Italian *studia* to forge a lay thesis of the world order furnished an intellectual groundwork of promising growth potential which helped to create the preconditions for the university movement in Italy. Against this background of intensified professional and polemical activity it is natural to ask why the schools of Bologna rather than those of Pavia and Ravenna, which had attained an earlier prominence, emerged as Europe's first fully-fledged university. Considerations of site may be tentatively adduced. It is clear that Bologna was excellently situated, forming as it did a cross-roads in northern Italy through which passed a floating population of some magnitude, including a steady concourse of pilgrims travelling to Rome.[3] As the plain of Lombardy had for centuries been an important exchange centre for merchants north of the Alps and Italian traders carrying Byzantine products, Bologna would have been exposed to social and economic cosmopolitanism from an early date.

While the site factor was favourable for the advancement of the Bolognese schools it is unlikely to have been crucial. Considerations of personnel and academic specialism were often of greater importance than situation in determining the location of the earlier *studia generalia*. A highly mobile academic society, which had not yet accustomed itself to the idea of permanent concentrations of masters and students on any scale, would not be particularly site-conscious: only when universities came to be specifically founded did site surveys assume priority proportions in the founding process and considerations such as adequate accommodation, food sup-

[1] Ullmann, *A History of Political Thought: The Middle Ages* (Pelican Books, 1965), p. 118.
[2] Loc. cit.
[3] D'Irsay, op. cit., i, p. 78; Knowles, op. cit., p. 159.

plies, a healthy climate, the availability of financial facilities and a reasonably stable environment enter into the final decision.[1] The Bologna law school seems to have crystallized from the private teaching enterprise of a nucleus of individual masters who effected a transition from education of a primarily literary character to one specializing in Roman law.[2] And it was the teaching residence of the most outstanding of these early jurists, Irnerius, who taught at Bologna between 1116 and 1140, which probably above all enabled Bologna to surpass the other Italian law schools. For it was Irnerius who, by commenting comprehensively upon Justinian's *Corpus Juris Civilis*, using a method of critical analysis reminiscent of the *Sic et Non* of Abelard, succeeded in evolving for students of civil law a more manageable synthesis of inherited public and private Roman law than had hitherto existed.[3] The basic Roman legal texts were now made available in a form suitable for professional study as a clearly defined area of higher education; and this emergence of a quasi-curricular basis for Roman law, allied to the apparently charismatic qualities of Irnerius as a teacher, established the pre-eminence of Bologna as a centre for civilian studies to which students began to congregate from distant parts of Europe. The entrenchment of Roman law at Bologna proceeded apparently unhampered by the theoretical dilemma which it posed. For Justinian, in the constitution *Omnem*, had sought to confine the teaching of law to the 'royal' cities of Rome, Constantinople and Beirut.[4] This problem for the Bolognese jurists had been circumvented by the early thirteenth century with the firm adoption of the legend that Bologna had been accorded the status of *civitas regia* by the Emperor Theodosius, an historical interpretation which, on the testimony of Odofredus, had been in general currency at the time of Azo and Johannes Bassianus.[5] From then onwards Bologna

---

[1] E.g. geographical considerations were of some importance in the decision to found a university at Pécs (papal bull of foundation issued 1367): see A. L. Gabriel, *The Mediaeval Universities of Pécs and Pozsony* (Frankfurt am Main, 1969), pp. 15 ff. On general prerequisites of university foundations see e.g. P. Classen, 'Die ältesten Universitätsreformen und Universitätsgründungen des Mittelalters', *Heidelberger Jahrbücher*, xii (1968), pp. 72 ff. at pp. 79–80.

[2] See recently J. K. Hyde, 'Early Medieval Bologna' in *Universities in Politics: Case Studies from the Late Middle Ages and Early Modern Period*, ed. J. W. Baldwin and R. A. Goldthwaite (Baltimore, 1972), p. 21.

[3] On Irnerius and Bologna see e.g. Rashdall, op. cit., i, ch. 4, pp. 87 ff.; d'Irsay, op. cit., i, pp. 85–6; H. Kantorowicz, *Studies in the Glossators of the Roman Law* (Cambridge, 1938), ch. 2, pp. 33 ff.

[4] See conveniently Hyde, op. cit., p. 27.

[5] Loc. cit.; also W. Ullmann, 'The Medieval Interpretation of Frederick I's Authentic

was regarded as the supreme *civitas regia*, the *nutrix et mater legentium*, a view reinforced by the reality that, because of the divisive political and religious situation, the law schools of Constantinople and Beirut had ceased to have much practical impact on western Europe.[1]

From the 1140s and 1150s the intensely lay character of Bologna was substantially qualified by the infusion of canon law studies and their rapid growth as a major academic counterpart to Roman legal thought. This development was spearheaded by the codifying achievement of the monk Gratian who was a teaching master of canon law at the Bolognese monastic school of San Felice. His *Concordia Discordantium Canonum* (the *Decretum*), completed *c.* 1140, performed for canon law a service similar to that which Irnerius effected for the Roman law by providing a convenient synthesis appropriate for academic consumption.[2] Just as Irnerius, who had perhaps a predecessor in the shadowy Pepo,[3] had helped to make Bologna the leading centre of Roman legal studies in the twelfth century, so Gratian rendered it an almost equally important focus for canon law. The papacy could henceforth rely upon a strong output of Bolognese trained canonists, the best of whom were themselves to contribute to canon law and who were among the main exponents of the hierocratic system. In the two centuries following the establishment of canon law at Bologna a high proportion of the popes were jurists, several of whom had been law professors at Bologna or at some other *studium generale*.[4]

The Authentic *Habita*[5] – the constitution issued by the Emperor

---

"Habita" ' in *L'Europa e il diritto Romano: Studi in memoria di Paolo Koschaker* (Milan, 1954), i, pp. 101 ff. at p. 114 and n. 3.

[1] Ullmann, art. cit., p. 115.

[2] On Gratian and Bologna see e.g. Rashdall, op. cit., i, ch. 4, pp. 126 ff.; d'Irsay, op. cit., pp. 89–90.

[3] On Pepo see H. Kantorowicz and B. Smalley, 'An English Theologian's view of Roman Law: Pepo, Irnerius, Ralph Niger', *Mediaeval and Renaissance Studies*, i (1941–3), pp. 237 ff.

[4] Ullmann, *A History of Political Thought: The Middle Ages*, cit., p. 119.

[5] For the Authentic *Habita* see Ullmann, 'The Medieval Interpretation of Frederick I's Authentic "Habita" ' in op. cit.; F. Koeppler, 'Frederick Barbarossa and the Schools of Bologna: Some Remarks on the "Authentic Habita" ', *E.H.R.*, liv (1939), pp. 577 ff.; Rashdall, *Universities*, i, pp. 143–5, 180–81; Denifle, *Die Entstehung der Universitäten des Mittelalters bis 1400*, cit., pp. 45 ff.; d'Irsay, op. cit., i, pp. 90–1; Hyde, 'Early Medieval Bologna' in op. cit., pp. 32 ff.; F. M. Powicke, 'Bologna, Paris, Oxford: Three *Studia Generalia*' in *Ways of Medieval Life and Thought* (London, 1949), pp. 149 ff. at pp. 153–7; P. Kibre, *Scholarly Privileges in the Middle Ages*, Mediaeval Academy of America (London, 1961), pp. 10–17. See further the critical remarks of A. Marongiu on Professor Ullmann's interpretation, 'A proposito dell' Authentic Habita' in *Atti*

Frederick I at Roncaglia in November 1158, apparently at the request of the *scholares* of Bologna, and inserted in the *Codex* of Justinian and confirmed by the papacy – came to acquire, by means of the sometimes elastic interpretations of medieval jurists, a fundamental academic significance which far transcended its original import. For the cumulative juristic interpretation of the *Habita* led to the formulation of a *privilegium scholarium* to rank equally alongside the older established *privilegium clericorum*.[1] In this respect, the *Habita* came to be venerated as the origin and fount of academic freedom in much the same way as Magna Carta became an indispensable reference point for English liberties. But when first proclaimed in 1158 (there is a dubious possibility that a draft of the *Habita* was circulated in 1155) Frederick's constitution had a more circumscribed purpose. The rapidly growing strength of canonistic studies at Bologna after the publication of Gratian's *Decretum* presented a serious competition to Roman law. As it was central to Hohenstaufen political ideology to promote Roman (civil) legal studies as an effective counter to the canonists, the chief propagators of papal hierocratic doctrine, it was necessary to afford an adequate protection to the non-Bolognese Roman law students who had gathered in such numbers to study in Bologna, but who, as aliens, were legally defenceless under city law.[2] The clerks pursuing canonistic studies were already protected by canon law, but the lay students of Roman law had none of these protective advantages.[3] By means of the Authentic *Habita* Frederick Barbarossa sought to confer on foreign Roman law scholars a greater measure of security when travelling to an academic centre and a protection within the university town from humiliations and malpractices such as reprisals for debt. The exemption of the Roman law scholars from reprisals was buttressed by heavy penalties against those who perpetrated them and against those officers who failed to effect restitution. In the course of time, the Authentic *Habita* was extended to embrace all lay scholars in whatever faculty.[4] The imperial grant (*beneficium*) to 'all scholars and especially those who profess the sacred and divine (civil) laws who are pilgrims for the sake of study (*causa studiorum peregrinantur*)'

---

del convegno internazionale di studi Accursiani, ed. G. Rossi, (Milan, 1968), i, pp. 99–112; and see Professor Ullmann's reply, ibid., pp. cvi f.

[1] E.g. Ullmann, art. cit., pp. 103–4.
[2] The most convincing explanation of the imperial motives which inspired the *Habita* is given ibid., pp. 104 ff.
[3] Ibid., esp. pp. 104, 106–7.
[4] Professor Ullmann discusses juristic opinion on this matter ibid., p. 132; see also Kibre, op. cit., p. 11, n. 28.

was scarcely innovatory since security of travel was covered by Justinian's codification.[1] Later juristic opinion endowed this provision with the meaning that scholars journeying to a *studium* were to be exempted from paying tolls, although this is nowhere stated in the *Habita*.

Hohenstaufen ideology is firmly embedded in the constitution.[2] It is expressly asserted that the study of Roman law (*sacrae et divinae leges*) will lead men to be obedient to God and to the emperor (*ad obediendum Deo et nobis*). The emperor is described as the minister or servant of God, a doctrine which postulates that imperial power was derived directly from God and not through the intermediary of the Church. This imperialist posturing, this propagandist hub of the document, must make us wary about the apparently altruistic motives which inspired the *Habita* in which Frederick is pointing to his concept of world dominance based on the primacy of the civil (Roman) laws over the canon law.

One of the most valuable privileges granted by the *Habita* was that which increased a scholar's choice of judicial authority.[3] A scholar, when sued, might choose as judge either his own teacher or the local bishop. The judicial option of the *podestà* remained intact since the *Habita* did not quash this jurisdiction: it added judicial choices to it. By the fourteenth century, the student rector had emerged as a fourth customary judicial option. For some time, it seems that the provisions of the *Habita* applied to criminal as well as civil cases involving scholars, but later its terms were restricted to civil suits.[4] Clerical scholars came under the jurisdiction of the bishop in the *studium*.[5] Although Frederick's constitution was designed primarily with Roman law scholars in mind, juristic opinion generally agreed that its benefits should be extended not only to *bona fide* students in other faculties, but also to their servants, and the scribes, booksellers and members of the various trades which served the academic population. This extension was based on the statement in the *Habita* that the imperial protection embraced the *nuntii* of the scholars.[6] These jurisdictional arrangements of the *Habita* developed an ecumenical application

[1] Ullmann, art. cit., pp. 110–11.
[2] Ibid., esp. pp. 108–10.
[3] On this subject see ibid., pp. 123 ff. Koeppler (art. cit., pp. 604–5) argues that Frederick's privilege was granted in 1155 minus this judicial section, but that these judicial clauses were added in 1158 in response to a worsening situation in Bologna. But the evidence for the alleged award of 1155 is tenuous.
[4] Ullmann, art. cit., pp. 125–6; Rashdall, op. cit., i, p. 180.
[5] For canonistic views on this point see Ullmann, art. cit., pp. 130–31.
[6] Ibid., pp. 133–4.

and became a basis for the rights of jurisdiction claimed by university authorities over their students throughout the medieval period. In the course of time, the powers of the bishops in the affairs of the universities were whittled away, and episcopal jurisdiction devolved upon the university courts, which became the normal tribunals for academic cases.

The Authentic *Habita* is a negative source for the degree of organizational maturity achieved at mid-twelfth-century Bologna. Although Frederick's constitution was a response to the Bolognese situation, it is couched in general terms and neither Bologna nor any other centre of learning is specifically mentioned. One may conjecture that the rather amorphous type of assembly of masters and scholars referred to in a papal letter of Clement III in 1189–91 was already a feature of Bologna when the *Habita* was issued;[1] but, if so, there was no precise imperial recognition of the fact in 1158. The most that can perhaps be extracted from the *Habita* is that by enabling students to select their teachers as judges the jurisdictional powers exercised by individual doctors over their own students were firmly consolidated. It may be that the Bologna doctors did not, at this early juncture, seek a formal imperial incorporation. The habit of academic mobility was too basic to be easily superseded by notions of institutional permanency. And the Authentic *Habita* left the Bologna *studium* a loosely structured confederation of individual doctors and their students supported by the minimum of concerted organization.

The socio-economic and political context within which the Bolognese university germinated cannot be easily reconstructed, but one may draw attention to the growth of the new political and social forms which emerged, phoenix-like, as a response to the waning effectiveness of the imperial government in northern Italy. German imperial power, superimposed upon the late Roman system, was drastically weakened by the events of the Investiture Contest which brought havoc and civil war to several of the Italian cities, including Bologna. In these near-anarchical conditions the formation of mutual protection associations, such as the tower societies and confraternities, was at a high premium. The most important type of collective reaction to the deteriorating situation was the commune.[2] Communes were generated in cities or wider areas as a spontaneous answer to a local power vacuum, and they were rapidly characterized by their demo-

---

[1] The pope ordered the letter to be read annually 'in communi audientia magistrorum atque scholarium': see Rashdall, op. cit., i, p. 148 and n. 2.
[2] For the characteristics of the north Italian communes see Hyde, 'Early Medieval Bologna' in op. cit., pp. 24–5.

cratic, anti-feudal nature. Initially, associations for the defence of their members, the communes gradually assumed governmental responsibility for defined territorial units. It was within the shadow of the emergent Bolognese commune[1] that the schools of Bologna acquired the legal concentration upon which the *studium* was founded. And the organizational form of the nascent university was shaped by immediate environmental considerations. For there is a close parallel between the efforts of the Bolognese law students to achieve a necessary protective organization and the initiatives of the Bolognese citizens who sought collective protection through the medium of the commune.[2]

It was from the protective organization called into being by the law students that there evolved the whole parade of student controls which is the especial distinguishing feature of Europe's first university.[3] When the conditions of student life in northern Italy in the second half of the twelfth century are examined, the growth of organizational student power becomes intelligible. A key to the understanding of the rise of the student-university at Bologna lies in the prevailing concept of Italian citizenship, a precious possession in a country increasingly fragmented by the communal movement.[4] As the status of citizen afforded personal protection and safeguarded property, non-citizens, lacking that legal security, were vulnerable in the face of city law. The students who had converged on Bologna from diverse regions of Europe were legal aliens and consequently the future of the Bolognese educational endeavour was placed at risk. In a society witnessing a mushroom growth in communes and urban craft and trade guilds, it was natural that the law students should band together to form protective associations or *universitates*, which subsequently sub-divided into nation groupings presided over by elected rectors.[5]

Originally, the Bolognese law students had no common organization and merely entered into contracts with individual teaching doctors.[6] They

[1] In existence, it seems by 1116: the evidence is discussed ibid., pp. 29–32.
[2] This parallel is well brought out in ibid., passim.
[3] Medieval student power is the subject of ch. 7, pp. 163 ff. Part of the following discussion on the student power situation at Bologna has been adapted from my article, A. B. Cobban, 'Medieval Student Power', *Past and Present*, no. 53 (1971), pp. 28 ff.
[4] See e.g. Rashdall's account, *Universities*, i, pp. 150 ff.
[5] For the probable influence of the municipal guilds on the student-universities see ibid., i, pp. 161 ff.; A. Sorbelli, *Storia della Università di Bologna*, i (Bologna, 1944), pp. 154–6; Hyde, 'Early Medieval Bologna' in op. cit., passim.
[6] On Bologna contracts see F. E. von Savigny, *Geschichte des Römischen Rechts im Mittelalter*, 2nd ed. (Heidelberg, 1834–51), iii, esp. pp. 254–60; also S. Stelling-Michaud,

later formed *societates*, loose associations which acquired a legal character by virtue of their collective responsibility for the debts of their members.[1] During this early phase, the natural authority of the masters over the students was preserved intact.[2] But this simple doctor-student relation was radically transformed when these fluid *societates* evolved into the higher structural form of the student guilds designed to give a more effective protection against potential enemies.

As far as one can judge, relations between the students and the doctors in the twelfth century were harmonious and both had an interest in discouraging encroachments of the commune. In 1182, however, the commune tried to exact an oath from the doctors which would have prevented them from teaching outside Bologna for two years.[3] This met with only partial success, but from 1189 the commune was able to impose an oath on the doctors whereby they had to restrict their teaching to Bologna and refuse to aid their students to study elsewhere in Italy.[4] The commune had come to appreciate the economic and prestigious advantages to be derived from the permanent settlement of the university in the city of Bologna;[5] and the oath was to be the instrument by which teaching and student stability would be ensured. The policy of the communal oath was the major turning point in the Bologna situation. It was the beginning of a process whereby the doctors were gradually deprived of their independent status vis-à-vis the commune.[6] If there had existed at this time a powerful doctoral college through which both Bolognese and foreign teachers could have presented a corporate resistance to the encroaching jurisdiction of the commune, the future of the *studium* might well have

---

L'Université de Bologne et la pénétration des droits romain et canonique en Suisse aux xiiie et xive siècles, cit., p. 26. (cited hereafter as Stelling-Michaud, *L'Université de Bologne*).

[1] The *societates* are analyzed by G. Rossi, ' "Universitas Scolarium" e Commune', *Studi e memorie per la storia dell'università di Bologna,* new ser., i (Bologna, 1956), pp. 175, 186-7. (cited hereafter as *Studi e memorie*). See also Stelling-Michaud, op. cit., loc. cit.

[2] Rossi, art. cit., p. 175.

[3] Savigny, op. cit., iv, pp. 312-14.

[4] Rossi, art. cit., p. 189; Stelling-Michaud, *L'Université de Bologne*, p. 27. See examples of the oath imposed by the commune on Bolognese doctors in the late twelfth and early thirteenth centuries in M. Sarti and M. Fattorini, *De Claris Archigymnasii Bononiensis Professoribus a saeculo xi usque ad saeculum xiv,* 2nd ed., C. Albicini and C. Malagola (Bologna, 1888-96), ii, pp. 26-7, 31, 33, 240.

[5] E.g. Rossi, art. cit., p. 181.

[6] See Stelling-Michaud, op. cit., p. 27 and the same author's 'L'histoire des universités au moyen âge et à la renaissance, au cours des vingt-cinq dernières années', cit., pp. 110-11.

followed a different course. But as the doctors were in no position to pose as the champions of academic freedom, this defensive mantle fell upon the student body. The students anticipated that in any clash with the commune the doctors would be led by their interests to range themselves with the municipal authorities. In these circumstances, the foreign law students assumed the initiative and certainly towards the end of the twelfth century and probably by 1193,[1] they appointed themselves a *universitas scolarium* which, in a remarkably brief interval of time, imposed its will on the doctors.[2] The pristine contractual arrangements between individual students and doctors were now superseded by organized and militant student guilds (*universitates*) sufficiently powerful to command doctoral obedience to their members. By 1204 the guilds of law students had probably grouped themselves into four *universitates*,[3] and by the mid-thirteenth century these had further coalesced into two confederations, the *universitas citramontanorum* for students of the Italian peninsula and the *universitas ultramontanorum* for the non-Italian students, each with its own elected student rector at its head.[4] The student-universities may have come into being without provoking overmuch immediate antagonism from the commune, but in the early thirteenth century relations became progressively strained. The generally hostile climate led to student migrations to Vicenza in 1204 and Arezzo in 1215.[5] In 1217 and 1220 the commune attempted to impose on the student rectors the oath prohibiting departure from Bologna for study in another city.[6] The rectors refused to comply on the grounds that such an oath would be a negation of academic freedom threatening the independent corporate status of the student body. But after a confused period in which the students appealed to the papacy, the matter was settled by compromise.[7] It seems that the commune was able to insist on the rectorial oath which, however, failed to eradicate the migratory drives of the *studium*. On the other hand, the persistent student unrest, allied to the political struggles including the conflict with the Emperor Frederick II,[8]

---

[1] Rossi, art. cit., p. 191 (adopting the conclusion of A. Gaudenzi).
[2] One of the best studies of the evolution of the *universitas scolarium* is that provided by Rossi, art. cit., passim.
[3] See Rashdall's discussion, *Universities*, i, pp. 154–6.
[4] For the Bologna nations see Rashdall, op. cit., i, pp. 154–61, 182–3; Kibre, *The Nations in the Mediaeval Universities* (Mediaeval Academy of America, Cambridge, Mass., 1948), chs. i, 2.
[5] Rashdall, op. cit., i, pp. 169–170.
[6] Kibre, *Scholarly Privileges in the Middle Ages*, cit., pp. 18–19.   [7] Ibid., pp. 19–20.
[8] Relations between the commune and Frederick II are traced by G. de Vergottini, 'Lo Studio di Bologna, l'Impero, il Papato', *Studi e memorie*, new ser., i, pp. 19 ff., passim.

forced the commune to adopt a more conciliatory policy; in the city statutes of 1250 there was a general recognition of the entrenched student position and, in particular, of the jurisdictional powers of the student rectors, so long as this did not extend to rectorial authorization to transfer the *studium* elsewhere.[1] And in 1252 and 1253 the statutes of the student jurist universities were officially recognized by the commune and the papacy.[2] By 1245, and perhaps by 1241–2, the vital concession of protection under city law had been granted to the foreign students:[3] that is to say, the foreign students were to enjoy the advantages of citizenship while being exempted from some of its burdens.[4]

In the opening years of the thirteenth century, the position of the law doctors was uncertain. They had initially no corporate organization with which to neutralize the student guilds. The fact that many of the doctors were Bolognese citizens, who already had adequate legal protection, presumably acted as a restraint on the formation of doctoral organization. A college of doctors of laws had emerged by the mid-thirteenth century and may have been in existence as early as 1215:[5] there would almost certainly have been a rudimentary association of doctors in the later twelfth century necessary for the regulation of examining procedure and the promotion to the mastership; but of this probable customary society there is no firm documentation. However weak, the doctoral organization of the thirteenth century enabled the doctors to maintain a hold over the conduct of examinations and admission to their professional circle, but did little to modify the near-monopoly control which the students came to exercise over the affairs of the *studium*. The exclusion of the doctors from the student guilds, although there may have been exceptions,[6] had not been an inevitable

---

[1] Rossi, art. cit., p. 189 and n. 2; Stelling-Michaud, *L'Université de Bologne*, pp. 27–8. The communal statutes of 1245, while forbidding the students to take oaths to obey a rectorial order to secede from Bologna, recognize the right of the foreign students to elect rectors: Rashdall, *Universities*, i, p. 172; Kibre, *The Nations in the Mediaeval Universities*, cit., p. 7.

[2] Kibre, *Scholarly Privileges in the Middle Ages*, p. 24.

[3] For a discussion of this complex matter see Rossi, art. cit., pp. 219–20; also Rashdall, op. cit., i, p. 172; Kibre, *The Nations in the Mediaeval Universities*, p. 8.

[4] Much information on the civic privileges and exemptions accorded to the foreign Bolognese students is given by Kibre, *Scholarly Privileges in the Middle Ages*, ch. 2, pp. 18 ff.; see also Ullmann, 'The Medieval Interpretation of Frederick I's Authentic "Habita" ' in op. cit., p. 113.

[5] Rashdall, op. cit., i, pp. 145 ff.

[6] See Hyde, 'Early Medieval Bologna' in op. cit., p. 40; Rashdall, op. cit., i, p. 158, n. 3. Doctors, who had full Bolognese citizenship (the majority) would, *ipso facto*, be excluded from the *universitates*.

student decision. But the doctors had shown themselves antithetical to the student guilds from the start,[1] partly for the human reason that the presence of these corporations constituted a threat to the pre-eminent position of the teachers in the *studium*. Instead of a cohesive academic community synthesizing, the students and doctors split asunder and the latter perceptibly gravitated towards the orbit of the commune.

If the doctors in the twelfth century controlled examining procedure and entry to their professional grouping, it is not clear that they actually granted the teaching licence. This may have been awarded by ecclesiastical authority, although the point has not been proven.[2] Whatever the case, ecclesiastical supervision of the licence was either instituted or confirmed by papal authority on 28 June 1219 when Honorius III decreed that no one might assume a teaching function in the city of Bologna unless he had first obtained the licence from the archdeacon of Bologna who was required to make a thorough examination of the candidate.[3] It may be that a main point of the document is the concern with a previous lack of rigorous examination.[4] For the careful archidiaconal examination was designed to prevent those from teaching who were *minus docti* and who had a detrimental effect on the doctoral title and on the scholars who were subjected to their inferior instruction. A very different interpretation is that which regards the central importance of the papal bull as an attempt to end the 'unfettered liberty' of the doctors by bringing the Bologna *studium* 'within the ecclesiastical system' and so into alignment with Paris and the clerically impregnated education life of northern Europe.[5] On balance, this is perhaps too dramatic a view and does not allow for the probable operation of some ecclesiastical influence over the affairs of the *studium* in preceeding years; nevertheless, the bull of 1219 unequivocally stressed what ecclesiastical connection there may previously have been and regularized the place of the Bolognese *studium* within the papal orbit. The archdeacon of Bologna came to be styled chancellor; and, though a lesser figure, he occupied a similar position with regard to the *studium* as did the

---

[1] The hostility of the doctors towards the student associations is revealed in Buoncompagno's *Rhetorica Antiqua* read at Bologna in 1215: see Rossi, art. cit., p. 187, n. 4 (on p. 188).

[2] See the *Additional Note* by Rashdall's editors in *Universities*, i, pp. 231–2.

[3] '... nisi a te obtenta licentia, examinatione prehabita diligenti ...' This bull of Honorius III is printed by Sarti and Fattorini, op. cit., ed. cit., ii, p. 15 and by Rashdall, op. cit., i, p. 586.

[4] The opinion of G. Manacorda: his argument is summarized in Rashdall, op. cit., i, p. 231.

[5] See Rashdall's discussion, ibid., i, pp. 221–3.

chancellor of the cathedral of Notre Dame to the masters' guild at Paris. Apart from a dispute in 1270,[1] relations between the archdeacon and the doctors and students appear to have been amicable.

Initially, the law student guilds at Bologna were essentially mutual benefit societies, charitable associations designed to maximize protection for their members under city law and as a general defence mechanism against hostile parties. The fraternal character of the student guilds is nowhere better illustrated than by the statutes and proctors' accounts of the German nation, the most privileged of the units of the ultramontane university.[2] The Bolognese student movement did not, *ab initio*, set out to gain dominion over the *studium* and its teaching staff. There was not here the striving of impatient student youth to organize university matters according to a formulated ideology. No blueprint plan was produced as to how ideally a university ought to be organized. Possibly the students never debated this sociological question. But, given the delicate and at times desperate situation in which they found themselves, their achievement of power was a logical progression. In order to survive, a trade union attitude was inescapable, and this motivated the students to carve out for themselves a bargaining strength counter within the university. Once this had been attained, once the organizational strength was there, the power momentum could not be circumscribed. In the course of the thirteenth century, the students were galvanized from the defensive to the offensive, and this resulted in their acquiring a controlling authority in the affairs of the *studium*, thereby effecting what might graphically be called the first student takeover bid in history. Because of the tenuous nature of the evidence, the details of this phased assumption of power cannot be easily pieced together. In general terms, however, the bid for student dominance was born of the antagonism which arose between the students and their teachers and between the students and the commune.

Both the commune and the doctors contested the alleged right of the students to organize themselves into a corporation with elected officers, statutes and independent legal status. The idea of a student-university was one which violated the professional sense of the teaching doctors.[3] It was agreed that the students by themselves did not constitute a profession and,

---

[1] Ibid., i, p. 222.
[2] See *Acta nationis Germanicae universitatis Bononiensis ex archetypis tabularii malvezziani* (ed. E. Friedländer and C. Malagola, Berlin, 1887). The statutes (1497) are printed pp. 1–15; the accounts, dating from 1289, pp. 35 ff. See also Rashdall, op. cit., i, pp. 159–61.
[3] See e.g. Rashdall, op. cit., i, p. 164.

ipso facto, had no legal right to elect rectors or to frame statutes. The students were merely the pupils (*discipuli*) of the doctors, the academic equivalents of trade apprentices, and, as such, were devoid of professional status. These views were propounded by Bolognese jurists of the calibre of Johannes Bassianus, Azo, Accursius and Odofredus: for example, Odofredus states, 'those who exercise a profession elect judges, but pupils (*discupuli*) do not exercise a profession, therefore they do not elect judges'.[1] The equation of students with artisans may have been polemically convincing, but it ignored the material difference in their circumstances; for whereas trade apprentices were economically dependent on master craftsmen, in the university context, the situation was reversed as the teaching doctors were the financial prisoners of the student population. The doctoral reluctance to give a *de iure* recognition to the student guilds and to rectorial jurisdiction merely accentuated student militancy: and the prolonged efforts to subject the office of student rector to the commune provoked violent student reaction and had to be abandoned.[2] With the temporary crumbling of communal resistance the teaching doctors were obliged to acquiesce in a university structure wherein they were manifestly employed as student functionaries.

It needs to be affirmed here that a fair number of the Bologna law students were older than the majority of modern undergraduates. It has been reckoned that their average age lay between eighteen and twenty-five and some of them were on the borders of thirty upon entry to the university.[3] Many of the Bologna students were already equipped with an advanced arts training before embracing their university studies;[4] and it is established that a sizable proportion held ecclesiastical benefices or offices upon their enrolment as law students.[5] That legal studies might

[1] Sarti and Fattorini, op. cit., ed. cit., i, p. 93, n. 1. Quotations from the commentaries of medieval civil lawyers with reference to this academic debate are given by Savigny, *Geschichte des Römischen Rechts im Mittelalter*, cit., iii, ch. xxi, p. 174, n. a. Rossi (art. cit., pp. 191–2) discusses, with extracts, the views of Bassianus, Azo and Odofredus.
[2] Savigny, op. cit., iii, p. 175.
[3] Stelling-Michaud, *L'Université de Bologne*, p. 81 and 'L'Université de Bologne et la suisse, à l'époque de la première réception du droit romain', *Studi e memorie*, new ser., i, p. 561.
[4] Loc. cit.
[5] Stelling-Michaud, *L'Université de Bologne*, pp. 81, 89–90 and art. cit., p. 556; also G. de Vergottini, 'Lo Studio di Bologna . . .', *Studi e memorie*, new ser., i, pp. 88 ff., 93–4. Barcelona cathedral canons are found at Bologna as early as 1218. Ramón de Torrelles (precentor at least from 1233–35) had been a student at Bologna in 1220–1: J. Miret i Sans, 'Escolars Catalans al Estudi de Bolonia en la xiiiª centuria', *Boletín de la Real Academia de Buenas Letras de Barcelona*, viii (1915–16), pp. 137 ff. at pp. 142–3, 147.

extend for five to ten or more years (and longer if interrupted by a migration) is a circumstance which further reinforced the mature nature of the student body. A significant number of the students in the thirteenth century were laymen which is reflective of the almost exclusively lay character that the Bolognese schools had possessed before the fixation of canon law studies in the 1140s. These lay students were sometimes affluent, living with an entourage in rented houses or apartments, and making a visible impact on city society. Many of them came from easy social backgrounds and were the sons of prosperous urban bourgeoisie or, like so many of the German students inscribed in the records of the German nation, were scions of noble families.[1] It is therefore apparent that a goodly proportion of the Bologna law students were young men of substance with experience of the world and accustomed to administering responsible offices in society. The elevated social plateau from which many of the law students emanated, their mature years, and the prior participation of some of their colleagues in community business, furnished a promising launching pad for the assumption of controlling power when the circumstances dictated that course of action to be unavoidable.

The Bologna students fashioned a type of university in which sovereign power was vested in the student community.[2] In conception, the Bologna *studium* was severely democratic, but, as will be demonstrated below, the everyday administrative business came to be concentrated in small executive committees comprising the student rectors and their supporting officials (*consiliarii*), who were the elected representatives of the nations. The teaching doctors were, for a good part of the thirteenth century, mere hirelings, elected annually by the students[3] and dependent upon student

Further examples of canons, priests and clerics from Spanish cathedral schools (mainly Gerona and Vich) will be found in *Chartularium Studii Bononiensis*, 10 vols. (Bologna, 1909–36), v (1921), nos. 1575, 1576; vii (1923), no. 2372; x (1936), no. 3999. Spanish scholars at Bologna in the thirteenth century are also cited by P. Linehan, *The Spanish Church and the Papacy in the Thirteenth Century* (Cambridge Studies in Medieval Life and Thought, 3rd. series, vol. 4 (Cambridge, 1971), pp. 78, 139, n. 3, 289, n. 4.

[1] On the lay element at Bologna see Stelling-Michaud, *L'Université de Bologne*, pp. 123–4 and art. cit., pp. 552, 556, 562. For the German students see *Acta nationis Germanicae . . .*, cit., passim.

[2] The constitutional features of Bologna are reconstructed by Rashdall, *Universities*, i, ch. 4, esp. pp. 176 ff.

[3] See e.g. the procedure for student election to chairs in the jurist statutes (1317–47) in *Archiv für Literatur- und Kirchengeschichte des Mittelalters*, iii, ed. H. Denifle and F. Ehrle (Berlin, 1887), rub. xl, pp. 304–8 and in *Statuti delle università e dei collegi dello studio bolognese*, ed. C. Malagola (Bologna, 1888), pp. 36–8 (cited hereafter as *Archiv* and *Statuti* respectively). See also the statutes of the university of arts and medicine (1405),

fees (*collectae*) for their university income;[1] the students seem to have elected their prospective teachers several months in advance of the beginning of the academic session in October.[2] Upon election, the successful doctors took an oath of submission to rectorial jurisdiction in all matters affecting the life of the *studium*.[3] The statutory controls imposed by the students on the doctors were formidably rigorous and, collectively, they amount to what, in a restricted sense, might be termed a quasi-totalitarian régime.

The earliest extant jurist statutes for Bologna are those of 1317 with additions up to 1347;[4] as already mentioned, jurist statutes were recognized by the commune and the papacy in 1252 and 1253 respectively. The statutes of 1317, drafted by a student committee of fourteen with the assistance of the canonist Johannes Andreae, do not constitute a complete code, but they are closely akin to the one produced in 1432. There is every reason to believe that the statutes of 1317 are a full-bodied reflection of the student governmental system as it had evolved in the thirteenth century. It is probable that they are a more accurate guide to thirteenth-century practice than to the power situation in the *studium* in the early fourteenth century. For by 1317, student dominion had undergone serious reverses at the hands of the commune which had led to a partial restoration of magisterial authority. The statutory evidence for Bologna is richly supplemented by the statutes of the university of arts and medicine of 1405.

Under the student governmental system the doctors were excluded from voting in the university assemblies, although they may have been allowed, by invitation, to attend as observers: yet all teachers had to obey the statutory wisdom that emanated from these student congregations. Student controls over the lecturing system were impressive. The lecturer's life must have proceeded in an anxious atmosphere of impending fines. A lecturer was fined if he started his lectures a minute late or if he continued after the prescribed time: indeed, if the latter occurred, the students had a

---

rub. l in *Statuti*, pp. 257–9. There is no statutory material extant for the thirteenth century.

[1] See Rashdall, op. cit., i, p. 208; also G. Post, 'Masters' Salaries and Student-Fees in the Mediaeval Universities', *Speculum*, vii (1932), pp. 192 ff.

[2] In the university of arts and medicine doctors were elected in May of each year: *Statuti*, rub. l, at p. 257. It is probable that the jurist arrangements were similar.

[3] For the oath sworn by the law doctors to the student jurist rectors see *Archiv*, iii, rub. xlii, pp. 308–10 and *Statuti*, rub. xxxiv, p. 247.

[4] The Bolognese statutes are described by Rashdall, *Universities*, i, pp. 173–4. The editions are cited in n. 69.

statutory obligation to leave the lecture room without delay.[1] At the opening of the academic session the students and the teaching doctors reached agreement on the material to be presented in the lecture courses and the way in which it was to be distributed over the year.[2] The material was divided up into a number of sections or *puncta*, each of which, at Bologna, had to be completed within the space of a fortnight, and which meant that the lecturer must reach stipulated points in the set texts by certain dates in the session. Failure to adhere rigidly to the *puncta* brought with it the threat of heavy fine.[3] It would hardly be an exaggeration to say that lecturing performance in thirteenth-century Bologna was continuously assessed by the students on both a qualitative and quantitative basis. A doctor who glossed over a difficulty or who failed to ascribe an equal emphasis to all parts of the syllabus would incur financial penalties for his lack of expertise.[4] Moreover, if a lecturer neglected to cover the ground by omitting a group of lectures, he was liable to repay some or all of his student fees, depending on the degree of his negligence.[5] As a surety for his lecturing conduct the lecturer, at the beginning of the session had to deposit a specified sum with a city banker, acting for the students. From this deposit a student review court, headed by the rectors, would authorize the deduction of fines incurred by the lecturer for infringements of the statutes. If the fines were of such an order of magnitude that the first deposit was used up, the lecturer was required to make a second deposit.[6] Refusal to comply was pointless: no lecturer, with fines outstanding, was permitted to collect fees, and thus his source of university income would be cut off. In any event, a recalcitrant doctor could be rendered less obstinate by means of the student boycotting machinery that was fundamental to the operation of the student-university. Even in normal circumstances, it seems that a lecturer was required to attract an audience of at least five students at every ordinary lecture and three at every extraordinary lecture: if, on any occasion, he failed to do so, he was deemed to be absent and incurred the stipulated fine.[7] This whole gamut of student controls was

[1] *Archiv.*, iii, rub. xliv, pp. 313–15; *Statuti*, pp. 41–3 (jurist), rub. xli, pp. 253–4 (arts and medicine).
[2] *Archiv.*, iii, rub. ci, pp. 379–80.
[3] As in n. 1.
[4] *Archiv.*, iii, rub. xlv, pp. 316–17; *Statuti*, pp. 43–4 (jurist).
[5] *Archiv.*, iii, rub. cv, pp. 387–9.
[6] *Archiv.*, iii, rub. xliv, pp. 313–15; *Statuti*, pp. 41–3 (jurist), rub. xliii, pp. 254–5 (arts and medicine).
[7] This is according to city regulations: Rashdall, op. cit., i, p. 196.

underpinned by a system of secret denunciations. That is to say, four students were secretly elected to act as spies on the doctors and were bound to report finable irregularities arising from such matters as bad lecturing technique and failure to complete the *puncta* or to give the specified number of disputations.[1] The rectors were obliged to act on the denunciation of only two of the students 'that the disobedience of the doctors may be punished'.

Student permission was required for almost every doctoral act. For example, if a doctor sought to absent himself from Bologna for a few days during term time he had to obtain the prior consent of his students, and then the permission of the rector and his officials. Upon leave being granted, the doctor was bound to deposit a sum of money against his promised return within the agreed time.[2] Students were urged, as part of their public academic conscience, to denounce doctors who absented themselves without leave or who acted in any other way contrary to the statutes. In this matter of doctoral accountability to the student body one imagines that the dividing line between a lecturer's public and private life could not always be clearly delineated. At Bologna, the student machine must have encroached upon the twilight areas of activity that were only marginally related to a teacher's public capacity. The students do not appear to have been concerned about these obtrusive overtones of the statutory régime.

Why were university teachers prepared to submit to this kind of student dominion? They rejected the legitimacy of the student-university and yet they consented to serve as its acolytes. Even if we allow that the actuality of the student government was not as inflexible as the statutory models depict, the employment of lecturers in a university situation whose *de iure* basis they could not condone needs some explanation.

The crucial reason for the submission of the teaching doctors to student power stems from the circumstance that in southern Europe student controls derived ultimately from the economic stranglehold the students had over their lecturers. Before the salaried lectureship became the established norm, the majority of teachers depended for their academic incomes on teaching fees collected from their students.[3] The threat of boycotting of lectures, which would extinguish that income, hung like the sword of

[1] *Archiv.*, iii, rub. xxii, p. 284; *Statuti*, pp. 23–4 (jurist), rub. lxviii, p. 270 (arts and medicine).
[2] *Archiv.*, iii, rub. xlviii, p. 323; *Statuti*, rub. xlvii, pp. 109–10 (jurist).
[3] See Post, art. cit., esp. pp. 192 ff. Sometimes the doctors lent money to their students and charged higher *collectae* by way of interest: Savigny, op. cit., iii, p. 257.

Damocles over the university teachers as a permanent reminder of where their economic interests lay. As a result, the money relationship between students and lecturers dictated the distribution of power. Against the disadvantages of student controls one has to balance the consideration that a successful lecturer in a populous university like Bologna could expect to earn a good remuneration from student fees,[1] although as Odofredus so vividly testifies, the students were not always willing to pay their dues.[2] As a group, university teachers did not easily put down roots: many of them stayed in one *studium* for only a year or two before migrating to another which offered better terms. Few of them seemed to regard university teaching as a permanent career, and they often divided their energies between bouts of academic and non-academic employment, for example as communal ambassadors.[3] The ease with which lecturers migrated from one *studium* to another or alternated between the university and the wider community may go some way towards explaining why teaching staff were prepared to put up with student controls for a limited period. Moreover, in medieval Italy, the subjection of those exercising public office to rigorous controls, such as the important communal officials, the *podestà*, and *capitani del popolo* and their judicial personnel, was not considered degrading, merely a healthy measure of accountability.[4] Similarly, university lecturers, as teachers, had an authority and respect deriving from their knowledge and professional expertise; but, as elected office holders, they were just as answerable to the students for the exercise of their academic trust as were their colleagues in the public sector to the general body of citizenry.

By the mid-fourteenth century the Bologna situation had been radically transformed. Arising from the establishment of lectureships salaried by the commune in the last quarter of the thirteenth century,[5] the students

---

[1] For the Bolognese situation see Stelling-Michaud, *L'Université de Bologne*, p. 44.

[2] '... scholars (*scholares*) are not good payers (*pagatores*) because they wish to learn but they do not wish to pay for it; all want to learn, no one wants to pay the price' (Odofredus): see Sarti and Fattorini, *De Claris . . .*, i, p. 166, n. 6; Savigny, op. cit., iii, ch. xxi, p. 254, n. c; Post, art. cit., p. 192 and n. 4.

[3] See the remarks on the Paduan law doctors by J. K. Hyde, *Padua in the Age of Dante* (Manchester, 1966), esp. pp. 125, 147. On the tenures of doctors at Florence University in the second half of the fourteenth century see G. A. Brucker, 'Florence and its University, 1348–1434' in *Action and Conviction in Early Modern Europe*, ed. T. K. Rabb and J. E. Seigel (Princeton, 1969), p. 231. On extra-university activity of Bologna doctors see Kibre, *Scholarly Privileges in the Middle Ages*, pp. 49–50, and p. 50 notes 154, 155.

[4] See the comments of Hyde, 'Early Medieval Bologna' in op. cit., pp. 41–2.

[5] The commune had contemplated introducing salaries in the 1220s, but this had not materialized: ibid., p. 44.

progressively lost their controlling power over the appointment of the teaching staff. By 1300, the salaried lectureship was an integral part of the life of the *studium*. For some time, the students continued to choose the doctors while the commune paid their salaries; this phase was superseded by direct nomination of teaching doctors by the commune, although the students were still entitled to propose candidates: by 1350, however, almost all the doctors were appointed and salaried by the commune.[1] In the second half of the fourteenth century the commune wielded a near monopoly control over the affairs of the *studium*. The authority of the student rectors was greatly diminished[2] and the bristling array of student controls was reduced to a titular set of hollow forms. In the fifteenth century the student-universities continued to exercise authority over certain external attributes of academic life such as those relating to the book industry in Bologna and to the regulation of money lenders and money changers (*feneratores* or *mercatores*).[3] The doctoral colleges, however, arrogated to themselves firm direction of the substance of academic affairs including the composition and arrangement of the lecture courses, the methods of lecturing and teaching, and degree requirements.[4]

In Bologna and in the student-universities of the Bolognese type the exercise of power tended to be more concentrated in the hands of a few long-tenured executive officials than in the family of magisterial universities based on the Parisian model. Even during the high noon of student dominion at Bologna the theoretically democratic form of government was offset by the consideration that the small executive committees or councils of the student rectors and their lieutenants, the *consiliarii*, who were the elected representatives of the nations (called proctors in the case of the German nation) functioned as the hub of daily administrative government. The student population would be assembled to vote on issues of major importance, but the cumbersome nature of this procedure, involving copious student numbers, made the summoning of the sovereign body a less frequent occurrence than at Paris where there were numerous congregations and therefore regular and active participation by members of the masters' guild. As a result, less reliance was placed at Paris upon administrative continuity and the turnover in executive personnel was more

[1] See Rossi, ' "Universitas Scolarium" e Commune', art. cit., p. 239.
[2] Ibid., p. 240. On the loss of student powers from 1350 onwards see G. Le-Bras, 'Bologne: Monarchie médiévale des droits savants', *Studi e memorie*, new ser., i, p. 16.
[3] See Kibre, *Scholarly Privileges in the Middle Ages*, p. 49.
[4] Loc. cit.

rapid than at Bologna, although tenures of Paris offices tended to lengthen from the later thirteenth century. In general, Bologna exhibited a clear cut governmental system, wherein administrative office at every level was subject to closely defined checks and balances ensuring a maximum degree of public accountability: but while embodying a model of extreme academic democracy, the Bolognese machine was nevertheless rather top-heavy in terms of effective power distribution. By contrast, Paris and its university derivatives were characterized by less legalistically precise and more variegated governmental forms where power was diffused over the component parts of the structure giving rise to a real if somewhat ramshackle democratic process.

The constitutional device of the nation, which was extensively woven into the medieval university fabric, was probably first crystallized at Bologna.[1] In origin, the nations were societies of the non-Bolognese law students which assumed a definite shape in the early years of the thirteenth century and which evolved from earlier spontaneous groupings of students who had come together for defensive purposes. It was from the combinations of these nation units that there emerged the guilds or *universitates* of foreign law students, which, by the mid-thirteenth century, had confederated into two major groupings, the *universitas ultramontanorum* and the *universitas citramontanorum*, each directed by its own student rector and supporting officers. As constituent parts of the student *universitates* the nations were initially concerned with matters of defence and the mutual welfare of their members. Only when, by the process already described, the student law guilds acquired the dominant voice in the affairs of the *studium* did the nations become channels for the expression of grass root student opinion on academic and governmental matters which, hopefully, would be registered in the university assemblies through the nation representatives, the *consiliarii*.[2] Even so, apart from this measure of democratic involvement by the ordinary non-Bolognese student through his nation, the policy making decisions, the real direction of the *studium* during the heyday of student power, resided not in the nations but in the controlling executive councils of rectors and *consiliarii*. Although the Bolognese nations provided a forum for canalizing the groundswell of student feeling, which may have contributed in some measure to the formulation of policy in the *studium*, their main importance, beyond fraternal functions, was to furnish

[1] For the Bologna nations see p. 57, n. 4.
[2] On the *consiliarii* see Kibre, *The Nations in the Mediaeval Universities*, pp. 10–14, 43–6, 49–50, 52–7, 59–60, 63.

the bases or representative units for the university guilds.[1] If the Bolognese nations were not designed to give the ordinary student a primary participating rôle in university government, the meetings of the sovereign body, the congregations of the two jurist universities and that of the later university of arts and medicine, did not substantially augment the *de facto* level of direct student involvement. For the summoning of these congregations was an administrative inconvenience and was not resorted to more than was necessary. As the consent of one rector and the majority of *consiliarii* was required for the calling of a congregation,[2] the legislative initiative lay firmly in the hands of the executive powers. And while every student member had the right to speak and vote at these assemblies the amount of innovation was limited in that the jurist statutes were designed to have a ten year permanency,[3] increased to twenty years by the statutes of 1432:[4] and even when an interim statutory change was mooted, the assembly merely registered consent to the detailed proposals approved first by the rectors and *consiliarii*, and then by a nominated committee of university members.[5] In these circumstances, the mass meeting was, for the average student, a means by which he was kept informed on the governmental and educational life of the *studium*; but although he could make his voice heard in these assemblies and vote secretly (using ballots – *cedulae* – or white and black beans),[6] most of the policy-making remained with the executive committees. The sovereign body must often have appeared a rather impotent assembly, a passive reflector of the decisions of conciliar government.

If the average non-Bolognese student was less directly involved in the management of the *studium* than would be suggested by the idea of student controls, his counterpart, the student who was a citizen of Bologna, was wholly excluded from the governmental process. Bolognese students, as citizens of the commune, were deprived of full membership of the guilds and nations, although they may have acquired a form of associated status.[7] The reason for exclusion was the subjection to communal jurisdiction which citizenship involved and which was considered incompatible with

---

[1] See Kibre's conclusions ibid., pp. 63–4 and, generally, chs. 1, 2.
[2] Rashdall, op. cit., i, p. 183.
[3] *Archiv.*, iii, rub. xx, p. 281.
[4] *Statuti*, pp. 76–7 (jurist).
[5] Rashdall, op. cit., i, p. 189.
[6] Much fascinating data on voting procedure at Bologna is given by Kibre, op. cit., ch. 2.
[7] See Rashdall, op. cit., i, pp. 157–8.

scholarly protection and privilege. Both the university guilds and the commune adopted a strong line over the jurisdictional quandry of the Bolognese students. As they did not take the oath of obedience to the rectors, the Bolognese students were not accorded voting rights in university assemblies and were not eligible for university offices. Even scholars who acquired full citizenship after ten or more years of residence were deprived of their former rights and privileges in the *studium*;[1] indeed, any student who appealed to communal jurisdiction from a rectorial ruling was liable to be deprived of his scholarly privilege:[2] the guilds were adamant that their members must be placed under the sole jurisdiction of the rectors. The commune's attitude was enshrined in a statute of 1245 which prohibited Bolognese students, as citizens, from taking the oath of obedience to the rector under threat of seizure of goods and banishment.[3] Bolognese students were, however, obliged to swear not to injure the university and their names were listed in a *matricula specialis*.[4]

The two-tier student system in which the Bolognese students were without governmental significance and were scarcely regarded as integral members of the university, must have reinforced the divisive nature of the *studium*. It is true that by the fourteenth century the two student jurist universities, though retaining a *de iure* distinction, had become almost fused with a common code of statutes and common congregations.[5] But when the university of arts and medicine, divided into four nations, was formed in the second half of the thirteenth century, a new entity had come into being which had no constitutional nexus with the law universities, beyond the fact that all students received their degrees from the common chancellor, since 1219 the archdeacon of Bologna.[6] At first, the jurist rectors had attempted to impose their jurisdiction on the university of arts and medicine: but in 1316 the independent position of the medical rector was recognized by the jurist universities and the city magistrates.[7] The structural cleavage in the *studium* was further intensified by the separate development of the doctoral joint college of arts and medicine and by the later faculty of theology. Before 1364, when the theological faculty was established at Bologna, the teaching of theology was vested largely in the conventual schools of the mendicants, which had no official linkage with the

[1] Kibre, op. cit., p. 8.   [2] Loc. cit.
[3] Loc. cit.; also Denifle, *Die Entstehung der Universitäten*, i, p. 144, n. 338.
[4] Kibre, op. cit., pp. 8–9; Rashdall, op. cit., i, p. 158, n. 1.
[5] Rashdall, op. cit., i, p. 176.
[6] On the university of arts and medicine see ibid., i, pp. 233 ff.
[7] Kibre, op. cit., p. 13.

studium.[1] During this time, Paris and the English universities, and it seems Florence from 1359,[2] retained their monopoly right of theological promotion, and students of theology at Bologna would have to graduate at one of these *studia*. But the inception of a theology faculty at Bologna did little to integrate theological studies into the mainstream of academic life because teaching and study continued to be predominantly a mendicant concern, although seculars might be admitted as students or teachers. The college of theological doctors remained apart from the other doctoral colleges and the student-universities and functioned under the authority of the bishop of Bologna. As perhaps befitting a university founded upon the primacy of law, the Bologna *studium* was an amalgam of separate jurisdictions, a series of self-contained empires which collectively had no focal personage analogous to the Paris rector or the Oxford and Cambridge chancellors. Neither the Bologna rectors nor the heads of the doctoral colleges nor the archdeacon of Bologna, as chancellor, symbolized and expressed the unity of the *studium* in which the constituent parts were more important than the whole.

The jurisdictional powers of the Bologna rectors stemmed from an authority vested in the guild statutes which all members of the *universitates* had to obey. This was bolstered by direct oaths of obedience to the rectors imposed upon all non-Bolognese students, the German nobles excepted, and the doctors of the *studium*.[3] By electing rectors, the students were acting analogously to established trades and professions, which, following Roman law, claimed the right to form societies presided over by their own elected officers. As the chief executive officer of the guild, the rector was bound to implement, without discretion, the prescribed penalties for statutory infringements involving a fixed hierarchy of fines, and deprivation or expulsion of a student or doctor. A rector's failure to perform his executive functions to the satisfaction of the guild would be dealt with by syndics appointed to inquire into his conduct at the expiry of his period of office.[4] The rectors exercised jurisdiction over cases in which both parties were university members or university servants and, in addition, claimed

---

[1] On theology at Bologna see Rashdall, op. cit., i, pp. 250–3 and F. Ehrle, *I più antichi statuti della facoltà teologica dell' università di Bologna* (Bologna, 1932).
[2] See the comments of Rashdall's editors, *Universities*, ii, p. 50, n. 1.
[3] E.g. see the form of doctoral oath to be sworn to the rectors, *Archiv.*, iii, rub. xlii, pp. 308–10; *Statuti*, p. 39 (jurist). On the Bologna rectors see G. Zaccagnini, *La vita dei maestri e degli scolari nello Studio di Bologna nei secoli xiii e xiv* (Biblioteca dell'Archivum Romanicum, 5, Geneva, 1926), ch. i, pp. 9 ff.
[4] *Archiv.*, iii, rub. viii, p. 263; *Statuti*, p. 11 (jurist).

exclusive jurisdiction over civil cases in which one of the parties was a scholar;[1] but the commune refused to concede the principle and there was a running conflict over this matter in which the university and city statutes embodied diametrically opposing standpoints.[2] It was not until the fifteenth century that the rectors attained a measure of criminal jurisdiction over cases where both parties were scholars. Rectorial jurisdiction extended beyond the guild proper to embrace public servants of the university, scribes, binders and illuminators and other groups of tradesmen who served the *studium* in various capacities,[3] and also landlords who let rooms or houses to university personnel.[4] This extended jurisdiction was made effective by the powers of interdict or boycotting which the university could bring to bear on those who transgressed the statutory provisions.

The rectors of the jurist universities were elected for a period of two years by a system of indirect election involving wax tablets or ballots.[5] From the late thirteenth century they were elected by groups of nations acting in fixed rotation, the German nation having the privilege of providing the rector every fifth year[6] (it lost this privileged status by the statutes of 1432). The rectors were required to be clerks, so that they might exercise jurisdiction over clerical scholars, unmarried, not professed of any religious order, with five years experience in the study of law, and at least in their twenty-fifth year.[7] Arrangements for the election of the rector of the university of arts and medicine were similar. The rectors were expected to live in considerable state, and until the fifteenth century, largely at their own expense. The financial burden of the office led to an unwillingness to assume the position,[8] and acceptance was made compulsory for suitable candidates with the requisite means.[9] The office often went to a member of an aristocratic family.[10] Because of the financial difficulties, and

---

[1] On the jurisdictional claims of the rectors see e.g. *Archiv.*, iii, rub. x, pp. 264–6; *Statuti*, pp. vii, x, 12–13 (jurist).

[2] Rashdall, op. cit., i, pp. 178–9 and p. 178, n. 5; Kibre, *The Nations in the Mediaeval Universities*, p. 51.

[3] See e.g. legislation on *stationarii* and the book trade *Archiv.*, iii, rub. xix, pp. 279–81; *Statuti*, pp. 20–1 (jurist).

[4] Rashdall, op. cit., i, p. 179.

[5] *Archiv.*, iii, rub. iv, pp. 258–9; *Statuti*, pp. 8–9 (jurist).

[6] *Archiv.*, iii, rub. v, pp. 259–60; *Statuti*, p. 9 (jurist).

[7] *Archiv.*, iii, rub. ii, pp. 256–7; *Statuti*, pp. 7–8 (jurist).

[8] Kibre, *The Nations in the Mediaeval Universities*, p. 47. Padua experienced similar difficulties in finding willing candidates for the rectorship: see Kibre, *Scholarly Privileges in the Middle Ages*, p. 74 and n. 100 (an illuminating case history).

[9] Rashdall, op. cit., i, p. 186.

[10] Kibre, *The Nations in the Mediaeval Universities*, p. 47.

with the decline in student power at Bologna, there was a tendency from the mid-fourteenth century to unite the two jurist rectorships in one individual.[1] By 1500 this had become the norm. With the demise of effective student controls in the later medieval period, the rectorship was increasingly reduced to an honorific office, real authority having been transferred to the doctoral colleges.

The history of the Bolognese *studium* pointedly underlines the turbulent and disruptive conditions in which the medieval student had to live and work. It has been claimed that co-operation was the normal and conflict the exceptional state of most medieval communities including the universities;[2] when applied to Bologna, this judgment is dubious. For in the thirteenth and fourteenth centuries the *studium* was subject to a prolonged series of academic stoppages and migrations, several of which resulted in the foundation of daughter universities, among them Vicenza in 1204, Arezzo in 1215, Padua in 1222 and Sienna in *c.* 1246: Pisa (1343) owed much to the Bolognese migration of 1338. The periodic cessation of lectures and subsequent migrations of colonies of doctors and students to rival cities arose either from direct conflict with the communal authorities, or because factious civic disorder made settled study too difficult, or, less frequently, it resulted from a reaction to unwelcome papal policy. On two occasions, between 1286-9 and 1306-9, the *studium* was closed down for three years following the imposition of a papal interdict on the city.[3] These were exceptionally long closures: nevertheless, there were at least thirteen cessations of the *studium* in the thirteenth and fourteenth centuries as well as some half dozen stoppages because of plague.[4] These are probably minimal figures as some cessations may have gone unrecorded. In any case, they represent only the high conflict points which are indicative of the electric undergrowth of tension and hostility enveloping the Bolognese academic community and which was ever ready to erupt into migratory defiance. The cost in terms of academic frustration, financial difficulty, and social disruption, throws into vivid relief the parlous instability of an Italian study régime of the medieval period. The fight for academic free-

---

[1] Rashdall, op. cit., i, p. 186.
[2] See F. M. Powicke, 'Bologna, Paris, Oxford: Three *Studia Generalia*' in *Ways of Medieval Life and Thought*, cit., p. 167.
[3] Kibre, *Scholarly Privileges in the Middle Ages*, p. 34.
[4] There were cessations and/or migrations in 1204, 1215, 1222, 1258, 1286-9, 1291, 1301, 1306-9, 1312, 1316, 1321, 1338, and 1376-7. Plague stoppages occurred in 1348, 1349, 1372, 1399, 1400 and 1401. (Figures derived from Kibre, op. cit., ch. 2 and Rashdall, op. cit., i, p. 589).

dom was one of depressing longevity. Eternal vigilance was required as positions conceded might go unrecognized by the city magistrates at some point in the future. It is hard to escape the conclusion that conflict figured just as prominently as harmonious co-operation in moulding Europe's first *studium generale*.

IV

Paris: magisterial archetype

As in the case of the Bologna *studium* the constitutional development of Paris University was in large measure a response to conflict. If these archetypal universities had been allowed an early placid existence, unfettered and unharassed by external controls, it is conceivable that they would have slipped quietly into a municipal or ecclesiastical ambit. But the need to combat external encroachments of a stifling nature helped to formulate more sharply views of corporate and individual academic freedom which were fundamental to the growth of the university as a separate estate in the medieval community. In northern Europe ecclesiastical and especially episcopal involvement in university affairs was one of the principal agencies of tension which served to promote an aggressively self-conscious image of the university as an independent republic of letters poised between the spiritual and temporal domains.

With respect to university-episcopal relations in the middle ages we might profitably borrow an analogy from the annals of British imperial history and distinguish between an early embittered 'imperial' era and a succeeding more constructive 'commonwealth' phase.[1] The later medieval episcopate, or 'commonwealth' bishops as we may call them, had come to an acceptance of the principle that the essence and core of a university was its autonomy: although the university might continue to function

---

[1] The substance of this paragraph is derived from my article, 'Episcopal Control in the Mediaeval Universities of Northern Europe', *Studies in Church History*, v (Leiden, 1969), pp. 1–2.

under the tenuous sway of an external authority, it was generally recognized that the academic guild was a legally constituted autonomous entity
standing outside the ecclesiastical structure. Within these terms of reference,
it was the duty of the episcopate to nurse its university offspring towards
maturity and full corporate independence. In many instances, episcopal
aid was a veritable *sine qua non* of university survival. For example, it is
hard to imagine that the fifteenth-century Scottish universities could have
survived at all without the sustained, enlightened treatment that they received at the hands of their episcopal sponsors. The Scottish bishops of the
fifteenth century had no thought of effecting a permanent episcopal
stranglehold over the universities they had brought into being. On the
contrary, they freely gave of their wealth and energies in the realization
that adequate endowments and organizational maturity would inevitably
bring full independent status to these university guilds. To this extent,
the bishops who founded the universities of St Andrews (1413), Glasgow
(1451) and Aberdeen (1494–5) are truly representative of the magnanimous
and liberal episcopal outlook which pervaded the university scene in
northern Europe towards the close of the medieval period. This contrasts
strikingly with earlier episcopal attitudes. For in the thirteenth and fourteenth centuries episcopal authority had all too often been channelled in
a direction antithetical to the growth of the corporate independence of
the university guilds. This turbulent 'imperial' era was characterized by
an episcopal outlook which tended to classify the north European university guilds as near ecclesiastical 'colonies', almost as the physical pos-
sessions of the local bishops and their representatives. The universities
were not regarded as evolutionary organisms: rather they were viewed as
natural ecclesiastical appendages, as the highest forms of educational
vehicle yet to emerge under the auspices of the Church. As such, they were
to be integrated into the existing ecclesiastical structure and subjected to a
permanent ecclesiastical governance. This dependent and static rôle cast
for the universities was one wholly at odds with the ideas and aspirations
of the guilds of masters and associated scholars. For this reason, much of
the history of university-episcopal relations is concerned with the complexities and stormy difficulties inherent in the slow transition from the
'imperial' to the 'commonwealth' phase.

Paris University provides both the earliest and the most dramatic example
in European history of the struggle for university autonomy in the face of
ecclesiastical domination. In this case, the immediate ecclesiastical barrier
to the exercise of university freedom was the chancellor and chapter of the

Cathedral of Notre Dame whose schools, dating from the eleventh century and situated in the enclosed area known as the *cloître*, were the primordial root of the Paris *studium*.

The students who attended the schools of the *cloître* on the *Ile de la Cité* were at first accommodated in the houses of the canons of the Cathedral from whose ranks the earliest teaching masters were commonly drawn;[1] the schools were entrusted to the jurisdiction of the cathedral chancellor who wielded delegated episcopal authority derived from the bishop of Paris. As these schools grew in reputation they were infiltrated by numerous outside students (*scholares externi*), and this development led to serious disorder within the *cloître*. When the bishop and chapter severely curtailed opportunities for study in the cathedral schools there followed a migration of students to the left bank of the Seine, the present Latin Quarter.[2] Although the centre of academic gravity had temporarily moved away from the *Ile de la Cité*, the schools on the area in front of the Cathedral, designated the *Parvis*, still retained a considerable importance.

In the twelfth century the Paris schools were widely dispersed, often ephemeral, and they embodied that spirit of anarchical turbulence so basic a prerequisite of the intellectual advances of the period. Apart from the cathedral schools, specializing in theology, schools, especially of grammar and logic, were established on and around the bridges of the Seine, such as those of the Petit-Pont; and on the left bank schools grew up round the collegiate church of Sainte Geneviève (on the *Montagne Sainte-Geneviève*) and in association with the canons regular of the abbey of St Victor which, in contrast to the older monastic communities, opened its schools to the reception of outside students. In the second half of the twelfth century, however, the majority of the Sainte-Geneviève external schools fell into decline and by *c.* 1200 most of the left-bank students had returned to the *Ile de la Cité* which again became the main educational focus.[3] In the early thirteenth century, however, there occurred a further exodus of arts scholars to the left bank. This circumstance gave rise to dispute between the

---

[1] On the schools of the *cloître* see A. L. Gabriel, 'The Cathedral Schools of Notre-Dame and the Beginning of the University of Paris' in *Garlandia: Studies in the History of the Mediaeval University* (Notre Dame, Indiana, 1969), pp. 39 ff., esp. pp. 41–4. The twelfth-century school situation at Paris is recently discussed by J. Verger, *Les universités au moyen âge* (Paris, 1973), pp. 25 ff. For the origins of Paris University see Rashdall, *Universities*, i, pp. 271 ff.; Denifle, *Die Entstehung der Universitäten des Mittelalters bis 1400*, cit., pp. 655 ff.; d'Irsay, *Histoire des universités* . . ., cit., i, pp. 53 ff.
[2] Gabriel, op. cit., p. 42.
[3] See Rashdall, op. cit., i, pp. 277–8 and notes.

chancellor of Notre Dame and the abbot of Sainte-Geneviève who claimed the right to grant the licence to the artists within his jurisdiction. The matter was apparently resolved by uneasy compromise.[1] The existence of an alternative source from which the arts licence could be obtained in the thirteenth century proved of considerable advantage for the masters' guild in its confrontation with the chancellor of Notre Dame.

In a general sense, the university which emerged at Paris towards the end of the twelfth century can be seen as a distillation of the city's multifarious school activity and of the particular intellectual achievements of the galaxy of outstanding scholars who raised Paris to the forefront of academic life in northern Europe. The left-bank schools, through masters such as Abelard, helped to elevate the study of logic to the dominant position in the arts hierarchy; and the school of the abbey of St Victor with its élitist brand of mystical theology and biblical exegesis,[2] expounded by Hugh of St Victor and his disciples, made a distinctive contribution to the standing of theological scholarship at Paris in the pre-university era. Nor should Hugh of St Victor's educational ideology be undervalued.[3] While the Victorine mystics placed the first priority upon the contemplative side of man's nature, they were also deeply learned in the liberal arts and they strove to harness secular learning to the service of theology and contemplation: by means of long and intensive preparatory study man might be led, by a series of well defined stages, into the sublime reaches of the mystical state. The educational programme of the Victorines, set out by Hugh of St Victor in the *Didascalion*, was idealistically encyclopaedic in scope: but the Victorine organization of knowledge into related and hierarchical categories was a valuable if rarefied addition to the curricular presentation of higher education which, on a lower and more practical plane, was being developed in the twelfth-century cathedral schools. Notionally it could be argued that the University of Paris was founded upon the rocks of logic and speculative theology: and, insofar as one could single out an individual from the host of celebrated masters who graced the Paris schools, the choice would fall upon the dazzling, meretricious figure of Abelard. It is doubtful, however, if the university would have crystallized but for the stabilizing effect of the Cathedral of Notre Dame. Amid all the vicissitudes

---

[1] Ibid., i, pp. 340–1; Gabriel, op. cit., pp. 52–3.
[2] See B. Smalley, *The Study of the Bible in the Middle Ages* (Oxford, 1952), chs. 3, 4.
[3] The educational ideas of Hugh of St Victor are discussed in ibid., pp. 86 ff.; see also Paré, Brunet and Tremblay, *La renaissance du xii⁰ siècle: les écoles et l'enseignement*, cit., pp. 218–29.

of the twelfth-century school situation in Paris it was the Cathedral which, in the event, furnished the sole enduring institutional framework around which the *studium generale* could coalesce. The left-bank schools had done much to establish Paris as a city of teaching masters and as a host to an exuberant international student population: but they depended overmuch on the individual teacher with powers of student attraction and, in this respect, they were in similar vein to numerous north European schools, including those of the cathedral cities of Chartres, Laon, Rheims, Tours, Lincoln, York and Hereford, which experienced fluctuating fortunes according to the unpredictable peregrinations of a mobile teaching force. At Paris, both in the cathedral *cloître* and on the *Montagne Sainte-Geneviève*, Abelard's dialectical brilliance had caused many aspirant scholars to crowd into the city: but this was a transient intellectual happening in no wise productive of institutional permanence. As an academic centre, Paris had many advantages to offer.[1] By medieval standards it was a salubrious city of considerable beauty and sufficiently capacious to provide accommodation for a large concourse of masters and students. While medieval population figures are notoriously speculative and the size of educational groupings largely conjectural, it has been recently estimated that the Paris academic community accounted for at least 10 per cent of the total population of the city which has been computed at between 25,000 and 50,000 during the reign of Philip Augustus: if these limits are in any way reliable, this would mean that in *c.* 1200 the nascent University of Paris had a population of between 2,500 and 5,000.[2] The siting of the university in the royal domain proved of immense advantage as the Capetian kings had a vested interest in promoting Parisian economic, social and political development: and they quickly recognized the value of the academic population in their midst and they early adopted a benign and positive attitude towards it which was of the highest importance for the emergence and survival of the Paris *studium* as an expression of academic freedom.

Over the twelfth century circumstances were apparently combining to produce a permanent centre of learning: a multiplicity of teaching masters, a large cosmopolitan student population, an advantageous location, the support of the French monarchy, and a European reputation in logic and

[1] On the attractions of Paris see Gabriel, 'The Cathedral Schools of Notre-Dame . . .' in op. cit., pp. 40–1 and 'English Masters and Students in Paris during the Twelfth Century' in op. cit., pp. 4–5. See further J. W. Baldwin, *Masters, Princes and Merchants: the social views of Peter the Chanter and his circle*, 2 vols. (Princeton, New Jersey, 1970), i, pp. 63–5.

[2] Baldwin, op. cit., i, p. 72 and ii, p. 51, n. 52.

speculative theology. In retrospect, it perhaps appears that events were moving towards the inevitable creation of a *studium generale*: but this would be misleading. For the intellectual dynamism which made twelfth-century Paris a key centre of dialectic and theology might well have dissipated had it not been for the encapsulating rôle of the Cathedral of Notre Dame.[1] Without the cementing capacity of the cathedral school apparatus it is conceivable that Paris would have joined the company of medieval towns whose school activity came within an ace of evolving a higher university form but whose development was prematurely arrested. At Paris, however, while the cathedral provided the institutional umbrella for the nascent *studium generale*, the university could not be confined to a mere extension of the Notre Dame schools: the emergent university far transcended the cathedral school and was something radically different in kind from the cathedral matrix which produced it.

During the twelfth century the Paris schools seem to have been subject to a degree of laicization with masters and students identifying themselves more with Parisian urban society than with established ecclesiastical forms,[2] a tendency arising from an awakening sense of academic freedom deemed incompatible with a rigid ecclesiastical control. But, in the event, the academic population proved too naturally differentiated to align successfully with urban trade and professional life, and in the situation of tension and conflict which developed between the academic and non-academic sectors the masters and students came to realize that their interests were best served by ecclesiastical surveillance and clerical status.[3] The Capetian monarchy was well disposed towards this movement because the Church would bear the major responsibility for the effective internal disciplining of the Paris schools. The clerical standing of the masters and students was presumably embraced and confirmed by the bull of Celestine III of 1194[4] which directed that secular cases involving all clerks at Paris be heard in ecclesiastical courts. More specifically, the charter of Philip Augustus of 1200[5] recognized the *privilegium fori* for masters and students: and subse-

---

[1] See Rashdall's stress on this point, *Universities*, i, pp. 275–8; Gabriel, 'The Cathedral Schools of Notre-Dame . . .' in op. cit., passim; G. Leff, *Paris and Oxford Universities in the Thirteenth and Fourteenth Centuries*, cit., p. 16.

[2] See Verger, *Les universités au moyen âge*, cit., p. 28.

[3] Ibid., p. 29.

[4] *Chartularium Universitatis Parisiensis*, i, introduction, no. 15; Rashdall, *Universities*, i, p. 291, n. 1; P. Kibre, 'Scholarly Privileges: Their Roman Origins and Medieval Expression', *A.H.R.*, lix (1954), pp. 543 ff., at p. 551.

[5] *Chartularium*, i, no. 1.

quent papal awards, including that of Gregory IX of 1231, *Parens Scientiarum*,[1] further added to and reinforced the degree to which the masters and students were subject to ecclesiastical protection.[2] But while this protective canopy was necessary to win a measure of basic security, when manifested at the local level through the bishop of Paris and the chancellor of Notre Dame, the threat to the attainment of full corporate independence by the academic guild became apparent.

The pivotal point of ecclesiastical control was the authority claimed by the chancellor, acting as the bishop's delegate, to grant or withhold the teaching licence, without which no master could legitimately teach. Papal legislation of the Third Lateran Council of 1179 relating to cathedral schools was partially designed to ensure that chancellors granted the licence free of charge to all properly qualified candidates.[3] Whether or not this legislation was issued with the cathedral school of Notre Dame prominently in mind is uncertain: nevertheless, it had a particular relevance for the position of the episcopal chancellor at Paris vis-à-vis the emergent guild of masters and scholars because the chancellor's monopoly control of and his exaction of fees for the licence was diametrically opposed to the masters' demand for automatic and free licensing of every suitable potential teacher. This conflict highlighted the polarized positions of the academic and ecclesiastical parties over the issue of university autonomy.[4]

An association of masters had probably evolved at Paris by the third quarter of the twelfth century and had presumably been in the process of formation a good deal earlier.[5] The charter of Philip Augustus of 1200, directed to the Paris scholars, did not formally recognize a legal corporation of masters, but it gave the community of scholars a privileged clerical standing with regard to the municipal authorities and bound each new provost of Paris to swear a public oath in the presence of the assembled

---

[1] Ibid., i, no. 79.

[2] See e.g. Verger, op. cit., pp. 29–30.

[3] *Chartularium*, i, introduction, no. 12. See the pioneer study by G. Post, 'Alexander III, the *Licentia docendi* and the rise of the universities' in *C. H. Haskins Anniversary Essays in Mediaeval History*, ed. C. H. Taylor and J. L. LaMonte (Boston, 1929), pp. 255 ff.

[4] For the conflict between the masters' guild and the bishop of Paris and the chancellor of Notre Dame see Rashdall, *Universities*, i, esp. pp. 304 ff.; Kibre, *Scholarly Privileges in the Middle Ages*, cit., ch. 4; Leff, *Paris and Oxford Universities in the Thirteenth and Fourteenth Centuries*, pp. 15–34. Gabriel, *Garlandia*, p. 58 minimizes the effect of the opposition to the chancellor on the corporate growth of the masters: no detailed argument is, however, adduced.

[5] See e.g. Verger, op. cit., p. 31.

scholars to uphold their privileges.[1] In 1208–9 Innocent III assumed the right of the masters to act as a body;[2] but witnesses such as Thomas Becket and John of Salisbury indicate the much earlier existence of a distinct corps of masters with *de facto* powers of collective action.[3] By 1215 the guild of masters and associated scholars had acquired the essential attributes of corporate status:[4] the right to elect officers, to engage judicially through proctors, and to frame governing statutes. The statutes granted to the masters and scholars of Paris in 1215 by the cardinal legate, Robert de Courçon,[5] give the best summary view of the stage of corporate development reached by the guild in the early thirteenth century. By these, the masters were authorized to make their own statutes, supported by penalty or oath, relating to murder or injury of scholars, the fixing of rents of lodgings, costume, burial, lectures and disputations, provided that the *studium* was not thereby dissolved or destroyed. This was a very clear confirmation of the right of the masters to act as a guild, as a *universitas magistrorum et scolarium*, with the power to devise statutes for its members and to enforce obedience to them.

The statutes also mark an important point in relations with the chancellor. They had been preceded by the conclusions of a papally-appointed committee of arbitration of 1212–13, which had attempted to curb the chancellor's jurisdictional powers in several key respects.[6] It was enacted that the chancellor must license any candidate in theology, canon law and medicine who was presented by the majority of masters in these disciplines and any candidate in arts proposed by six masters in that faculty. Although the chancellor might continue to license independently of the masters, he was forbidden to exact any fee or oath of obedience and was deprived of his alleged right to imprison any master or student. The statutes of 1215 made a general embodiment of these provisions and stipulated that the chancellor was to grant the licence without condition or payment. But despite the papal support for the masters, the bishop of Paris and the

---

[1] *Chartularium*, i, no. 1. See the discussion of the charter by Rashdall, *Universities*, i, pp. 294–8 and by Kibre, op. cit., pp. 86–7.

[2] *Chartularium*, i, no. 7; Leff, op. cit., p. 24.

[3] See Gabriel, 'English Masters and Students in Paris . . .' in op. cit., pp. 1 ff., passim.

[4] On the development of magisterial legal corporate status see G. Post, 'Parisian Masters as a Corporation, 1200–1246', *Speculum*, ix (1934), pp. 421 ff. Post regards the University of Masters as a papally recognized legal corporation by 1215 at the latest.

[5] *Chartularium*, i, no. 20. These statutes are analysed by Rashdall, *Universities*, i, pp. 309, 357, 440–1, 450, 471–2; Leff, op. cit., pp. 25–7, 138–9.

[6] *Chartularium*, i, no. 16. See the discussion by Rashdall, op. cit., i, pp. 308–9 and Leff, op. cit., pp. 25–6.

chancellor did not relax in their efforts to smother the growing corporate independence of the university. After a prolonged conflict marked by much bitterness and protracted litigation the bull of Gregory IX of 1231, *Parens Scientiarum*, effectively broke the attempted dominance of the local ecclesiastical authority over the masters' guild.[1] The chancellor's powers of criminal jurisdiction were virtually nullified: he was forbidden to maintain a prison, the bishop alone retaining the authority to imprison criminous scholars. Concerning the vexed question of the *licentia docendi* the chancellor was bound to license only worthy candidates; and, within three months of the licence being sought, he was obliged to consult with relevant masters about the qualifications and qualities of the applicant: the chancellor was further bound not to exact any oath of obedience, caution, emolument or promise from the recipient of the licence. While conflicts with the chancellor continued throughout the thirteenth century and beyond, in retrospect, *Parens Scientiarum* is seen as decisive in ensuring that the autonomous claims of the Paris masters would prevail over the negative, blinkered stance of the bishop-chancellor.

As a result of the papal espousal of the masters from the early thirteenth century and the subsequent contraction of the chancellor's activities by papal statutory controls, the papacy, in conjunction with the Capetian monarchy, has to be considered a major force in shaping the autonomy of the Paris guild. But apart from the legislative and interventionist assistance of these two guarantors of independence, the masters, in their struggle against the chancellor's arbitrary exercise of licensing power, possessed a potent weapon in the requirement of inception, the professional right of granting or refusing a candidate admittance to the guild. Even if the Paris masters could not always prevent the chancellor from licensing an unsuitable candidate, they could effectively render the latter an outcast by non-admittance to their academic society. For this reason, admission by inception to the masters' association came to be as necessary to the aspirant teacher as receipt of the chancellor's licence.[2] It is improbable that the chancellor on the one hand and the masters and associated scholars on the other had ever formed two distinct and independent entities:[3] from the time of the emergence of the *studium generale* at Paris the chancellor had been recognized as its head, although his exact relation to the guild is

---

[1] *Chartularium*, i, no. 79. The bull is examined by Rashdall, op. cit., i, pp. 338–40; Leff, op. cit., esp. pp. 31–3; Kibre, op. cit., pp. 95–6.
[2] See Rashdall's commentary on inception at Paris, *Universities*, i, esp. pp. 283–7, 305–6.
[3] See the cautionary remarks of Rashdall's editors, op. cit., i, p. 306, n. 2.

unclear. But with the gradual emasculation of the chancellor's powers consequent upon his abortive attempt to check magisterial evolutionary growth, the masters succeeded in forcing him into an external and isolated position as nominal head of the *studium* retaining only an increasingly formal bestowal of the licence.

One of the central features of Paris University was the size of the faculty of arts and the dominant position which it came to occupy within the *studium*. The masters and scholars of the arts faculty formed by far the most numerous single body, comprising about two-thirds of the total university membership in the thirteenth century.[1] By comparison, the combined number in the superior faculties of theology, canon law (civil law was prohibited by Honorius III in 1219), and medicine was relatively small.[2] Because of this, the masters of arts appear to have taken the initiative in the trial of strength with the episcopal chancellor. Before 1219 the masters of the four faculties are found acting as a body; they did so again in 1229, 1230–1, 1237 and on later occasions. Nevertheless, after 1219 the masters of arts often acted on behalf of the entire university and began to evolve a strong corporate identity and eventually became the most powerful constitutional unit in the *studium*.[3] The distinguishing feature of the arts faculty was the division of its masters (and by extension its associated scholars) into the four nations, French, Norman, Picard and English-German, each with its own elected proctor.[4] By 1249 there was a single rector of the nations who presumably was then regarded as the head of the faculty of arts (although he is not thus expressly styled until 1274) and who, by virtue of the numerical superiority of the artists and the lead which they assumed in university affairs first against the chancellor and then against the mendicants, succeeded in emerging as the common head of the guild of masters.[5]

---

[1] Leff, *Paris and Oxford Universities* . . ., p. 52.
[2] Rashdall, *Universities*, i, p. 315. Philip II's anti-imperial motivation in securing the papal prohibition of civil law at Paris is discussed by W. Ullmann, *Principles of Government and Politics in the Middle Ages*, ed. cit., p. 199, n. 4, and Ullmann, 'Honorius III and the Prohibition of Legal Studies', *Juridical Review*, lx (1948), pp. 177 ff. See also Baldwin, op. cit., i, p. 87.
[3] E.g. Rashdall, op. cit., i, pp. 315 ff.
[4] For the Paris nations see Kibre, *The Nations in the Mediaeval Universities*, chs. 1, 3; Rashdall, op. cit., i, esp. pp. 311–20, 406–15; Leff, op. cit., pp. 51 ff. For the English-German nation see the valuable study by G. C. Boyce, *The English-German Nation in the University of Paris during the Middle Ages* (Bruges, 1927).
[5] For the Paris rector see Kibre, op. cit., chs. 1, 3, passim; Rashdall, op. cit., i, esp. pp. 312–20, 325–34, 402–6; Leff, op. cit., esp. pp. 60 ff. See also Gabriel, 'The English-

The situation in the mid-thirteenth century was thus one in which the faculty of arts, divided into its four nations, had attained a full corporate status with an emerging common head or rector; outside this organization lay the superior faculties which, one may assume, had from the early thirteenth century held separate meetings to regulate their studies and to recommend candidates for the licence. But it seems that when the organization in the faculty of arts had reached maturity that of the superior faculties was as yet in a rudimentary form. Because of this organizational disparity, the rector of the artists became the most convenient representative of the entire university. It was the rector who summoned and presided over the university congregations and who, in conjunction with the nations and the superior faculties, directed university finances. Aided by the proctors, the rector conducted much of the university's litigation, exercised civil jurisdiction over members of the *studium*, and executed the university's decrees. Outside the *studium* he acted as its chief external representative.

It was only after custom had established the *de facto* headship of the artists' rector that the superior faculties developed their internal organization in the second half of the thirteenth century, with their deans, assemblies, statutory-making powers and so on.[1] Natural tensions arose between the rector and the deans; gradually, however, the rector came to be accepted as head of the university, not merely *de facto* but *de iure* as well, a process completed by the mid-fourteenth century. But even when the headship of the rector was universally accepted, there was no question of rectorial meddling in the government of the superior faculties which remained independent and self-contained. The *studium* was a federation of its four faculties: in the general congregations each nation of the arts faculty and each of the three superior faculties had one vote, and a majority of the seven votes determined the issue. In these proceedings the rector's rôle was confined to pronouncing the collective mind of the congregation: he had no vote himself and throughout he acted as an impartial chairman. One must not, therefore, put rectorial powers out of focus: rectors held office for very brief tenures (one month or six weeks, later extended to

---

German Nation at the University of Paris from 1425–1494' in *Garlandia*, cit., pp. 170–2. The nations of the artists were not completely identifiable with the faculty of arts which had its own corporate statutes and administrative machinery. Nevertheless, nation business occupied the major part of its affairs. For the express recognition of the rector as head of the arts faculty in 1274 see *Chartularium*, i, nos. 447, 485.

[1] The position and organization of the superior faculties are discussed e.g. by Rashdall, *Universities*, i, pp. 321 ff.

three months) and they were ever directly accountable to the scrutiny and control of the university assemblies. Clearly, however, it was the rector who kept the complicated university structure together and who both symbolized and expressed its corporate unity. And when one remembers the diverse elements of which the *studium* was composed – the inferior faculty of arts, divided into four nations each with its own proctor and business machinery, the superior faculties with their deans and separate organization, the quite-frequent assemblies of the sovereign body made up of the masters in all the faculties, the daily regimen of lectures and disputations, the complex of university administration and litigation, the legion of colleges and halls – it is of some remark that the *studium* cohered as well as it did.[1]

As previously indicated,[2] in student-universities of the Bologna type, despite their pretentiously democratic form, the exercise of power was, in reality, more centralized in a small executive than in the magisterial *studia* of Parisian derivation. Even in the heyday of student dominion at Bologna the daily administrative machine was run by executive committees of student rectors and *consiliarii* who were the elected choices of the nations. Because of the inconvenience of summoning the sovereign body in large populous student-universities of the Bolognese type, congregations were less commonly resorted to than at Paris where they were a frequent occurrence; and this enabled the members of the masters' guild to participate actively and regularly in university business. Executive tenures were shorter at Paris than at Bologna: the rector held office for a month or six weeks, later extended to three months,[3] and the proctors were elected on a monthly basis, later increased to two or three months.[4] Administrative continuity was not at a high premium in a university geared to a rapid turnover of personnel which allowed a greater proportion of members of the guild to assume responsible office than was the case at Bologna with its rather circumscribed power distribution. While the Parisian constitution did not emulate the precise legalism of Bologna, and was far less vociferous in its

---

[1] See the remarks of F. M. Powicke, 'Bologna, Paris, Oxford: Three *Studia Generalia*' in *Ways of Medieval Life and Thought*, cit., pp. 171–2.

[2] See above, ch. 3.

[3] Kibre, op. cit., p. 106. The rector's tenure of office was extended to three months in 1266 by the papal legate, Simon de Brie, to counteract the unrest occasioned in the *studium* by too frequent rectorial changes. The three months' term became the norm for over three hundred years.

[4] Ibid., p. 69 and notes 28, 29. During the summer vacation elections were normally suspended.

expressions of democratic involvement and control, in practice, the democratic process penetrated the component parts of the *studium* to a more impressive degree and in a more diffuse manner than is apparent in the daily operation of the Bolognese archetype.

Nation groupings were probably more important in the genesis of Bologna University than in the origin of Paris. At Bologna, the two jurist guilds coalesced from the nations which were primary creative ingredients of the *studium*. At Paris, voluntary associations of masters and students of similar geographical origin are detectable in the late twelfth and early thirteenth centuries.[1] Whether these loose confraternities were the direct antecedents of the nations of the faculty of arts, first specifically mentioned in 1222,[2] is problematical because of the lack of documentation covering the transition from the informal to the formal nation phase. It is not until 1249 that there is unequivocal evidence for the fourfold nation division of the faculty of arts: this is found in an agreement recorded between the French nation and the other three (Picard, Norman and English-German) following a disputed rectorial election, the concordat being sealed with the individual seals of the four nations.[3] Unlike the student nations at Bologna, the magisterial nations at Paris embraced masters of both foreign and indigenous derivation.[4] Although there were no nations in the faculties of theology, law or medicine, masters of arts who were studying for higher degrees were reckoned members of the nations until they acquired doctorates or masterships in a superior discipline.[5] Students below the rank of master of arts were disqualified from full membership of a nation: they seem to have been loosely embraced by the guild by virtue of association with their own regent masters, but they were excluded both from voting and participating in the discussions of faculty or nation assemblies.[6] In contrast to the relative lack of autonomous standing of the Bologna nations, which tended to sink part of their identity in the jurist guilds, the four nations of the faculty of arts at Paris attained a high degree of autonomy. Each Paris nation formed a distinct corporate society, having its own elected officers and proctor at its head, statutes and archives, finances, seal, schools, assembly point, and feast days. The separateness and pride

[1] Ibid., p. 16.
[2] In a bull of Honorius III, *Chartularium*, i, no. 45. The pope forbade the scholars, 'according to their nations, to place at their head, anyone to avenge injuries done to them' (trans. Kibre, p. 17). The nature of the officials alluded to is obscure.
[3] *Chartularium*, i, no. 187.
[4] Kibre, *The Nations in the Mediaeval Universities*, p. 15.
[5] Loc. cit.   [6] Loc. cit.

of each nation inculcated a sense of loyalty to the nation rather than to the faculty of arts or to the university as a whole, and this often led to bitter inter-nation feuding which, at times, assumed the character of open warfare causing serious disruption of the *studium*. Two recurrent reasons for these quarrels were conflicts over the geographical areas from which the nations recruited their members and disputed elections to the rectorship;[1] these dissensions between the nations persisted with regularity throughout the thirteenth and fourteenth centuries making necessary, on occasion, the intervention of the papal legate and the French king.

The nation turbulence of Paris was a commonly repeated theme in French provincial universities and caused secular and ecclesiastical authorities alike to look with a jaundiced eye upon these volatile manifestations of academic fraternity and led, in some places, to their attempted suppression.[2] But counter-productive and even self-destructive as the nations sometimes appear, they were among the most fundamental of medieval academic institutions perhaps because they were the most immediate realizations of group psychological needs in the earlier phase of university life. Their nearest surviving approximation is to be found in the student nations of Aberdeen University where the indirect method of electing to the rectorship is true to the spirit of the medieval procedure.[3]

The proctors who directed the Paris nations were more powerful personages than the equivalent Bolognese *consiliarii*.[4] In their executive capacity, they were required to enforce not only the regulations and statutes of the nations but those of the faculty of arts and the university as well; they were therefore key figures in welding together the component parts of the *studium* into some semblance of unity. Judicially, each proctor might act as a court of first instance and, collectively with the rector, they formed a faculty of arts tribunal for dealing with disciplinary cases and breaches of the statutes. It was each proctor's function to summon meetings of his nation, to preside over its business and to represent it in the faculty of arts assembly and in the general congregation of the university. But in these assemblies the proctor acted only as the delegate of the nation and, to this extent, he was the agent of corporate magisterial democracy. As at Bologna, executive nation officials were directly responsible to nation assemblies:

[1] On nation conflict at Paris see ibid., pp. 21–7.
[2] See below, pp. 185–6.
[3] Kibre, op. cit., p. 183; see also W. M. Alexander, 'The four nations of Aberdeen University and their European background', *Aberdeen University Studies*, no. 108 (Aberdeen, 1934), pp. 5–6.
[4] Much information on the proctors is supplied by Kibre, op. cit., ch. 3.

but because of the more autonomous nature of the Paris nations and their stronger internal structuring, the measure of control exercised over elected officials and the ,opportunities for democratic participation by individual members were probably greater than in the comparable Bolognese situation.

A prominent difference between the Bologna and the Paris nations was the degree to which the latter were involved in regulating teaching in the *studium*: the Bologna nations did not contribute in this direction. At Paris, each nation maintained its own arts schools, located mainly in the Rue du Fouarre on the left bank of the river, where the majority of schools of the faculty of arts were concentrated. The schools were given close and regular supervision by the nations;[1] they were allocated to *bona fide* regent masters on an annual basis; fees from those attending were collected by the proctors; and, until the second half of the fifteenth century, these schools provided the core of the teaching in the faculty of arts. By 1500, however, the nation schools were being progressively superseded by the colleges which, in the early sixteenth century, became the *foci* of arts teaching in the *studium*.[2] Apart from running their individual schools, the nations, acting collectively as constituents of the faculty of arts, determined the regulations governing the arts course: the subject content, the timetable, the qualifications for the M.A. and the licensing arrangements, all these came within their purview.[3] Moreover, the nations were directly concerned with the bachelor's degree in arts: they stipulated the necessary qualifications, elected the examiners and admitted candidates to the degree.[4] The Paris chancellor was not concerned with the awarding of the bachelor's degree which was conducted under the auspices of the nation.

The nations remained a vital force in the life of the university until at least the mid-fifteenth century after which they went into a state of decline. This was partly due to the falling numbers of foreign students attending the *studium*, a phenomenon which is apparent from the late fourteenth century. The Hundred Years War depleted the ranks of the English-German nation: there were only a few members left in 1383 and only two masters are recorded in 1438.[5] The decrease in the numbers of foreign

[1] See the legislation of the French (Gallican) nation of 1328 relating to the detailed supervision of its schools, *Chartularium*, ii, no. 871.
[2] See below, pp. 130–1.
[3] Kibre, op. cit., pp. 97–8.
[4] Ibid., pp. 99–100. For details relating to bachelors in the English-German nation see Gabriel, 'The English-German Nation . . .' in *Garlandia*, pp. 176–8. For the statutes of the English-German nation concerning bachelors see *Chartularium*, i, no. 202.
[5] Ibid., p. 108.

scholars was also a consequence of the mushroom growth in the later medieval period of university foundations in provincial France, Germany, the Low Countries, Bohemia, Poland, Hungary, Scandinavia, Scotland and Spain which encouraged scholars to seek university education in their home territories. The undermining of Paris as an international university prepared the ground for its 'nationalization' in the form of subjection to monarchical control in the fifteenth century culminating in the edict of Louis XII of 1499 which rescinded the university's right to suspend lectures,[1] papally confirmed by Gregory IX in *Parens Scientiarum*, 1231, and which was tantamount to a modern trade union's weapon of strike action. The reduction of the Paris *studium* from a seething cosmopolitan university to one of narrower dimensions rendered nation groupings less relevant, and their function as essential organs within the faculty of arts gave way to an increasingly bureaucratic rôle as units of administrative convenience: they were finally suppressed by decree of the National Convention in 1793.

Thus in the thirteenth and fourteenth centuries the four nations of the faculty of arts were central to the functioning of the Paris *studium*. As administrative, educational and fraternal units they provided the immediate framework for the life and work of the masters of arts who composed the majority section of the teaching force; and, through the latter, nation benefits were extended, though how far is not satisfactorily known, to the associated students in arts. The nations played a lion's share in the university assemblies in that they commanded the majority voting in the congregations (four votes out of seven) and furnished the presiding rector. As practitioners of a form of constitutional government, wherein elected executive officials were responsible to the membership and short periods of office were designed to frustrate the over-concentration of power, the Paris nations provided good opportunity for democratic involvement by the individual arts master.

By the mid-thirteenth century the Paris *studium* had achieved a sound measure of governmental democracy and autonomous control. Intervention by external authorities had been reduced to the minimum and the powers of the episcopal chancellor whittled down to largely ceremonial functions. The French monarchy was as yet benign and a positive aid to the advancement of university interest, especially with regard to the municipal authorities. An urban corporation, the Paris *studium*, as most universities were to do, had sought to escape from the restraints and obligations

---

[1] Kibre, *Scholarly Privileges in the Middle Ages*, cit., p. 225; Rashdall, *Universities*, i, p. 430; Verger, *Les universités au moyen âge*, cit., p. 168.

imposed on the rest of the urban population by building up an armoury of privileges and exemptions; and in this it had been singularly successful. Although the Paris masters had thrown off the yoke of local ecclesiastical control, they continued to seek the protection of the papacy which had done so much to ensure their privileged and autonomous status. But from the mid-thirteenth century there emerged the second major challenge to the independence of the masters' guild: this stemmed from the position of the mendicant orders within the *studium* and the elongated conflict amply and traumatically demonstrated to the university that it could no longer rely upon the automatic papal espousal of its fundamental interests in matters which had wider implications for the Universal Church.

In essence, the conflict with the mendicants centred on the position which the friars were to occupy within the *studium* in relation to the secular masters.[1] The educational life of the two main mendicant orders, the Dominican and Franciscan, was served by a hierarchy of schools most fully developed among the Dominicans, ranging from elementary to advanced level and teaching a wide coverage of subjects in arts, philosophy and theology. Each order could be said to contain a decentralized university structure which catered adequately for the needs of the majority of its members; but, inevitably, the reputation of Parisian theology led the orders to send their ablest scholars to their schools at Paris to study for theology degrees under their own mendicant masters. There was here no attempt made to integrate with the university: the friars desired to remain a distinct enclave within the *studium*. They would only associate with the faculty of theology, and they refused to allow their members to take the arts course, arguing that their students were already sufficiently versed in arts from the prior training received in mendicant schools, where, moreover, arts subjects could be presented free of the alleged profanities which marred the university course. At a time when the arts faculty had assumed a leading part in university government, the bypassing of arts degrees by the friars violated the guild's sense of corporate unity. More specifically, by avoiding inception in arts the mendicants thereby avoided taking an oath to the magisterial guild for the observance of the university statutes. What was here at issue was the right of the masters' guild to demand an

---

[1] On the mendicant dispute see Rashdall, op. cit., i, pp. 370–97; Leff, op. cit., pp. 34–47; Verger, op. cit., pp. 83–91; see also J. C. Murphy, 'The Early Franciscan Studium at the University of Paris' in *Studium Generale: Studies offered to Astrik L. Gabriel*, ed. L. S. Domonkos and R. J. Schneider, Texts and Studies in the History of Mediaeval Education, no. xi (Notre Dame, Indiana, 1967), pp. 159 ff. at pp. 190–203.

oath of obedience from all those who would enjoy the privileges of the university: but the friars seemingly desired to exercise the privileges of membership without submitting to the authority of the guild. The mendicants were concerned primarily with their own affairs and not with the problems of the university: they wished to be guided only by the decisions of their superiors and not by the orders of the masters' guild. Apart from matters of principle and the disunifying presence of the mendicants within the *studium*, tensions were further exacerbated when the secular masters began to feel their very livelihood threatened by the activities of the friars. During the dispersion of the university, 1229–31, the mendicants remained at Paris and, first under Roland of Cremona and then under Hugh of St Cher, the Dominicans opened their schools to the reception of secular students. This first Dominican chair in the theological faculty was retained on the return of the seculars in 1231, and the pattern was set for the infiltration and eventual monopoly control of the teaching of theology at Paris by the mendicants and other religious orders. Eminent secular theologians, such as John of St Giles and Alexander of Hales, were attracted to join the mendicants and a growing number of students preferred the schools of the friars to those of the secular masters in theology. By 1254 the secular masters held only three of the fifteen chairs in the theological faculty.

In 1253 the guild demanded from any master in any faculty, under penalty of expulsion, an oath of obedience to observe the statutes of the university and to participate in a cessation of academic activities when ordered to do so by the guild.[1] The mendicants refused to comply and, in addition, they remained teaching in Paris during the cessation of 1253; and this resulted in their expulsion from the university. The friars appealed to Pope Innocent IV and for the next eight years the dispute raged with increasing acrimony. The grievances of the secular masters were set forth with some feeling and at some length in a general letter of 1254 addressed to the secular clergy at large and to all scholars in Christian society.[2] Among other things, the masters accused the Dominicans of duplicity in acquiring their chairs by underhand methods, and they pointed to the threat which the mendicants, unless controlled and subjected to university authority, posed to secular livelihood in the theological faculty. Innocent IV was generally inclined to favour the magisterial standpoint, but his successor, Alexander IV, waged a full frontal attack on the fundamental rights of the guild which had been won with papal support in the previous half century. His bull, *Quasi lignum vitae*, 1255, was a thorough apologia for the conduct

[1] *Chartularium*, i, no. 219.   [2] Ibid., i, no. 230.

of the mendicants[1] which showed little grasp of the way in which the university had evolved and the meaning of academic freedom. Cessations in future were to be legal only if voted by a two-thirds majority of each faculty, a decree which would give the mendicants, who comprised more than a third of the theological faculty, an effective veto. The pope, with obscurantist obstinacy, also asserted that the chancellor had the power to license whomsoever he thought fit, thereby giving him control over admissions from the religious orders to the faculty of theology. In support of these measures, which struck at the autonomous root of the guild, Alexander IV in the following years extensively intervened in university affairs with the delicacy of a sledge-hammer, treating the university not as an independent corporation devoted to the pursuit of scholarship but as an instrument of misguided papal policy. Towards the end of his pontificate Alexander somewhat moderated his attitude and after his death in 1261 the way was mercifully open to compromise.[2] The mendicants were re-admitted into the bosom of the university, although they were not to be members of the faculty of arts (which would not have caused them much concern); the Dominicans were permitted to hold two of the theology chairs and the other religious orders one each; and the privileges of the university were fully confirmed. By 1318 the secular masters were strong enough to impose on the friars the oath of obedience to the university statutes. The mendicants submitted to the oath apparently without much opposition, and thus the main point at issue was eventually resolved in favour of the secular masters. Disputes with the friars continued at Paris throughout the later medieval period, but these did not assume the proportions of the conflicts of the thirteenth century.[3]

The university's dispute with the mendicants, which was reproduced on a smaller scale in Oxford and Cambridge, was not without advantages for the Paris *studium* in the thirteenth century.[4] The need to organize maximum resistance to the friars resulted in a greater measure of internal cohesion. The faculty of arts was further reinforced in its position as the leading power unit within the *studium*; and the theological faculty, faced with the mendicant pressure, was moved to reduce its customs to a written statutory form and to integrate more closely with the arts masters. The high costs of the conflict (for example, the frequent appeals to Rome and the

[1] Ibid., i, no. 247.
[2] For details of the compromise, which are not clear in every respect, see Rashdall, op. cit., i, pp. 392–3.
[3] See the *Additional Note* of Rashdall's editors, i, pp. 396–7.
[4] See ibid., i, pp. 393–5; Verger, op. cit., pp. 90–1.

subsequent litigation) caused the university to develop an internal graded tax system and other forms of revenue collecting, which in turn added to the authority of the rector who was responsible for university finances. Nevertheless, the papacy, especially in the person of Alexander IV, had demonstrated that university privileges were not sacrosanct and that academic freedom was an ephemeral possession which was not made easily compatible with the exercise of external organized power, whether that of the Church or the centralized monarchy.

The temporary subjection of the Paris *studium* to the papacy was not, however, repeated. But from the late thirteenth century the university came increasingly within the orbit of the kings of France.[1] As French royal authority became more firmly centralized and theocratic in character, papal influence in France underwent a corresponding decline, and it was natural that the university should turn to the monarchy as the guardian of its privileges. As the university lost something of its international character, it tended to rely on the Paris *parlement* rather than the pope for arbitration in university cases:[2] in 1446 Charles VII tried to carry this development to a logical conclusion by enacting the automatic removal of all such disputed cases to the *parlement*,[3] an element of compulsion which was ill-digested by the *studium*. In the fourteenth century Paris University was already involved in French politics. University delegates participated in the States General: at times, the university's opinion was sought in political matters (for example, during the Schism), and generally it ranged itself behind royal policy. But in the fifteenth century, during the turmoil of civil war between the Armagnac and Burgundian factions and the period of the Anglo-French 'double monarchy' instituted by the Treaty of Troyes, 1420, the university played an indecisive, faltering rôle marked by many changes in direction born of short term expediency. Throughout, the university was preoccupied with the defence of its privileges, and its consistent pacifism was dictated, not by the political realities of the situation, but by the adherence of its doctors of theology and canonists to traditional theological notions and the threat which war posed to its academic privileges and revenues.[4] The weakness and ineptitude of the university in the political sphere in the fifteenth century rendered it vulnerable to monarchi-

---

[1] See e.g. Verger, op. cit., pp. 159–62, 167–9 and 'The University of Paris at the End of the Hundred Years' War' in *Universities in Politics*, cit., pp. 47 ff.; Rashdall, op. cit., i, esp. pp. 425 ff.; d'Irsay, *Histoire des universités . . .*, cit., i, pp. 205 ff.
[2] See Leff, op. cit., pp. 49, 71.
[3] Kibre, *Scholarly Privileges in the Middle Ages*, p. 213.
[4] See Verger's arguments, art. cit. in op. cit., passim.

cal control. From a royal standpoint, the Paris *studium* was something of an anachronism in a centralized fifteenth-century state. For the university held rather aloof from nationalistic sentiment and matters of current concern, being concerned, even obsessed, with its own privileges and corporate nature and its function as a defender of the values of the Christian society as traditionally conceived. The assertion that the university's privileges were ecumenical in character had to succumb to the monarchical and theocratic version that they had been granted by royal concession and were subject to the direct control of the king's justice. In 1446 a prosecutor of Charles VII ruled as follows: 'To the king in his kingdom, where he is emperor and not subject to any man, it belongs – and not to the pope or any other – to create corporate bodies. He has created the university and endowed it with privileges, as was meet. And the university is his daughter, bound to him in reverence, honour and subjection'.[1] This is a neat summary of the relation of the Paris *studium* to the monarchy as it evolved in the fifteenth century. The reduction of the university to a strict royal dependence was underlined by the repeated (and often ill-considered) interventions in university affairs by Charles VII, Louis XI, Charles VIII and Louis XII. When, in 1499, Louis XII abolished the university's right of cessation[2] (it had been abrogated by the papacy in 1462) the Paris *studium* lost its ultimate bargaining counter. Although the Paris masters retained the essence of their individual privileges, such as financial and military exemptions, as a corporate body they were now deprived of the substance of their hard-won autonomous being. The denial of the right to suspend academic life and to make a diplomatic exodus from the city in the time-honoured way, marks, more than anything, the transition of the Paris *studium* from a mesmeric international university, the founder of the magisterial type in Europe, to a circumscribed national institution, a mere shadow of its former self but in alignment with the more settled, more regionally insular pattern of university development in the later middle ages. When buildings and material things and matters of national prestige are rated more highly than academic freedom and the untrammelled pursuit of scholarship beyond artificial frontiers, the universities had entered a new and perhaps lesser phase of being. But even in its falling state the University of Paris was an academic occasion which its twentieth-century north European successors have not found easy to emulate.

[1] Quoted in ibid., pp. 61–2 (trans. Verger) and in Verger, *Les universités au moyen âge*, p. 168.
[2] See above, p. 90, n. 1.

V

1. Oxford

In the course of the twelfth century the centre of educational gravity in Europe passed from the monasteries to the cathedral schools, thereby bringing secular education more into accord with the needs of an increasingly urbanized society. As Paris University was the direct outcome of the cathedral school movement, one might expect to find a similar English university development. But the Parisian pattern was not implanted in England: no cathedral city produced a lasting *studium generale*, although several came within an ace of so doing,[1] and the universities of Oxford and Cambridge were established in towns which had no cathedrals. The cathedral school movement was perhaps less entrenched in England than on the Continent: monasticism was for long so dominant in English society that the secular cathedrals tended to be less affluent and influential than their European counterparts, and consequently they claimed a proportionately smaller stake in educational life. In the English situation it is not easy to isolate and categorize a definite cathedral school phase as an evolutionary stage in the transition from the monastic to the university era.

The claims that Oxford University was founded by Alfred the Great or by Charlemagne or by exiles from Troy are the product of a gullible antiquarian scholarship which has long since been consigned to the realms of mythology. Equally, there is no truth in the allegation that Cambridge was founded by King Arthur in 531 or by a Spanish prince Cantaber of obscure

[1] See R. W. Hunt, 'English Learning in the late Twelfth Century', *T.R.H.S.*, 4th ser., xix (1936), pp. 19 ff., passim, reprinted, with revisions, in *Essays in Medieval History*, ed. R. W. Southern (London, 1968), pp. 160 ff.

origin and uncertain chronology.[1] Oxford and Cambridge, like Bologna and Paris, were not specifically founded but evolved over a period of time. A twelfth-century observer would have been very perceptive indeed if he had selected either Oxford or Cambridge as the locations of the future English universities. For there were a variety of educational centres in the twelfth century from which a fully-fledged *studium generale* might have emerged. The cathedral school of Lincoln, for example, came near to becoming a *studium generale* in the twelfth century.[2] By 1176, it seems that Lincoln had a reputation as a centre for law, for in that year it was grouped, in a letter of Peter of Blois, with Bologna, Paris and Oxford, as a legal focus: towards the end of the century, however, theology may have emulated or surpassed law as the principal study. Exeter was likewise a magnet for students in theology and law.[3] Hereford is particularly interesting: according to the poem (*c.* 1195–7) of Simon du Fresne, canon of Hereford, all the seven liberal arts were taught there along with geomancy and legal studies.[4] The schools of York were of some prominence, and those of London, described by William Fitzstephen *a.* 1183, seem to have specialized in arts, including both written and spoken rhetoric.[5] Above all, Northampton has a good claim to be regarded as a temporary *studium generale*, at least for a short duration in the reign of Henry II when it was just as important as Oxford and perhaps even more so.[6] But, in the event, none of these schools evolved into full-scale universities; and by the end of the twelfth century Oxford had attained a definite educational primacy and had emerged as the only *studium generale* of a permanent nature.

Rashdall considered that Oxford owed its primacy especially to a migration of English masters and students from Paris in 1167 arising out of an incident in the Becket controversy.[7] He contended that before this date, although there were individual masters teaching in Oxford, there is no

[1] On the mythological origins of Oxford and Cambridge see Rashdall, *Universities*, iii, pp. 5–6, 276 and notes.
[2] Hunt, art. cit., pp. 21–2 (*Essays in Medieval History*, pp. 107–8); see also K. Edwards, *English Secular Cathedrals in the Middle Ages*, 2nd ed. (Manchester, 1967), pp. 185–6.
[3] Hunt, art. cit., p. 28 (*Essays in Medieval History*, p. 114); Edwards, op. cit., pp. 186–7; see also S. Kuttner and E. Rathbone, 'Anglo-Norman Canonists of the Twelfth Century', *Traditio*, vii (1949–51), pp. 279 ff. at p. 321.
[4] The poem is edited by Hunt, art. cit., pp. 36–7 (*Essays in Medieval History*, pp. 121–2.)
[5] See William FitzStephen's 'Descriptio Londoniae' in *Materials for the History of Thomas Becket*, ed. J. C. Robertson, Rolls Series, iii (London, 1877), pp. 4–5, 9.
[6] See H. G. Richardson, 'The Schools of Northampton in the Twelfth Century', *E.H.R.*, lvi (1941), pp. 595 ff.
[7] For this thesis see Rashdall, *Universities*, iii, pp. 11 ff. and A. F. Leach's criticisms and Rashdall's response printed ibid., iii, appendix i, pp. 465 ff.

evidence of more than one master teaching at a time; and until a plurality of masters can be determined Oxford cannot be reckoned a *studium generale*. But the existence, soon after 1167, of several masters teaching in more than one faculty, with powers of attracting students from a wide geographical area, led Rashdall to conclude that the real beginnings of Oxford as a *studium generale* date from the settlement consequent upon the exodus of scholars from Paris.

Rashdall's thesis was based first on a letter of 1167 of the exiled John of Salisbury where he speaks of events fulfilled in accordance with an astrological prophecy including the expulsion of alien scholars from France; and secondly, on a series of ordinances of Henry II aimed against Becket's followers and which contained the provisions that royal consent was required for English clerks passing to and from the Continent and that beneficed English clerks should return home within three months if they were to safeguard their revenues.[1] Rashdall assumed that English scholars would form a proportion of those who migrated from Paris in 1167 and that there would be a sizeable number of English beneficed clerks studying in Paris who would return to England to secure their benefices. Although the edict relating to the beneficed clerks cannot be precisely dated, Rashdall argues that it probably belongs to 1167 (this is largely speculative) and was a main reason for the exodus mentioned in John of Salisbury's letter. The thesis is open to objection on several counts. Rashdall seemingly exaggerated the number of English beneficed clerks studying in the Paris schools in the mid-twelfth century:[2] and the 1167 dating of the edict relating to their return to England is not easily supported by any specific incident in the Becket dispute which would explain its issue at this particular time. Moreover, Rashdall too conveniently assumed that the majority of the returning scholars would be absorbed by Oxford, some perhaps after temporary stay in other towns, instead of being scattered among the various centres of learning in England or resorting to their benefices. But even if Oxford had absorbed all the migrant scholars which, in itself, is unlikely, the numbers involved were probably insufficent to have raised the Oxford schools to a position of clear ascendancy. In his attempt to show that the Oxford *studium* was launched from the traumatic effects of the Paris migration Rashdall thereby minimized a gradual evolutionary interpretation of the process

[1] For John of Salisbury's letter and Henry II's ordinances see ibid., iii, pp. 12–16 and qualifying notes.
[2] See H. E. Salter, 'The medieval University of Oxford', *History*, xiv (1929–30), pp. 57 ff. at p. 57.

by which Oxford achieved university status. Rashdall was impressed by the apparent suddenness with which Oxford after 1167 shot into prominence and could ascribe this only to an external cause. As the early period of university history holds many examples of *studia generalia* founded by migrations, Rashdall argued that Oxford might well provide one of the pioneer instances. (This would perhaps have been the earliest example in European history.) That Oxford, with adaptations, broadly followed the organization of the Paris *studium* was another circumstance which led Rashdall to doubt an evolutionary pattern and to postulate a wholesale importation of Parisian institutional features by the migrant settlers of 1167.[1]

Rashdall's thesis, though valuable in drawing attention to the possible boost which the Oxford schools received from the Paris exodus, seems too radical to fit the known vicissitudes of educational life in twelfth-century England. In particular, it fails to take cognisance of the Northampton schools which appear to have developed into a temporary *studium generale* in the period following the Paris migration. The cumulative evidence, set out by H. G. Richardson,[2] convincingly indicates that for a time during the reign of Henry II the Northampton *studium*, subject to the jurisdiction of the bishop of Lincoln, eclipsed the Oxford schools and became a chief centre of learning wherein, in preference to Oxford, Henry maintained, between 1176 and 1193, a protégé of his daughter, the queen of Spain.[3] From 1193, however, clerks supported by the king were sent to Oxford, and Richardson explains this by reference to the insecurity of the Northampton scholars who, because of Richard I's absence on crusade, were unable to secure protection against a hostile town and who may subsequently have migrated in some numbers to the comparative safety of Oxford: a possible date for this migration would be 1192.[4] If Richardson's thesis is valid, it shows that the Paris exodus of 1167 did not, by itself, transform the Oxford schools into a *studium* surpassing all others and that the university was probably the outcome of a more gradual evolution, in which the Northampton migration formed a coping stone, than is compatible with Rashdall's insistence on the Paris migration, which is best seen as an important link in a chain of continuous development extending over the whole of the twelfth century.

Favourable siting can be adduced as one factor in the development of

[1] On the extent to which Oxford departed from the Parisian constitutional model see below, pp. 101, ff.
[2] Richardson, art. cit., passim.   [3] Ibid., p. 597.   [4] Ibid., pp. 603–4.

the Oxford schools.[1] It is true that Oxford was not the seat of a bishopric, but it was strategically placed. It occupied a central position in the kingdom midway between Northampton and Southampton, and it was a meeting point of routes from several important towns including London, Bristol, Bedford, Worcester and Warwick; and it had easy access to the south coast. It was therefore within reach of most parts of England and was not too inaccessible from the Continent. With the royal palace of Woodstock, built by Henry I *c.* 1100, only a short distance away, and with the coming of St Frideswide's Monastery in 1121 and Oseney Abbey in 1129, Oxford would have been open to influential political and ecclesiastical contacts. Attempts to establish a connection between the Oxford schools and the monastery of St Frideswide's, Oseney Abbey, the church of the canons secular of St George-in-the-castle, or any other religious body have not proved convincing.[2] Had there been an organic relationship then, presumably, the masters and students would have been placed under the jurisdiction of some religious officer; but the chancellor who came to direct the academic guild was an elected official of the masters, one of their own number, exercising a delegated authority derived from the bishop of Lincoln, and in no wise dependent on any religious body in Oxford; and there is no evidence that the masters had been previously subject to a local religious authority from which they had gained emancipation.

In the first half of the twelfth century there is no concrete proof of university organization at Oxford; but there is definite evidence that Oxford schools were able to attract scholars of international repute and to provide at least sporadic teaching in law and theology.[3] The earliest recorded teacher is Theobaldus Stampensis who, having taught it seems at Caen, began to teach at Oxford before 1117 and perhaps as early as 1094. The Oseney chronicle records that Robert Pullen, one of John of Salis-

[1] For the early development of Oxford University see e.g. Rashdall, *Universities*, iii, pp. 5 ff.; T. E. Holland, 'The University of Oxford in the Twelfth Century', *Collectanea II*, ed. M. Burrows (Oxf. Hist. Soc., xvi, 1890) pp. 137 ff.; H. E. Salter, *Medieval Oxford* (Oxf. Hist. Soc., c, 1936), esp. pp. 90 ff. and 'The Medieval University of Oxford', art. cit., pp. 57 ff.; C. E. Mallet, *A History of the University of Oxford*, i (London, 1924), ch. i 'The Origins of Oxford', pp. 1 ff.; Strickland Gibson, 'The University of Oxford', *V.C.H.* (Oxford), iii, ed. H. E. Salter and M. D. Lobel (London, 1954), pp. 1 ff.; Leff, *Paris and Oxford Universities in the Thirteenth and Fourteenth Centuries*, cit., pp. 76 ff.
[2] But H. E. Salter, art. cit., pp. 57–8, has stressed the academic connections of St George-in-the-Castle, but no direct link can be established with the Oxford schools which seem to have grown up round the Church of St Mary.
[3] For this paragraph see the references cited in n. 1. Oxford as a centre of law is discussed by Kuttner and Rathbone, art. cit., pp. 323–7.

bury's masters at Paris, began to teach theology at Oxford in 1133 and continued in this for five years; Geoffrey of Monmouth was resident in Oxford between 1129 and 1151; Walter, archdeacon of Oxford (*c*.1112–*c*. 1151), provost of St George's, was a patron of Geoffrey and was himself a scholar of no mean repute; and Vacarius, the Italian jurist, may have taught civil law at Oxford in 1149. The earliest specific evidence for the existence of several faculties and a large concourse of masters and students at Oxford derives from the account of Giraldus Cambrensis *c*. 1185 of the reading of his *Topographia Hibernica* before the assembled scholars, a feat which occupied three days. In *c*. 1190 Oxford is described as a *studium commune* by a Friesland student then studying in Oxford: before the term *studium generale* acquired a technical precision *studium commune* was used as one of several alternatives;[1] and therefore by this time it seems safe to say that Oxford was regarded as a *studium generale ex consuetudine*, specializing in arts, law and theology. This is reinforced by the known presence in Oxford, towards the end of the century, of a number of celebrated scholars, including Daniel of Morley and Alexander Nequam, who lent distinction to the nascent *studium*, thus helping to stabilize its position of primacy in England's educational life.

The dating of Oxford University must clearly be placed in the twelfth century. Rashdall's Paris migration thesis has to be set within the wider context of the slow evolutionary process by which the *studium* was generated. In view of the evidence for the Northampton schools, one must be wary of antedating Oxford as the chief centre of studies in England. As far as can be determined, the Oxford schools had no organic dependence on any religious body in Oxford and, in this respect, there is a closer affinity with the Bolognese than with the Paris situation.

In a general sense, the Parisian system supplied the model for the Oxford constitution. Nevertheless, there are several significant points of difference which indicate a measure of indigenous growth. The most fundamental of these lay in the position of the chancellor. The first reference to a university chancellor occurs in the award of the papal legate, Nicholas, cardinal bishop of Tusculum, granted to the Oxford scholars in 1214,[2] which paved the way for the re-opening of the schools after their closure in 1209. This charter was in similar vein to that given to the Paris scholars by Philip II

---

[1] See above, p. 24 and n. 3.
[2] Printed by H. E. Salter, *Mediaeval Archives of the University of Oxford*, 2 vols. (Oxf. Hist. Soc., lxx, 1920–1), i, pp. 2–4. The charter is examined e.g. by Kibre, *Scholarly Privileges in the Middle Ages*, cit., pp. 268–9.

in 1200 and, as in the case of Paris, it defined the ecclesiastical standing of the members of the university according them a protected status vis-à-vis lay jurisdiction. The charter contains three references to a chancellor; they are so framed, however, that it is unclear if the office of chancellor is already in existence but vacant, or if it is being instituted by this document, or if it is a projection to be implemented at some point in the future.[1] On balance, the wording suggests that the chancellorship is a new office and that the bishop of Lincoln may soon appoint a chancellor over the scholars. It is not known when the first chancellor was appointed, but there is a good probability that master Geoffrey de Lucy was chancellor at some date between 27 June 1214 and August 1216 and that he was one of the earliest chancellors, and perhaps even the first.[2] One cannot overlook the mention of a *magister scolarum Oxonie* in 1201[3] which implies an earlier form of the chancellorship: indeed, from analogy elsewhere, the *magistri scolarum* may have conferred the teaching licence under the authority of the bishop of Lincoln, although equally this task might have been entrusted to the arch-deacon of Oxford.[4] Whatever the case, it is credible that the position of chancellor had some kind of precedent in the conditions before 1209 (the university was suspended between 1209 and 1214–15) and that it had been established by August 1216.[5] That Hugh of Wells, bishop of Lincoln, apparently forbade Robert Grosseteste, reportedly an early chancellor, to use the title *cancellarius* but only that of *magister scolarum*[6] is perhaps a fore-taste of the bitter jurisdictional feuding that was to develop between the masters' guild and the bishop of Lincoln over the independent standing of the chancellorship.

Originally, the English chancellors were officials of the bishops of Lincoln and Ely exercising delegated episcopal powers.[7] At an early juncture,

[1] The first reference is as follows: '. . . de consilio venerabilis fratris Hugonis tunc Lincolniensis episcopi et successorum suorum vel archidiaconi loci seu eius officialis aut cancellarii quem episcopus Lincolniensis ibidem scolaribus preficiet, . . .'

[2] See the often overlooked but important article by M. G. Cheney, 'Master Geoffrey de Lucy, an early chancellor of the University of Oxford', *E.H.R.*, lxxxii (1967), pp. 750 ff.

[3] *Snappe's Formulary and other records*, ed. H. E. Salter (Oxf. Hist. Soc., lxxx, 1924), p. 318 and *Medieval Oxford*, cit., p. 93.

[4] Rashdall, *Universities*, iii, p. 38 and n. 1.

[5] The terminal date of Geoffrey de Lucy's apparent appointment: Cheney, art. cit., p. 735.

[6] *Snappe's Formulary*, cit., p. 52. Grosseteste was probably chancellor in 1221: Strickland Gibson, 'The University of Oxford', *V.C.H.* (Oxford), iii, p. 2.

[7] For the Oxford chancellor see Strickland Gibson, *Statuta Antiqua*, cit., pp. lxx–lxxiv; for the Cambridge chancellor see the excellent discussion by G. Peacock, *Observations*

however, the chancellor came to be elected by the masters who merely submitted their choice for confirmation by the bishop.[1] In this way, the masters made the *de facto* election (viewed as a 'nomination' by the bishop) and the bishop retained the *de iure* right of appointment. Thus, from being an officer set above and apart from the masters, the chancellor quickly became in every sense one of their number and the champion and embodiment of the autonomy of the guild. The bishop did not excessively intervene in the daily administration of the *studium*, but this did not nullify his legal right to do so. As the chancellor was the vicegerend of the diocesan, the bishop was within his legal rights to supersede the chancellor's authority at any moment of his choosing. In England, the fight for university emancipation centred on the bishop's tenacious claim to confirm the chancellor-elect. After a protracted and acrimonious struggle Oxford won its case in 1367 when Urban V dispensed with the right of episcopal confirmation. A similar dispensation was gained for Cambridge in 1401. In 1395 Oxford acquired a complete exemption from ecclesiastical jurisdiction, and Cambridge did so by decision of the Barnwell Process in 1432.[2] Throughout these struggles the English chancellors had spearheaded the campaign for university freedom from ecclesiastical control and by doing so they further cemented chancellor-guild cohesion. It is the identification of the English chancellor with the masters' guilds and the lead taken by them as the defenders and promoters of university interests which, above all, demarcates the English chancellorship from that of Paris. Whereas the Paris chancellor became alienated from the magisterial guild and at times seemed to be a major obstacle to its growth and autonomous being, the English chancellors acted as buffers between the university and external ecclesiastical authority and summed up the independent aspirations of the academic body. Because of this, because there was no power vacuum, there was no

---

on the *Statutes of Cambridge University* (London, 1841), esp. pp. 17–18 and p. 18, n. 4 and M. B. Hackett, *The Original Statutes of Cambridge University: the Text and its History* (Cambridge, 1970), esp. pp. 104–18.

[1] See Strickland Gibson 'Confirmations of Oxford Chancellors in Lincoln Episcopal Registers', *E.H.R.*, xxvi (1911), pp. 501 ff. and R. M. T. Hill, 'Oliver Sutton, Bishop of Lincoln, and the University of Oxford', *T.R.H.S.*, 4th ser., xxxi (1949), pp. 1 ff.; for Cambridge see Rashdall, op. cit., iii, pp. 280–2; Hackett, op. cit., pp. 107–8.

[2] On Oxford's extended conflict with the bishop of Lincoln see Hill, art. cit., pp. 1 ff.; and much detailed information on the relations between the chancellor and the bishop of Lincoln will be found in Kibre, *Scholarly Privileges in the Middle Ages*, cit., ch. ix, passim; for Cambridge see A. B. Cobban, *The King's Hall within the University of Cambridge in the Later Middle Ages*, cit., pp. 108–11 and 'Episcopal Control in the Mediaeval Universities of Northern Europe', art. cit., pp. 16–21.

motivation for the emergence of a separate rector in the English situation, and the faculty of arts, although very prominent in English university government, did not have the opportunities to achieve the equivalent dominance attained at Paris.[1]

English chancellors wielded considerably greater power than either the Paris chancellor or the Bologna rector.[2] The English chancellorship was an office *sui generis*: it combined extensive spiritual, civil and criminal jurisdiction in a way which gave the English dignitaries a more concentrated authority than their continental counterparts. Spiritual jurisdiction, derived from the bishop of the diocese, was translated into the ecclesiastical powers of the chancellor's court which was conducted on canonical lines. Through his court, the chancellor exercised ordinary jurisdiction (as a *iudex ordinarius*) and quasi-archidiaconal powers over the scholars as clerks, which embraced such matters as discipline, correction of morals and probate of wills of members of the university who died within its precincts; his authority was underpinned by threat of deprivation of academic privileges, including the licence, and, if necessary, by sentence of excommunication. By a serious of royal grants the chancellor also acquired cognisance in many categories of mixed cases involving scholars and townsmen, although these mixed cases were the subject of perennial jurisdictional dispute; and as the resident presiding head of the university he was, rather like a modern vice-chancellor, ultimately responsible for the supervision of all the manifold strands of educational and administrative life of the *studium*.

Another basic difference between the constitutional development of the English universities and that of Paris was the relatively insignificant functions of the nations at Oxford and Cambridge.[3] Following the Paris example, magisterial nations were reproduced in the arts faculty in the English *studia*, although very little has been discovered of the Cambridge nation groupings. But the English nations were subject to a truncated growth. In the more insular English situation the need for defensive organizations of this kind was far less necessary than in a large cosmopolitan university. Originally, Oxford may have had a fourfold nation division (after the manner of Paris: the evidence is not very strong), but because of the small

---

[1] I am not wholly convinced by the common statement that the Oxford arts masters attained an even greater stake in university government and life than at Paris (e.g. Leff, op. cit., p. 101).

[2] See references in p. 102, n. 7.

[3] The Oxford nations are discussed by Kibre, *The Nations in the Mediaeval Universities*, cit., pp. 160–6: Cambridge nations receive one paragraph (pp. 166–7); also Leff, op. cit., pp. 98–100.

number of scholars from outside the British Isles a dual pattern stabilized based on an internal geographical distinction between the northern and southern British: English masters from north of the Nene[1] comprised the northerners or *boreales* and those from south of the Nene the southerners or *australes* (the Scots belonged to the northerners and the Welsh, Irish and foreign scholars to the southerners). The Oxford nations do not appear to have had much autonomous standing and no rector emerged at their head; and they made little impact on academic matters. Perhaps only in the sphere of nation turbulence and inter-nation dissension had the English nations much in common with those of the faculty of arts at Paris. The gang-warfare activities of competing academic bands which afflicted the streets of Oxford and Cambridge were lesser echoes of Parisian nation feuding. The elaborate concordance of 1252, drawn up after a fierce dispute between the *boreales* and the Irish scholars, gives some idea of the scale of the nation disturbance at Oxford.[2] The frequency and intensity of these conflicts led in 1274 to the abolition of the Oxford nations by amalgamation. But even after the supression of the nations the northern/southern division remained a fundamental feature of Oxford life, and racial disharmony continued well into the sixteenth century. On a more positive note, the university endeavoured to rationalize local regional antipathies by ensuring an equal representation as between north and south at most levels of the administrative machine. For example, A. B. Emden has shown that until at least 1509 one of the proctors was always a northerner and the other a southerner; and that as many as thirty-four university offices (but not including the chancellor, bedels, or registrar) were subject to this geographical basis of appointment.[3] This long-term policy is an interesting instance of how a medieval university tried to accommodate racial loyalties and prejudice by directing them into constructive channels which avoided discrimination.

It is therefore clear that the Oxford nations, and seemingly those of Cambridge too, were but pale imitations of their Parisian equivalents. They had little stake in the university constitution: as they had no sustaining *raison d'être* to lend them a permanent life, they withered away as superstructural irrelevancies on the academic scene.

[1] A. B. Emden, 'Northerners and Southerners in the Organisation of the University to 1509', *Oxford Studies presented to Daniel Callus* (Oxf. Hist. Soc., new series, xvi, 1964), pp. 1 ff. at pp. 4–5 has shown that the river Nene, not the Trent, was taken as the point of division between north and south.
[2] The agreement is printed in *Statuta Antiqua*, cit., pp. 84–7.
[3] Emden, art. cit., passim.

With the suppression of the Oxford nations the proctors, two in number as opposed to four at Paris, were concerned wholly with the administration of the *studium* in association with the chancellor.[1] Their range of activities was impressive and made them omnipresent figures in the daily life of the university. They were responsible for the execution of the public business of the university (*publica universitatis negocia*), including the summoning of congregations and the advising of the chancellor on their agenda, the supervision of the exercises leading to degrees, the academic timetable, the management of the elections of the chancellors and bedels, the enforcing of university discipline and the administration of the finances of the *studium*. The concentration of so much business in the hands of the chancellor and the proctors, allied to the fact that the superior faculties had no competing independent organization, as they came to have at Paris, meant that the Oxford central congregations absorbed much of the business performed by the Paris faculties and nations. The Oxford *studium* was thereby rendered more centralized, more unitary in government than the federalized Parisian structure.

The sovereign body at Oxford was the congregation of regents and non-regents or 'congregatio magna', composed of masters and doctors in all the faculties.[2] As the supreme legislature it had the power to make, repeal or amend statutes, and it was summoned according to need. Because of the rather unwieldy nature of the sovereign body the day-to-day administration was managed by the congregation of regents or 'congregatio minor', made up of all the masters and doctors actually teaching in the schools. This assembly could not make statutes; its functions were to apply university legislation to particular cases and to interpret the statutes where necessary. The earliest dated surviving ordinance of the assembly belongs to 1278.[3] It especially dealt with matters relating to degrees, graces, statutory dispensations and electoral procedures, and it met with some frequency.[4] A third assembly, the congregation of artists or 'congregatio

---

[1] On the functions of the proctors see *Statuta Antiqua*, pp. lxxiv–lxxvii; W. A. Pantin, *Oxford Life and Oxford Archives* (Oxford, 1972), ch. vii; Leff, op. cit., pp. 100–1. For legislation relating to proctors see *Statuta Antiqua*, pp. 63–7, 121–3, 149–51, 195–8.

[2] On the congregations of the university see Strickland Gibson, *Statuta Antiqua*, pp. xxi–xxxix and for legislative material relating to the congregations see ibid., pp. 18–19, 124–5, 127–8, 291–3.

[3] Ibid., p. 106.

[4] The type of business dealt with by this assembly is well illustrated from the earliest extant register of congregation: see *The Register of Congregation 1448–1463*, ed. W. A. Pantin and W. T. Mitchell (Oxf. Hist. Soc., new series, xxii, 1972) which contains mainly the proceedings of the congregation of regents.

nigra', reflected the numerical superiority of the artists in the *studium* and institutionalized their privileged claim to deliberate separately on proposed legislation before it reached the sovereign body, the 'congregatio magna'.[1] Just how important this assembly was and how often it met is unclear. By the fifteenth century, the 'congregatio minor', with its majority of regent masters of arts, had achieved a prominence equal to that of the 'congregatio magna' in university affairs; and this probably explains the decline of the separate congregation of artists in the later medieval period.

It would clearly be a simplification to regard the Oxford constitution as a diluted replica of the Paris system. For the position and functions of the Oxford chancellor, nations and higher faculties differed substantially from their corresponding rôles at Paris. The absence of a cathedral school origin and the relative insularity of Oxford's academic population are at least two of the factors which generated features of indigenous growth. It is true that, with adaptations of some importance, the Paris curriculum of studies and degree structure were reproduced in Oxford, but this alone was insufficient to detract from the distinctive character of Oxford's constitutional development.

Just as Bologna was based on the primacy of law and Paris on logic and speculative theology, so Oxford achieved, in the first half of the thirteenth century, a European reputation in mathematics and the natural sciences founded upon the vast corpus of new Aristotelian material absorbed piecemeal into Europe in the century or so after *c.* 1150. As previously indicated,[2] Englishmen in the twelfth century had been conspicuously engaged in the discovery of scientific data, and their pioneer advances in mathematics and the natural sciences found an institutional haven in the nascent University of Oxford. The twelfth-century English scientific tradition was allowed a full development at Oxford because the *studium* was unaffected by the papal ban on the teaching of the New Aristotle imposed at Paris in the early thirteenth century, a policy designed to maintain the purity of Paris as the leading stronghold of speculative theology. Moreover, there was at first no firm speculative, dialectical cast to Oxford studies to counter this growing interest in *quadrivium* subjects.[3] Robert Grosseteste, now seen to be the key figure in the Oxford scientific movement,[4] was bishop of Lincoln from

---

[1] See *Statuta Antiqua*, pp. 127–8. [2] See above, p. 17.
[3] See Knowles, *The Evolution of Medieval Thought*, cit., pp. 280–1.
[4] For Grosseteste's contribution see A. C. Crombie, *Robert Grosseteste and the Origins of Experimental Science*, cit., passim and Crombie, 'Grosseteste's Position in the History of Science' in *Robert Grosseteste: Scholar and Bishop*, cit., pp. 98 ff. See also Leff, op. cit., pp. 272 ff.

1235 to 1253, and apparently an early chancellor of the university. His translation and absorption of a sizeable bulk of the new Aristotelian material was the groundwork for the evolution of two procedural principles of enduring value for the study of science in the middle ages; namely, the application of mathematics to the natural sciences as a means of description and explanation, and the stress upon observation and experiment as the essential method of testing a given scientific hypothesis. These principles transformed the study of scientific data from a fairly random exercise to an integrated mathematical inquiry into physical phenomena based upon the tripartite cycle of observation, hypothesis and experimental verification. As first lector to the Franciscan school at Oxford Grosseteste transmitted his interests and methodology to the Minors who before 1250 confirmed the mathematical and scientific bent of Oxford learning. Later in the thirteenth century, however, this Oxford concentration was lessened: this was due partly to the international nature of the friars who gradually increased the amount of Parisian-based theological matter and techniques of study in Oxford academic life, and partly to the constant interchange of regent masters between Paris and Oxford which did much to effect a greater standardization of intellectual pursuits on both sides of the Channel.[1] Nevertheless, mathematical and scientific researches were still commonly combined with theological studies at the highest levels in fourteenth-century Oxford as the careers of Thomas Bradwardine and other fellows of Merton College adequately testify.

Generally speaking, the English universities were far less disturbed by the theological and political controversies which made of Paris an academic microcosm of Europe.[2] For example, the disputes with the mendicants, which were fought out with such intensity at Paris, found only a moderate reflection at Oxford and Cambridge; the struggle for university emancipation from episcopal control was of a far milder variety at Oxford than at Paris, and even more so at Cambridge; and direct intervention of the English universities in the Great Schism cannot compare with the entanglement of the Paris *studium*, although it has recently been shown that Cambridge was more significantly involved than was formerly realized.[3]

[1] Knowles, op. cit., p. 281.
[2] See the remarks of F. M. Powicke, 'Bologna, Paris, Oxford: Three *Studia Generalia*' in *Ways of Medieval Life and Thought*, cit., p. 175.
[3] See W. Ullmann, 'The University of Cambridge and the Great Schism', *J.T.S.*, ix (1958), pp. 53 ff.

The pace of life in the English universities was less hurried than on the Continent, less prone to be thrown out of gear by a European crisis. From the thirteenth to the sixteenth centuries Oxford and Cambridge benefited from the consistent support of the English monarchy and, when necessary, from the papacy; and this measure of security allowed for quiet evolution.

V

2. Cambridge

It is well known that only a small corpus of material relating to the medieval University of Cambridge has survived by comparison with the copious records which are available for medieval Oxford.[1] Even so, until recently,[2] Cambridge historians have not evinced a proper interest in the history of their own university. The result has been that Cambridge University, at least for the period before 1400, has suffered from a low European reputation being generally assigned to the lower end of the league table for medieval universities,[3] and often hurriedly passed over in general accounts of university development. English academic history in the middle ages is frequently viewed through Oxford eyes with Cambridge regarded as an inferior derivative of the Oxford *studium* following its progenitor in every essential respect. Research of the last fifteen years, however, would appear to make a revision of these traditional views necessary and would indicate that the medieval University of Cambridge is significant for academic history in several important respects.

The evidence for the origins of Cambridge University is of the most fragmentary kind. The attempt to see the *studium* as an outgrowth of the town's twelfth-century grammar schools, fostered and augmented by the activities of the monks of Ely, Croyland and Barnwell, is a thesis which is

---

[1] See e.g. Cobban, *The King's Hall* . . ., cit., p. 2.
[2] For examples of recent progress on the history of the medieval University of Cambridge see ibid., p. 2, n. 1.
[3] See e.g. Rashdall's disparaging remarks, *Universities*, iii, p. 284: but see also A. B. Emden's qualification of Rashdall's harsh judgment, loc. cit., n. 2.

too speculative to carry much weight.[1] By 1200, there is no indication of an embryonic *studium* of higher learning in Cambridge; this seemingly emerged only after the migration of Oxford masters and scholars to Cambridge following the *suspendium clericorum* in 1209. One must therefore accept that the university owed its foundation primarily to the Oxford exodus.[2] Some of the migratory masters may have been natives of Cambridge and of East Anglia and this would provide a tentative reason as to why Cambridge was selected by a section of the Oxford exiles in 1209.[3] The noticeable number of *magistri* connected with Eustace, bishop of Ely, 1197–1215, including some who had definitely been Oxford masters, may furnish another pointer to the choice of Cambridge.[4] The period of the closure of the Oxford *studium*, 1209–14/15, apparently saw the firm establishment of the Cambridge schools. By 1225 a chancellor is recorded[5] which denotes that the masters and scholars now formed a distinct corporation within Ely diocese. The earliest recognition of Cambridge University by the papacy seems to be an indult of Gregory IX of 14 June 1233 addressed to the 'chancellor and university of scholars at Cambridge'[6] and which conceded to Cambridge the essential university judicial privilege of the *ius non trahi extra*, which was granted to Paris only in 1245 and to Oxford in 1254.[7] It is therefore clear that by 1233 the Cambridge *studium* was firmly recognized as a corporate juridical entity functioning under the direction of a chancellor who, by 1250 and probably a good deal before, was elected by the regent masters. The earliest extant enactment of the chancellor and regent masters dates from 1246;[8] and the earliest dated statute of the university was promulgated on 17 March 1276 which presupposes a high degree of university organization and advanced state of learning.[9]

The recent discovery by Dr Benedict Hackett of a MS in the Biblioteca

---

[1] See G. Peacock, *Observations on the Statutes of the University of Cambridge*, cit., pp. 14–15 and J. B. Mullinger, *The University of Cambridge*, 3 vols. (Cambridge, 1873–1911), i, p. 324; Rashdall, op. cit., iii, p. 277 and notes 1, 3.
[2] See recently Hackett, *The Original Statutes of Cambridge University*, cit., p. 44.
[3] See ibid., pp. 45 ff.
[4] Loc. cit.
[5] Ibid., pp. 47–8.
[6] *Register, Gregory IX*, ed. L. Auvray (Paris, 1896), i, p. 779, no. 1389.
[7] See Hackett, op. cit., p. 53.
[8] Printed in ibid., p. 55.
[9] The significance of this statute for the early history of Cambridge University is discussed by W. Ullmann, 'The Decline of the Chancellor's authority in medieval Cambridge: a rediscovered statute', *Historical Journal*, i (1958), pp. 176 ff.

Angelica, Rome, containing undated folios, bearing the title of *Constitu-ciones Universitatis Cantebrigiensis* has important implications for the organi-zational maturity and degree of indigenous growth of the Cambridge *studium* in the thirteenth century.[1] Dr Hackett's thesis is that these folios contain the only surviving copy of the first constitution of Cambridge University, and that from these it is now possible to reconstruct the text of the original statutes. From internal evidence he concludes that the text of the original constitution was compiled *c.* 1234–54 and advances 'by *c.* 1250' as a convenient working date. He further alleges that these *Constitu-ciones* comprise a complete code of statutes, the first of any medieval uni-versity. These *Constituciones* comprise thirteen chapters of varying length relating to such basic matters as a chancellor, rectors, regent masters, bedels, convocation, judicial procedure, dress, discipline, hostels and the rents of houses, the commemoration of benefactors, and funerals of mem-bers of the university. Of special interest are the brief directives concerning the admission of scholars to the master's degree, regulations about lectures and disputations, and the chapter on the terms of the academic session. Unfortunately, there is nothing on the curriculum or prescribed texts and reference is made only to the three faculties of arts, canon law and theology, there being no mention of civil law or medicine.

By comparing these *Constituciones* with the early statutes of Oxford and other thirteenth-century *studia generalia* and tracing their evolution right down to the sixteenth century, Dr Hackett has assembled a wealth of detail illustrative of the constitutional and academic development of the medieval University of Cambridge which amply demonstrates that one cannot view Cambridge's constitution as a mere derivative: the problem must be set within the wider context of international university history. Moreover, if his dating is accurate, Dr Hackett has added much new material to convince that Cambridge was a fully-extended *studium generale ex consuetudine* by the mid-thirteenth century. It is not so clear, however, whether Dr Hackett has proved his point that these *Constituciones* measure up to a complete statutory code, the first among medieval universities.[2] It is possible that there are early statutes here but equally some of the items are perhaps no more than written customs which only later acquired statutory form. The absence of a preamble, embodying a declaration of intent, the terse eco-

[1] Dr Hackett's findings are published as *The Original Statutes of Cambridge University,* cit.
[2] See my review of Dr Hackett's valuable book in *E.H.R.,* lxxxvii (1972), pp. 167–8; also the more detailed review by W. Ullmann, *Journal of Ecclesiastical History,* xxii (1971), pp. 134–9.

nomy of the text at several crucial points, the tangled textual, juristic, academic and dating problems and the fact that the Angelica text had no official standing but was probably privately commissioned must make us hesitant about the unqualified acceptance of Dr Hackett's conclusions in this respect.

It has been widely assumed that Pope John XXII officially conferred the status of *studium generale* upon the University of Cambridge in 1318.[1] The assumption is that, before this date, Cambridge had not yet acquired a status equal to that of Oxford, which had been recognized as a *studium generale ex consuetudine* for over a century. But a re-examination of the letter of John XXII, based on a more accurate text than previously utilised,[2] makes it clear that the papal award was nothing more than a confirmation of Cambridge as a *studium generale*, without in any way improving upon its status. This has important bearings for the history of the medieval university. For it signifies that at no time did the pope confer, even officially, the status of *studium generale* upon the University of Cambridge, but intervened only to strengthen it by apostolic confirmation. From this, it follows that throughout at least part of the thirteenth and early fourteenth centuries Cambridge had already been recognized as a *studium generale* in the widest sense of the term and not merely *respectu regni*: a view which Dr Hackett's researches would seem to endorse. As Cambridge had not been recognized as 'general' by papal authority, it must have been treated as 'general' by custom. One may therefore assert that even if Cambridge did not then possess a European reputation as great as that of her more prominent and larger English counterpart, she nevertheless enjoyed a status in every way equal to that of Oxford. Indeed, there is now justification for ranging the Cambridge *studium* with all those older *studia* such as Paris, Bologna, Oxford, Padua and Orléans, which had attained positions as *studia generalia* by custom (*ex consuetudine*) and not by formal papal enactment. And as a supplement to this picture of the standing of medieval Cambridge, it should be stressed that by the beginning of the fifteenth century the university appears to have acquired a European renown as a university of the first league. In support of this contention can be adduced, for example, the

---

[1] Denifle, *Die Entstehung der Universitäten des Mittelalters bis 1400*, cit., esp. pp. 352–3, 375–6 (Dr Hackett, op. cit., p. 177 seems to me to slightly misrepresent Denifle's view of this papal award); Rashdall, *Universities*, iii, p. 283; J. P. C. Roach, 'The University of Cambridge', *V.C.H.* (Cambridge), iii, ed. J. P. C. Roach (London, 1959), p. 154.

[2] The letter of John XXII is re-examined by A. B. Cobban, 'Edward II, Pope John XXII and the University of Cambridge', *B.J.R.L.*, xlvii (1964), pp. 49 ff. at pp. 68 ff.: the revised edition of the letter is printed as an appendix, pp. 76–8.

revealing circumstance that at the conclusion of the Council of Constance in 1417 the cardinals took the trouble to send a special letter to the University of Cambridge to inform it of their choice of a new pontiff. As far as is known, there is no such corresponding announcement to the Oxford *studium*.[1]

And in the realm of collegiate history too Cambridge University made a not inconsiderable contribution to English academic life. Details are given in chapter six of some of the areas in which this academic impact was made. In this respect, the royal College of the King's Hall, Cambridge, had a dual significance. Apart from its innovatory character in a number of important academic spheres, it stands out as an institution *sui generis* among English academic societies of the middle ages.[2] It had its origins in an extension of Edward II's chapel royal set in the University of Cambridge. For over two hundred years the King's Hall functioned as the intensely personal instrument of the Crown: the Society was maintained throughout by royal exchequer grant, and successive English kings retained the patronage in their own hands, every fellow and warden being a crown appointee. These exceptional constitutional features set apart the King's Hall from all other categories of English colleges with royal associations. It is no exaggeration to say that the Society was something of a landmark in English university history. For it called into being the first royal colony of clerks to be established in a university context and inaugurated the earliest institutional link between the royal household and the English universities. This college-government connection was later expanded to embrace all 'royal' colleges at Oxford and Cambridge; but because of its unique relationship to the royal household, the King's Hall remained the sheet-anchor of this nexus between the universities and the court throughout the middle ages. As a kind of educational prop to the central government, this royal society apparently had as one of its chief functions the provision of a reservoir of educated personnel for ecclesiastical and governmental service. It is noteworthy that, 'of the superior disciplines, civil law was the main academic concentration at the King's Hall: and from the early fourteenth century English kings had fostered this study at the college. Their success can be gauged from the fact that the

---

[1] For a detailed analysis of this whole subject see W. Ullmann, 'The University of Cambridge and the Great Schism', *art. cit.*, with edition of text of the cardinals' letter, pp. 75 ff.

[2] The conclusions in this paragraph are derived from Cobban, *The King's Hall . . .*, cit., passim.

college became the most important cradle of civil law graduates in Cambridge. Under direct royal patronage and stimulation, the King's Hall was intended to play a central rôle in the perpetuation and renaissance of civil law studies at the English universities prompted perhaps partly by the need to meet an increased demand for civil law graduates arising from movements such as the Hundred Years War and European Conciliarism, and partly to engender a climate of legal thought generally favourable to the more theocratic aspects of kingship. Further researches may well reveal that the King's Hall was only one of several such *foci* sponsored by the Crown to promote civilian studies in medieval England.

The direction of recent research has been to revise and largely to reject the traditional image of Cambridge University in the thirteenth and fourteenth centuries. Whether from the standpoint of organizational growth and degree of indigenous evolution, or legal status, or the importance of its collegiate development, or its powers of attraction of prominent schoolmen, the University of Cambridge is now seen to be a major force in medieval English academic life.

V

3. Late medieval universities

The history of the later medieval universities, which followed the period of spontaneous university creation, has yet to be written.[1] It is an area of study which forms an uncertain mosaic wherein broad generalizations co-exist uneasily with the findings of monographic research. A reason for past neglect of this subject has been the assumption that the later universities were watered down and inferior versions of Europe's archetypal *studia* and manifested the symptoms of organizational and intellectual decline. But difference is not necessarily decline: and the readiness with which the later universities adapted to meet changing social needs suggests that the university movement continued to be a vibrant force and not a petrification of a once living ideal. Contemporaries would probably not have viewed the universities of the fourteenth and fifteenth centuries as exhibiting marks of decay just because they failed to emulate the position attained by Bologna, Paris, Oxford, Padua, or Montpellier in the early phase of university development when scarcity value led to easier distinction. If there were between fifteen and twenty universities functioning in 1300, there were about seventy in 1500,[2] which, by any criterion, was a

[1] For the later medieval universities see e.g. S. d'Irsay, *Histoire des universités* . . ., cit., i; Rashdall, *Universities*, ii; J. Verger, *Les universités au moyen âge*, cit., pp. 105 ff.; H. Koller, 'Die Universitäts-Gründungen des 14. Jahrhunderts' *Salzburger Universitätsreden*, no. 10 (Salzburg, 1966).

[2] See the 'university map' in Rashdall, op. cit., i, p. xxiv and in V. H. H. Green, *Medieval Civilization in Western Europe* (London, 1971), pp. 264-5. The problem of computing numbers of universities is complicated by the fact that it is not always possible to know if some universities were functioning at a particular point in time, or even if they had progressed beyond the stage of paper foundation.

sign of buoyant optimism in the university condition. Even allowing for substantial redistribution of the student population of the older *studia*, this massive university expansion presupposes a sizeable increase in Europe's student numbers[1] and teaching force. This rising academic stake in the community was reflected in the growing splendour of university buildings which were being designed to have a prestigious permanence: solidly enmeshed in their urban environments, the later medieval universities could not easily employ the threat of migration; and this marks a fundamental departure from the era when instability was the hallmark of university life and intermittent nomadism one of the perils of the academic profession. The diffusion of intellectual talent over so many widely dispersed *studia* broke the monopolistic sway of the old-established universities; but the fragmentation of these cosmopolitan academic concentrations did not necessarily mean a lessening of university standards: it may only have resulted in a levelling over a broad geographical canvas. Although these matters are beyond measurement, one should avoid the automatic assumption that because the archetypal *studia* suffered population and intellectual reverses, the new universities must have partaken in a corresponding diminution.

There is a rich profusion of documentation for the study of the later universities and some of it is different in kind from that available for the older *studia*. The main interpretative lines for the history of the archetypal universities, at least in their formative stage, were based largely upon the official documents such as statutes, charters, bulls and the like and combined with intellectual assessments of the outstanding schoolmen. For the new universities there is more material of an administrative and business nature including records of university government, books of account, and matriculation and degree lists. These are supported by collegiate records, letters, sermons, and legal, ecclesiastical, state and municipal categories of archive which, directly or indirectly, have a bearing on universities and can perhaps provide a better insight into university life at the average level than is obtainable from the records of the thirteenth-century *studia*. But the examination and publication of this material is very far from complete and synthesis is not yet possible.[2]

The majority of the fourteenth- and fifteenth-century universities were founded by secular rulers or by municipalities and confirmed by the papacy: Treviso (1318), Pavia (1381), Orange (1365) and Prague (1347–8)

[1] E.g. Verger, op. cit., p. 105.
[2] See the remarks of Verger, ibid., pp. 106–9.

were imperial foundations, although Prague was nevertheless submitted for papal approbation.[1] While considerations of prestige loomed large among the motives for foundation, unless the proposed university was rooted in real need and was favourably sited, its chances of survival were not good. The University of Grenoble, founded in 1339, was badly placed in the Dauphiné whose territory was disputed between the Empire and the French monarchy; it never prospered and was eventually replaced by the University of Valence in 1452.[2] Moreover, there was often a long gap separating the initial foundation step and the time when the university came into active being. For example, a university was projected at Nantes, with papal backing in 1414, and again in 1449; but it was not until 1461 that a university was actually opened.[3] In addition, a number of stillborn or entirely paper universities were projected which were sanctioned by papal bulls conferring *studium generale* status. In most of these cases, the reasons for abortive growth are unclear. Among this category of *studia* are included the proposed universities of Dublin, Lucca, Orvieto and Gerona.[4]

The multiplication of universities in Italy, France, Spain, Portugal, Germany, Scotland and Scandinavia radically altered Europe's university geography. There was now far greater opportunity for students to attend a local university and this helped to accentuate the position of the universities as agents of secular government. Just as Paris and Bologna in the later medieval period succumbed to increasing state control, so the new foundations, from the circumstances of their inception, were accommodated to national, regional or municipal interests from the start. The celebrated exodus of 1409 from Prague University of the German masters and students, who comprised a majority of the academic population, following the alteration of the constitution by King Wenceslas to ensure the Bohemian masters a rigged commanding voice in all university assemblies, is only an outstanding instance of the way in which nationalistic concerns began to infiltrate the European *studia*.[5] Universities lost their supranational character and were increasingly regarded as integral parts of political territorial units, designed to serve the needs of national institutions and to be

[1] See Rashdall, *Universities*, ii, pp. 43–4, 51–3, 184–6, 213 ff.
[2] Ibid., ii, pp. 183–4; Verger, op. cit., pp. 140–1.
[3] Rashdall, op. cit., ii, pp. 203–5.
[4] 'Paper universities' are discussed ibid., ii, appendix i, pp. 325 ff.
[5] For the Czech-German struggle at Prague see ibid., ii, pp. 222 ff. and H. Kaminsky, 'The University of Prague in the Hussite Revolution: The Role of the Masters', *Universities in Politics*, cit., pp. 79 ff.

of benefit to those living in the locality. In the late medieval German universities, for example, many of the masters approximated to the rank of state
officials, and this led to a close fusion of the professional intellectual ethos
with that of the professional civil servant.[1] By definition, a cosmopolitan
academic gathering, especially one wherein the foreign element was noticeably
large, was held to be at odds with the centralized pattern of secular government which was so pronounced a trend in the late middle ages. There is
nothing to indicate that the universities exhibited organized resistance to
their rôle as protégés of secular authority: they must long since have
realized that academic freedom, in any purist sense, was a chimera and that
society would not tolerate or financially support academic groupings without exacting some kind of quantitative return.[2] In these circumstances, it is
not surprising that the proportion of lay masters and students was augmented appreciably, especially in the *studia* of Italy and southern France
where there had always been a significant lay tradition.[3]

If the later medieval universities were trapped within the orbit of secular
control, they were far freer than their predecessors from ecclesiastical dominion. This is particularly true of the fifteenth-century *studia*. For by that
time the hard-fought struggle with the ecclesiastical authorities had been
won and the 'commonwealth' episcopal era begun.[4] Most of the fifteenth-
century French *studia* such as Aix (1409), Dôle (1422), Poitiers (1431),
Valence (1452, 1459), Nantes (1460) and Bourges (1464) were almost entirely free from attempts by local ecclesiastical powers to infiltrate and
control the university corporation. Likewise, episcopal dominion is not
really a live issue in the universities of Germany, Bohemia, and the Low
Countries of the late fourteenth and fifteenth centuries. Many of these,
such as Prague (1347–8), Vienna (1365), Heidelberg (1385) and Leipzig
(1409) owed their inception to the actions of the local rulers.[5] Others such
as Cologne (1388) and Rostock (1419) were brought to fruition as a result
of municipal enterprise. Würzburg (1402) was an episcopal foundation,
and it was fairly common practice in this group of universities to appoint

[1] See L. Boehm, 'Libertas Scholastica und Negotium Scholare: Entstehung und Sozialprestige des Akademischen Standes im Mittelalter' in op. cit., p. 47.
[2] See the highly utilitarian and changeable attitude adopted by the Florentine Signoria
towards the University of Florence in G. A. Brucker, 'Florence and the University,
1348–1434' in *Action and Conviction in Early Modern Europe*, cit., pp. 220 ff.
[3] E.g. Verger, op. cit., p. 111.
[4] See Cobban, 'Episcopal Control in the Mediaeval Universities', art. cit., esp. pp. 13–14.
[5] Leipzig owed its foundation to Frederick and William Landgraves of Thuringia,
who invited a section of the German scholars who migrated from Prague in 1409 to
establish a *studium* in this city.

a bishop or archbishop as chancellor. But where this was done, the chancellor's authority was to be largely nominal and his jurisdictional powers were, from the start or at a conveniently early stage, conferred upon the governing body of the university, usually represented by a rector.[1] The universities of Germany, Bohemia and the Low Countries were thus conceived in an intensely secular milieu, and this provided a solid limitation to the exercise of ecclesiastical authority. In Scotland, as previously mentioned,[2] episcopal initiative in university foundation was a wholly benevolent force, and one entirely compatible with an inevitable advance towards independent status. As far as one can judge, the same holds true for the situation in fifteenth-century Scandinavia.[3]

The broad constitutional features of the French provincial, Spanish and Italian universities are outlined in chapter seven; and the evolution of the college-university as a focal point of university development in Germany and Scotland is discussed in chapter six. These aspects need not therefore be examined here.

The archetypal universities of Bologna and Paris formed the models upon which the twofold pattern of late medieval university organization was based, the former giving rise to the notion of the student university and the latter to that of the masters' university. Generally speaking, the north European *studia* followed the framework of Paris and those of southern Europe the direction of Bologna. But few universities reproduced these patterns without adaptations. Even the German universities, which were closely influenced by the Paris model, show important departures. The earliest of these, Prague and Vienna, initially allowed scope for student participation, although these Bologna elements were later phased out.[4] The position of rector ceased to have much significance in the German

---

[1] E.g. at Prague the archbishop was chancellor and exercised considerable authority in the early years. In 1397, however, the university obtained a complete exemption from all episcopal and archiepiscopal jurisdiction (Rashdall, ii, pp. 218, 220). At Würzburg (1402) the bishop became chancellor but, by the founder's charter of privileges of 1410, both spiritual and temporal jurisdiction over all students were conferred on the rector (Rashdall, ii, p. 257). The bishop of Merseburg was made chancellor at Leipzig (1409) and delegated jurisdiction over the students to the rector at an early stage; here, degrees were usually conferred by a vice-chancellor (Rashdall, ii, p. 259). The chancellor at Rostock (1419) was the bishop of Schwerin, but by 1468 the rector had acquired extensive jurisdictional powers from the bishop (Rashdall, ii, p. 261 and n. 2).
[2] See above, p. 76.
[3] See the accounts of the universities of Upsala (1477) and Copenhagen (1478) in Rashdall, op. cit., ii, pp. 298–300.
[4] On the nations of Prague and Vienna see Kibre, *The Nations in the Mediaeval Universities*, pp. 167–76; Rashdall, op. cit., ii, p. 281.

situation. It lost its Parisian connections with the faculty of arts and the rector could be chosen from any quarter. Sometimes the office was accorded to a young aristocrat on a largely honorary basis as it was to the advantage of many German universities to encourage aristocratic patronage.[1] Several universities evolved features of such a hybrid nature that they formed a third constitutional category whose inspirational base was a combination of Bologna and Paris. Some of the French provincial *studia* were cast in this mould. The institutional permutations were manifold; and the chain of archetypal borrowing, adaptation and borrowed adaptation becomes so complex that it is not always possible to work out the constitutional pedigree of several of these later *studia*. Nation groupings were usually less important in the later universities than in those of the thirteenth century, presumably a symptom of the diminishing international university order.[2] In some universities, for example Orange, Dôle, Caen, Cahors, Perpignan, Nantes, Bordeaux, Erfurt and Cologne, there was no system of nations at all,[3] and in other *studia* such as Heidelberg they were quickly abolished.[4] Where nations survived, they did so primarily as administrative units and not as governmental or educational organs. The artificial and formal nature of the nations in the late medieval period represents a compromise between respect for a fundamental pioneer force in university development and a progressive need to fade out the nation unit as a central feature of the academic landscape. The nations had become something of an albatross: they were democratic embarrassments from a bygone age. Their centrifugal character could not be allowed to deflect from the more unitary style of university government that was emerging in the late middle ages.

[1] Rashdall, op. cit., ii, p. 281; see J. M. Fletcher, 'Wealth and Poverty in the Medieval German Universities' in *Europe in the Late Middle Ages* (ed. J. R. Hale, J. R. L. Highfield and B. Smalley, London, 1965), pp. 410 ff.
[2] For the nations in the later medieval universities see Kibre, op. cit., chs. iv, v.
[3] Ibid., pp. 156, 177.
[4] Ibid., p. 177.

VI

European collegiate movement

The colleges of the medieval universities do not always receive the emphasis they deserve. In the past, the college history has often amounted to little more than an evaluation of the founder's statutes, a biographical survey of its *alumni*, and a description of its architectural features.[1] This work has sometimes been undertaken by an ex-member of the college who might be an amateur in matters historical. As the colleges were destined to occupy a commanding position in the universities of northern Europe, they merit more sympathetic treatment. The partial avoidance of collegiate studies by professional historians has had unfortunate results. It has meant that the 'pious memorial' approach has been a good deal in evidence; and there has often been a disregard of the historical forces of change which underlay and largely determined the major upheavals and deflections in this field of study. Consequently, the interpretative lines of collegiate history have suffered here and there from the blight of parochialism. The insular type of investigation which presents college history as a labour of love, a tribute to a shrine, and which fails to utilize comparative material, does injury by channelling collegiate studies into a patchwork mould which is an obstacle to the emergence of a reliable integrated pattern.

It is only right that the colleges of the medieval universities should receive the same close attention that has been given to the monastery or the baronial household. For the colleges were the main secular supports of the students in the superior faculties of law, theology and medicine, and,

[1] See the remarks of W. A. Pantin, 'College muniments: a preliminary note', *Oxoniensia*, i (1936), pp. 140 ff. at p. 140.

in company with the mendicant orders, harboured generations of the abler and most creative talents in the universities. Presumably, these were the students with the greatest potential social and professional value; and before we can properly evaluate the place of the university as a functional entity in medieval society we shall have to know far more about the colleges which housed them than we do at present. Only when collegiate organization and life have been microscopically examined and considered on a comparative basis shall we be in a position to estimate, with any degree of probability, the conditions in which the majority of the advanced students, at least in northern Europe, had to live and work. Moreover, one must stress that from relatively insignificant beginnings the colleges grew to have a fundamental bearing on the direction and character of the old-established universities of Paris, Oxford and Cambridge. For in the later middle ages the Parisian and English colleges were the heirs to the system of public instruction of the university schools, a system which progressively degenerated for reasons that are not entirely clear. The emergence of the colleges as self-sufficient educational units completed that movement whereby teaching came to be decentralized in the colleges which then were recognizably the focal points of secular academic life on both sides of the Channel; from this stage onwards, the study of Parisian and English university history is inseparably bound up with the collegiate movement. At the same time, it would hardly be an exaggeration to assert that several of the fourteenth- and fifteenth-century universities in Germany and Scotland might not have survived at all but for the stabilizing and enriching effects of the collegiate establishments in their midst. There is therefore no shortage of reasons for the promotion of college studies; they should be assigned a position commensurate with their creative historical rôle and not, as is sometimes the case, dismissed with subordinate and cursory treatment.

The secular medieval college was not simply an advanced version of the academic hall or hostel. In its most mature form the college was an autonomous, self-governing, legal entity, firmly endowed and with its own statutes, privileges and common seal.[1] But many colleges, especially in Continental Europe, fell a good deal short of this definition. For example, corporate status would be severely qualified if the society were denied the right of co-optation of members or full supervision of its administrative

---

[1] See the definition by A. L. Gabriel, 'Motivation of the Founders of Mediaeval Colleges', *Beiträge zum Berufsbewusstsein des mittelalterlichen Menschen* (Miscellanea Mediaevalia, 3, 1964), pp. 61 ff. at p. 61.

and governmental affairs. And there are many instances among the Parisian and French provincial colleges where the founder vested the patronage and ultimate control of government in an external body such as an archbishop, bishop, the head of a religious house or board of university officials.[1] It is abundantly clear that the academic colleges in the medieval universities subsumed a diversity of types ranging from the autonomous, self-governing, landowning model usual in England to the humble institution frequently found in France and Italy, which was little more than a lodging house for students. The common factor underlying this wide spectrum of collegiate differentiation was the act of endowment made for educational purposes. It is the endowed status of the college that decisively distinguishes it from hall or hostel, setting up the conditions of a permanent and stable existence within the university community. Only this element of endowment can provide the connecting thread between sophisticated, highly-organized and prosperous societies such as Merton College, Oxford, or the King's Hall, Cambridge, or the College of Navarre, Paris, and the primitive boarding establishments which flourished in profusion at the lower end of the collegiate scale.

Although the college movement was primarily a contribution to secular need in the universities, it would be misleading to undervalue the spiritual and charitable motives behind this European-wide enterprise. For colleges were, to some extent, an offshoot of the growth of collegiate churches of secular canons with their schools of grammar and song attached. The difference between the academic college and the collegiate church was one of functional emphasis: whereas the *raison d'être* of the college of secular canons was a religious one with education a secondary purpose, in the case of the academic college the position was self-evidently reversed. Nevertheless, many secular colleges partook strongly of the chantry foundation. Generally speaking, the founders of university colleges, whether kings, queens, high-ranking ecclesiastics and statesmen or wealthy members of the lay aristocracy, regarded the foundation of a college as a charitable and pious concern whereby a permanent shrine would be erected to their

---

[1] E.g. the supreme government of the College of the Sorbonne, Paris, was entrusted to the archdeacon and chancellor of Paris, the doctors of theology, the deans of the two other superior faculties, and the rector and proctors of the university (Rashdall, *Universities*, i, p. 508); at Toulouse, the college founded by Vidal Gautier in 1243 was committed to the supervision of the bishop and the prior of the Dominicans (Fournier, *Statuts*, i, no. 517): and the College of Montlezun, founded by two brothers of that name in 1319, was vested in the combined hands of various university and ecclesiastical authorities (Fournier, op. cit., i, nos. 549, 699).

memory in which masses would be said for their souls and those of their relatives. That is to say, the fellows were obliged to take upon themselves the duties of chantry priests. Some colleges were more obviously utilized as chantries than others. In the English situation, for example at King's College and St Catharine's College, Cambridge, and Queen's, New College and All Souls, Oxford, the fellows or scholars had heavy chantry duties to perform;[1] by contrast, the statutes of the King's Hall, Cambridge, enjoin only a minimal stress upon the religious obligations of the fellows.[2] But the personal chantry motive was normally combined with the founder's desire to carry out a useful act of long term consequence. Europe's first group of college founders in the Paris of the late twelfth and early thirteenth century was motivated by the need to alleviate the distress of poor students.[3] The De disciplina scholarium, a treatise written between 1230 and 1240 and widely read in the universities, preached the responsibility of university masters to ensure that student poverty be not a barrier to academic progress.[4] This increasing awareness in academic circles of the need to admit liability for the social and economic welfare of students was one of the main intellectual impulses which launched and sustained the earliest collegiate wave at Paris University. And from the simple conception of a boarding house as a support to poor students there soon evolved the more positive notion of the college as an academic centre where students from a particular region or at specified levels of study might live together in a spirit of harmonious amity and stimulating intellectual exchange.[5] A Christian community embodying spiritual, moral and academic excellence was the kind of model projected by college founders of the thirteenth century, and for whose realization the giving of private wealth was an attractive form of spiritual investment.

The charitable motive underlying the foundation of colleges remained

[1] The chantry regulations for Cambridge fellows will be found in the college statutory codes in *Documents relating to the University and Colleges of Cambridge* (3 vols., ed. by the Queen's Commissioners, London, 1852) (cited hereafter as *Camb. Docs.*); for St Catharine's, *Documents relating to St Catharine's College in the University of Cambridge*, ed. H. Philpott (Cambridge, 1861); for the Oxford fellows, *Statutes of the Colleges of Oxford*, 3 vols., ed. by the Queen's Commissioners (Oxford and London, 1853) (cited hereafter as *Statutes*). An excellent discussion of this chantry theme in academic environments is provided by F. Ll. Harrison, 'The Eton Choirbook', *Annales Musicologiques*, i (1953), pp. 151 ff.
[2] See the King's Hall statutes in W. W. Rouse Ball, *The King's Scholars and King's Hall* (privately printed, Cambridge, 1917), p. 65.
[3] Gabriel, art. cit., p. 62.
[4] Loc. cit.
[5] Ibid., pp. 63-5.

a constant in the medieval period, but the concrete objectives into which it was translated altered according to the changing social and intellectual climate. In general, the thirteenth-century collegiate system served especially to promote arts and theological studies, while in that of the fourteenth and fifteenth centuries civil and canon law were accorded a greater prominence,[1] although at Paris this legal concentration was necessarily truncated by the prohibition of civilian studies by Honorius III in 1219. During the Hundred Years War some founders, both in France and England, were concerned that colleges should be mobilized to fill the depleted ranks of the secular clergy and ensure a supply of competent teachers for the community.[2] And when humanistic values infiltrated the universities, college founders of the late fifteenth and early sixteenth century increasingly reflected the alternative culture in their societies.[3] Whatever objectives lay uppermost in the minds of medieval college founders in different places and at different times the fusion of subjective spiritual expression with objective educational purpose is a fixed ingredient of the collegiate movement.

Paris must be regarded as the home of the university collegiate system in the sense that academic colleges of a kind arose there earlier than anywhere else. The common aim of the founders of the first Parisian colleges was simply to provide endowed accommodation for poor students who could not afford to pay for their own board and lodging. The earliest European college about which there is information is that of the Collège des Dix-Huit which had its beginnings at Paris in 1180.[4] This very rudimentary college was an outgrowth of the Hospital of the Blessed Mary of Paris, known as the Hôtel-Dieu, situated near the Cathedral of Notre Dame. It

[1] On the provision of canonists in medieval Paris colleges see Gabriel, 'Les Collèges parisiens et le recrutement des Canonistes', *L'Année Canonique*, 15 (1971), pp. 233 ff.; see also Gabriel, 'The College System in the Fourteenth-Century Universities' in *The Forward Movement of the Fourteenth Century*, ed. F. L. Utley (Ohio, 1961), pp. 79, ff. at p. 82.

[2] See e.g. Gabriel, 'Motivation of the Founders of Mediaeval Colleges', art. cit., pp. 69–70, and 'The College System in the Fourteenth-Century Universities' in op. cit., loc. cit.

[3] For the English situation see M. H. Curtis, *Oxford and Cambridge in Transition 1558–1642* (Oxford, 1959), pp. 70–72, 105–6 and passim; J. K. McConica, *English Humanists and Reformation Politics* (Oxford, 1965), ch. 4, pp. 76 ff.; J. Simon, *Education and Society in Tudor England* (Cambridge, 1966), esp. pp. 81–9.

[4] The foundation charter of this college is printed in *Chartularium Universitatis Parisiensis*, i, no. 50. The college is discussed by Gabriel, 'The Cathedral Schools of Notre-Dame and the Beginning of the University of Paris' in *Garlandia: Studies in the History of the Mediaeval University*, cit., pp. 39 ff. at p. 56.

had been customary to set aside a single room in this hospital for 'poor clerks', and in 1180 a certain 'dominus Jocius de Londoniis' on his return from a pilgrimage to Jerusalem bought this room and endowed it for the perpetual use of eighteen poor clerks. We are here dealing with a most elementary type of collegiate establishment. Apart from the provision concerning the religious duties of the clerks, there were apparently no regulations made for internal government or for domestic economy. Indeed, only by virtue of its endowment can it be properly styled a college at all. Nevertheless, this can be reckoned the first of some sixty or seventy known Parisian colleges of the medieval period,[1] and the first of any European university.

Foundations of a similar nature such as the Collège de Saint Thomas du Louvre, the Collège des Bons-Enfants de Saint Honoré and the Collège des Bons-Enfants de Saint Victor followed in quick succession, and by the mid-thirteenth century Paris was studded with endowed colleges which had, as yet, little constitutional connection with the university.[2] The early Parisian founders do not appear to have prescribed studies and academic duties, and, like the Collège des Dix-Huit, several of these charitable societies were closely akin to medieval hospitals: moreover, some of them were not initially confined to students but provided also for clerks who were not engaged in university study. As far as is known, most early foundations were designed either for the maintenance of grammar boys or for young men who had completed their grammatical training and had embarked upon the arts course. In modern terminology, they were for advanced schoolboys or university undergraduates or both.

A wholly new departure in European collegiate history came with the foundation of the College of the Sorbonne founded c. 1257/8 by Robert de Sorbon, chaplain to Louis IX.[3] The novel feature of this college lay in the fact that it was planned for graduates, for scholars who had already acquired the degree of M.A. and were about to undertake the onerous course leading to the doctorate in theology. And it is precisely this College of the Sorbonne, this purely graduate college which was later to give its name to the University of Paris, that supplies the essential link between the Parisian and English colleges about which more will be said below.

[1] A tentative list of the Paris colleges, including those of the monastic orders, is given by Rashdall, *Universities*, i, pp. 536–9.
[2] For these early foundations see ibid., i, pp. 501 ff.
[3] See Gabriel, 'Robert de Sorbonne', *Revue de l'Université d'Ottawa*, 23 (1953), pp. 473 ff. and P. Glorieux, *Les Origines du Collège de Sorbonne*, Texts and Studies in the History of Mediaeval Education, no. viii (Notre Dame, Indiana, 1959).

As far as one can judge, about nineteen colleges were founded at Paris before 1300,[1] and about twice that number, at least thirty-seven, in the fourteenth century which was the century *par excellence* of collegiate expansion in western Europe.[2] Eleven or so were founded in the fifteenth century, though it must be stressed that these figures are probably incomplete: because of the instability of the Paris collegiate scene, it is possible that several colleges which enjoyed no more than a fleeting existence have gone unrecorded. At the height of college-founding at Paris in the fourteenth century almost every type of society was represented. As already indicated, some were conceived exclusively for grammar boys and others for students launched upon the B.A. course, and several were for grammarians and artists combined. There were purely graduate societies for the promotion of studies in the superior faculties, and there were mixed institutions, such as the College of Navarre, where undergraduates and graduates lived a life in common pursuing their studies at their appropriate levels. Nor should we overlook the numerous colleges founded for the benefit of foreign students at Paris. Prominent among these were the colleges established by Swedish and Danish cathedral chapters for the maintenance of their fellow countrymen, for example the College of Upsala, Skara House, the College of Linköping and the College of Dacia.[3] Colleges for Scottish and German students and for other national groupings added to the ethnic variety of collegiate enterprise at Paris. Moreover, it is possible that there were several provincial colleges which had links with particular colleges at Paris University. One such was the college founded at Soissons by Aubert de Guignicourt (statutes 1345) for students studying grammar:[4] in 1349 Aubert instituted a scholarship whereby one of his students might proceed to the College de Laon in Paris for advanced study.[5] The extent to which there were provincial collegiate 'feeders' for the Paris colleges is a subject which might well repay further investigation. In general, a rich diversity, a measure of instability, a wide divergence of function and a

[1] This figure and those following are derived from Rashdall's list of Paris colleges referred to in p. 127, n. 1.
[2] It has been reckoned that about eighty-seven colleges were founded in fourteenth-century universities compared with about fifty-eight colleges of the thirteenth and fifteenth centuries: Gabriel, 'The College System in the Fourteenth-Century Universities', art. cit., pp. 82–3.
[3] See Gabriel, *Skara House at the Mediaeval University of Paris*, Texts and Studies in the History of Mediaeval Education, no. ix (Notre Dame, Indiana, 1960), pp. 15 ff.
[4] See F. Pegues, 'The Fourteenth-Century College of Aubert de Guignicourt at Soissons', *Traditio*, 15 (1959), pp. 428 ff.
[5] Ibid., p. 434.

markedly roisterous nature were among the chief characteristics of the medieval Paris colleges.[1]

Constitutionally, the Paris colleges differed considerably from their English counterparts.[2] In the main, the English colleges were self-governing, democratically-run societies. With the notable exception of the King's Hall, Cambridge, the fellows had the right of co-opting to fellowships and of electing to the headship.[3] All important business was decided by majority vote of all the fellows, and the administration lay with college heads and small committees of fellows. These independent societies jealously guarded their autonomous position, and the right of intervention by external ecclesiastical or university powers was reduced to the minimum. At Paris, however, the typical college was not an independent entity but one whose supreme governship lay with one or more external authority. For example, the government of the College of the Sorbonne was vested in the archdeacon and chancellor of Paris, the doctors of theology, the deans of the faculties of law and medicine, and the rector and proctors of the university.[4] While the daily administration of the internal affairs of the Paris colleges was, subject to intervention, usually entrusted to internal officers, external authorities were responsible for the patronage – that is to say, the appointment to the headship and the filling of vacant fellowships or *bursae*; and the property of the colleges was often wholly or partially managed externally. Another basic difference between the Paris and English colleges was the extent to which the former were subject to university surveillance. For at Paris the university, through the chancellor or its faculties or nations, acquired a substantial amount of control over the college system which might manifest itself in the internal arena, in the removal of unsatisfactory personnel, in property matters, or in any deficient aspect of collegiate life where remedial action had not been taken by the appointed governors. Whether in the person of its chancellor or a particular nation, the university was here assuming a visitatorial function vis-à-vis the colleges. There is no reason to suppose that this was regarded as a usurpation of collegiate autonomy, because the university had often been vested with numerous statutory rights of intervention by college founders themselves or their later representatives.[5] The need for university help in the maintenance of

[1] See Rashdall's discussion, *Universities*, i, pp. 501 ff.
[2] On the main features of the Paris colleges see ibid., i, pp. 511 ff. and Gabriel, 'The College System in the Fourteenth-Century Universities', pp. 89 ff.
[3] For the English colleges see below, pp. 132 ff.   [4] See above, p. 124, n. 1.
[5] On this point see the *Additional Note* to Rashdall's treatment of the Paris colleges in *Universities*, i, pp. 533–6; see also Gabriel, art. cit., p. 94.

discipline and in grappling with the legion of problems stemming from disruptive warfare and other turbulent sources made the surrender of college autonomy easier to bear.

As in England, the Paris colleges until the fifteenth century catered for only a minority in the university community. The majority of students in the thirteenth and fourteenth centuries lived either in hospices supervised by regent masters of the university or as 'martinets', as students were called who boarded with townspeople. Initially, the colleges were little concerned with teaching, at least in any formal sense, which was the preserve of the faculties and the nations.[1] But if the colleges at first occupied a relatively insignificant position within the Paris *studium* and in the English universities, by the time of the Reformation they had completely transformed their character.

It is likely that teaching was provided at an earlier date in the Parisian colleges than in England[2] because an undergraduate element was an integral part of numerous Paris colleges from the start, whereas in England the majority of colleges did not house undergraduate students before the fifteenth century. Collegiate instruction in the form of academic exercises and an embryonic lecture system was conceived as supplementary to the teaching of the regent masters in the university schools. But with the infiltration into the colleges of undergraduate pensioners or commoners as non-bursarial members and also of non-boarders who came for instruction, movements of some proportions in the fourteenth century and of considerable magnitude in the fifteenth,[3] the colleges were stimulated to expand their teaching facilities to an extent that they first rivalled and then surpassed the university system of public lectures. For example, in the fifteenth century courses in canon law were staged in several of the Paris colleges;[4] although the faculty of canon law reacted with anxiety and tried to arrest this development, collegiate courses in this subject became thoroughly entrenched in the sixteenth century.[5] The fact that many of the colleges were more comfortable and better heated than the university schools[6] is not a point to be lightly dismissed. As more teaching masters

---

[1] For the academic functions of the Paris nations see P. Kibre, *The Nations in the Mediaeval Universities*, cit., pp. 90–7.

[2] See the discussion of the staging of disputations and extracurricular programmes in the fourteenth-century colleges at Paris and other universities by Gabriel, art. cit., pp. 98–101.

[3] Rashdall, *Universities*, i, pp. 515 ff.

[4] Gabriel, 'Les Collèges parisiens et le recrutement des Canonistes', art. cit., pp. 242–3.

[5] Ibid., p. 243.   [6] Ibid., pp. 242–3.

were drafted into the colleges these became the centres of instruction within the *studium*; and in the sixteenth century the university schools were so reduced that they served as vehicles largely for acts of formality such as determinations and inceptions.[1]

The decentralization of teaching among the Parisian and English colleges had a profound fragmentary effect on their respective universities. For now the constituent parts were more important than the whole, and the university had almost withered away except as the body which through the chancellor conferred the licence, and through incorporation by the masters of the faculties completed the degree-awarding process. The decentralizing movement was, however, less diffused at Paris than in England. Whereas at Oxford and Cambridge instruction devolved upon fellow tutors in the majority of colleges, large and small alike, undergraduate teaching at Paris came to be concentrated in several of the larger collegiate establishments. The difference probably stems from the greater financial and functional divergence among the Parisian colleges than was current in England; and the numerous modest boarding establishments in Paris at the lower end of the collegiate scale could not afford the additional regents necessary to cope with extensive intramural teaching. The smaller colleges (and the unendowed hospices) were consequently encouraged to send their members to attend the lectures staged by the larger institutions which could support an adequate number of regent masters to take fee-paying students through the entire educational gamut. At Oxford and Cambridge even the smaller colleges would normally provide nuclear teaching supplemented perhaps by drawing upon the resources of their wealthier neighbours. But, in the main, England avoided the two-tier collegiate system of Paris whereby the majority of colleges were educationally dependent on a minority of prominent institutions. By the end of the fifteenth century the number of Parisian colleges which furnished a complete instruction in arts (*collèges de plein exercice*) had been reduced to eighteen, about a third of the colleges then known to exist.[2] Parallel with this development in arts, theology at Paris too came to be centred in a few institutions, in the religious houses and the secular colleges of the Sorbonne and Navarre.[3] The growth of this inter-collegiate educational system at Paris in the later medieval period probably made for more effective utilization of teachers and resources than the rather atomized, insular collegiate arrangements in England. Inevit-

---

[1] Rashdall, op. cit., i, p. 520 (commenting on arts teaching).
[2] On this inter-collegiate system at Paris see ibid., i, pp. 528–9.
[3] Ibid., i, p. 528.

ably, in the fifteenth century, there was at Paris a measure of constitutional confusion over the relative positions of college and university regents during the transition from university to college teaching as the Parisian norm. But well before 1500, it appears that college lectures had achieved a recognized status equivalent to the 'ordinary' lectures of the university schools[1] which previously provided the staple instructional diet. The college regents themselves, though nominated by collegiate heads, were appointed and removable by faculty authority and, to this degree, the university retained a supervisory rôle in the transformed teaching system which might extend, it seems, to powers of inspecting the standard of college instruction.[2] This element of university control over the Parisian college system forms yet another point of contrast with the English situation where the colleges developed as teaching islands with only the minimum of university direction.

The Paris colleges were suppressed at the French Revolution, and the university never reverted to collegiate lines. The untidy, variegated nature of Parisian college history is reflective of the unstable, cosmopolitan turbulence of this great medieval university, just as the ordered, conservative character of the English collegiate landscape is indicative of a more quiescent, sober and insular university environment. If some of the Paris colleges were hastily fashioned for ephemeral use, all of the English colleges were purpose-built to last. Too many sets of Paris college statutes remain unpublished, and a definitive view of Parisian college history is not yet possible. The recent publication of a scholarly edition of the three medieval sets of statutes of the College of Autun[3] has caused us to assign a more important place to this college, founded at Paris in 1341 by Cardinal Pierre Bertrand (c. 1280–1348), than had hitherto been suspected. This is so because the author convincingly demonstrates that the statutes of 1341 and 1345 (those of 1491 are concerned mainly with disciplinary affairs) were used as models for several of the Parisian colleges of the fourteenth and early fifteenth centuries. Here is just one pointer to the amount that waits to be discovered in the area of comparative Parisian college history.

Colleges were later phenomena in the life of the English universities than at Paris. And when they did emerge, and right down to the late fifteenth century, they were, with exceptions, primarily designed for a privi-

[1] Ibid., i, pp. 530–1.
[2] Ibid., i, p. 531.
[3] D. Sanderlin, *The Mediaeval Statutes of the College of Autun at the University of Paris*, Texts and Studies in the History of Mediaeval Education, no. xiii (Notre Dame, Indiana, 1971).

leged minority of graduate fellows. Colleges and undergraduates are relatively late bedfellows, and unless this is appreciated English university history will be put out of focus. English colleges were by no means coeval with the birth of Oxford and Cambridge; they have not always been an essential part of the university situation; and they have not always housed, taught and attempted to discipline the undergraduate population.

Initially, the universities of Oxford and Cambridge owned little or no property and could be described as groups of masters and associated students living as best they could in hired premises. Generally speaking, there were three ways in which a student might be domiciled. He might take a room in a tavern or a chamber in a townsman's private house. If he were rich enough, he might rent a whole house for himself and his entourage, though such instances were probably not too common in England. Thirdly, for the undergraduate of moderate means, there was the hall or hostel,[1] which was a house leased from a town landlord for a specified duration often by a master of arts of the university.[2] It served the dual purpose of providing accommodation and limited teaching facilities for students at a modest profit. The hall or hostel became the usual type of accommodation for all but the poorest or richest or most unclubbable of students.[3] It was also the one most favoured by the university authorities. For the perennial problem facing the university was how to control and discipline this

[1] Academic terminology differed at the English universities. At Oxford, rented premises run by (normally) graduate principals for the reception of fee-paying students were designated halls: at Cambridge, they were called hostels: A. B. Emden, *An Oxford Hall in Medieval Times* (Oxford, 1927), pp. 43–5. For a useful summary of the main features of the halls see H. E. Salter, 'The medieval University of Oxford', *History*, xiv (1929), pp. 57 ff. at p. 59: see also, W. A. Pantin, 'The Halls and Schools of medieval Oxford: an attempt at reconstruction', *Oxford Studies presented to Daniel Callus*, Oxf. Hist. Soc., new series, xvi (1964), pp. 31 ff. For the Cambridge hostels see H. P. Stokes, 'The mediaeval Hostels of the University of Cambridge', *Cambridge Antiquarian Society* (Octavo Publications, xlix, 1924).

[2] At Oxford, it was not until 1432 that legislation was enacted to enforce the graduate status of hall principals: *Statuta Antiqua*, pp. 243–4. In the early stages of university development it seems that even manciples and other scholars' servants might be principals as these were specifically excluded from holding principalships *a.* 1380: *Statuta Antiqua*, pp. 182–3. Nevertheless, it is probable that from the thirteenth century the majority of principals were graduates though some, presumably, were only of bachelor status.

[3] In *c.* 1410 Oxford made residence in a hall compulsory for all scholars, and in 1420 this was confirmed by a statute of Henry V: *Statuta Antiqua*, pp. 208–9, 226–7. This was one of the devices by which the university hoped to eliminate the 'chamberdeacons', the students who lived beyond the university's control in unlicensed lodgings and who, according to the legislation of 1410, slept by day and haunted taverns and brothels by night intent on robbery and homicide.

sprawling academic population scattered throughout the town. It first tried to do this by insisting that every student must have his name inscribed on the *matricula*, or roll of a definite master, whose ordinary lectures he was supposed to attend in the schools; the master would then undertake to protect, discipline and be answerable for the conduct of his charge at all times.[1] But this personal system of university control proved ineffective as the lecture room could provide only a temporary and occasional unit of discipline; and the authorities came to realize that the university could hope to exercise a far greater measure of control through the licensed houses where the undergraduates lived and studied.[2] Thus it was that the burden of responsibility for the maintenance of student good conduct was transferred from the shoulders of the teaching body to the principals of the halls or hostels. As their number multiplied, so they gradually absorbed the vast majority of the undergraduates. By this means, Oxford and Cambridge built up a tenuous control over their potentially unstable societies which was reasonably successful in stemming the worst excesses of chronic disorder, violence and murder which had been endemic in the thirteenth century. It is clear, however, that whereas halls and hostels managed to absorb the undergraduate population, the limited provision that they could offer to graduates went little or no way towards solving what was one of the most urgent problems facing university society in the pre-Reformation era.

In an age bereft of state post-graduate scholarships, it was often financially impossible for the B.A. or M.A. graduate of moderate means to remain at university to take a degree in one of the superior faculties of law, theology, or medicine. The trouble lay in the length of the courses leading to the higher degrees. For example, at Cambridge the doctoral degree in theology took some sixteen years from the student's first entry into university.[3] Because of the length and expense of the courses in the superior faculties, there was in the thirteenth and fourteenth centuries an overwhelming need to provide accommodation and financial support for secular scholars capable of study beyond a first degree. And here was the original *raison d'être* for the English medieval colleges which, at the same

[1] See the statute of *a.* 1231, ibid., p. 82: and for later legislation on this theme, pp. 60–1, 83.

[2] This point is discussed by W. A. Pantin, *Oxford Life in Oxford Archives*, cit., pp. 2–3.

[3] Before the reign of Elizabeth the minimum period for the D.Th. degree at Cambridge seems to have been sixteen years made up as follows: from first entry to M.A.: seven years; from M.A. to B.Th.: five years; from B.Th. to D.Th.: four years: see G. Peacock, *Observations on the Statutes of the University of Cambridge*, cit., appendix A, xlvi, n. 1.

time, furnishes the essential link with the Sorbonne, the first European model of the purely graduate secular college. Considerations of piety apart, these collegiate establishments were founded primarily to promote higher faculty studies in the English universities: they were designed not to provide a general arts education but a régime of higher study allied to specialized professional need and, for those of intellectual distinction, an opportunity to research deeply into aspects of a chosen discipline. The exact provisions varied in each case according to the interests or prejudices of the founder. Oxford led the way with Merton's foundation of 1264 which ranks as the prototype of the English 'graduate' college of the pre-Reformation era.[1] It was followed by University College c. 1280 and by Balliol in 1282.[2] At Cambridge, the only thirteenth-century college, Peterhouse, was established by Hugh de Balsham, bishop of Ely, in 1284.

The typical English medieval college was a self-governing community of fellows organized on democratic lines. In every college, founded before 1500, with the exception of the King's Hall, Cambridge,[3] the right of electing the warden, master, president or provost was conferred by statute on the fellows themselves. Although this election usually required confirmation by an external authority, such as the bishop of the diocese or the university chancellor, where this was so it was normally specified that the confirmation was to be of a nominal character.[4] Similarly, most codes of English college statutes make provision for the removal of an unsuitable

---

[1] It is relevant to point out here that De Vaux College, founded at Salisbury by Bishop Bridport in 1262, has some claim to be regarded as 'the first university college in England': K. Edwards, 'College of de Vaux Salisbury', *V.C.H.* (Wiltshire) (Oxford, 1956), iii, pp. 369 ff. at p. 371; see further A. F. Leach, *A History of Winchester College* (London, 1899), p. 86. An award of 1279 between the chancellor and subdean of Salisbury cathedral 'shows that most of the essentials of a *studium generale* or university then existed at Salisbury': Edwards, 'The Cathedral of Salisbury', op. cit., iii, p. 169, and *The English Secular Cathedrals in the Middle Ages*, ed. cit., p. 194. The nascent university was evidently not sustained, but De Vaux College remained until its dissolution in 1542, and throughout its history a fair proportion of its fellows are known to have taken degrees at Oxford and elsewhere. For a detailed examination of this college see Edwards, op. cit., iii, pp. 369–85.

[2] Although the scholars of John de Balliol were settled in Oxford before June, 1266, the college dates as a legal corporation from the issue of the first statutes in 1282. See H. W. C. Davis, *A History of Balliol College*, 2nd ed. by R. H. C. Davis and R. Hunt (Oxford, 1963), pp. 8–9.

[3] On the position of the King's Hall warden see A. B. Cobban, *The King's Hall within the University of Cambridge in the Later Middle Ages*, cit., pp. 148–9.

[4] See, from numerous examples, the statutes of Michaelhouse printed by A. E. Stamp, *Michaelhouse* (privately printed, Cambridge, 1924), p. 46 and the statutes of Trinity Hall in *Camb. Docs.*, ii, p. 421.

master:[1] the details vary from code to code, but the basic point is that the constitutional machinery existed for this purpose and could be set in motion by the fellows of the college. These inviolable statutory rights of election to the headship and the power of removal vested in the *comitia* (the collective body formed by all the members on the boards of the foundation) constituted two of the three indispensable preconditions of the self-governing English college society of the middle ages. The third was the right of co-optation of members. In at least three of the English colleges the French practice of vesting control of the patronage in an external body found, for a time, a pale reflection.[2] The statutes of 1282 of Dervorguilla, widow of John de Balliol, placed the principal and scholars of Balliol College under the supervision of two external procurators (a Franciscan friar and a secular masters of arts).[3] Although their powers steadily diminished, the procurators, or rectors as they came to be styled, persisted until the end of the fifteenth century; but, by the new statutes of 1507, their offices were abolished. Similarly, in her first code of statutes, Mary de Valence, countess of Pembroke, subjected her Cambridge college to the authority of two annually elected external rectors, with restricted powers of visitation, but charged with the duty of admitting newly-elected fellows. No trace of these rectors occurs in the later fourteenth-century code, and it is to be assumed that their powers were transferred to the master and fellows of the college.[4] The situation was paralleled at Peterhouse where at first the bishop of Ely, as founder, retained the patronage of the college for himself; but in 1338 this was partially resigned to the master and fellows.[5] From these details, it is clear that what measure of French influence there was on early English collegiate development was of a transitory character and so obviously unpopular that the Parisian 'external' attributes were soon discarded in favour of the indigenous Mertonian pattern of internal self-government with full powers of co-optation of members vested in the fellows. In the broad context of English academic history of the pre-Reformation era it is arguable that, with respect to

---

[1] See e.g. the statutes of Clare and Trinity Hall, *Camb. Docs.*, ii, pp. 128–9, 426.

[2] For a discussion of the Parisian collegiate influence on the Oxford colleges of the thirteenth century see J. R. L. Highfield, *The Early Rolls of Merton College, Oxford*, Oxf. Hist. Soc., new series, xviii (1964), pp. 67–8.

[3] Rashdall, *Universities*, iii, p. 181; R. W. Hunt, 'Balliol College', *V.C.H.* (Oxford), iii, p. 82.

[4] A. Attwater, *Pembroke College, Cambridge*, ed. S. C. Roberts (Cambridge, 1931), p. 9; Rashdall, op. cit., iii, p. 305.

[5] H. Butterfield, 'Peterhouse', *Victoria History of the County of Cambridge and the Isle of Ely*, iii, ed. J. P. C. Roach (London, 1959), p. 335.

patronage arrangements, the King's Hall, Cambridge, affords the one lasting parallel with the French colleges; for, from the foundation of the Society of the King's Scholars *c.* 1317 (which became the endowed College of the King's Hall in 1337) to the dissolution of the College in 1546, the patronage lay entirely with the kings of England who appointed every fellow individually by writ of privy seal as well as appointing to the wardenship, thus preventing evolution towards full corporate independence.[1]

While ultimate sovereignty in English medieval colleges resided in the fellows acting together as a body or corporation, day-to-day administrative business was usually conducted jointly by the head of college and committees of elected fellows. In most collegiate societies, though not perhaps in all, the organization was so designed that the majority of fellows who stayed for any length of time, at some point in their tenure would play a part, however small, in the running of college affairs. For example, the statutes of Queen's College, Oxford, enjoin that every fellow, the provost and the doctors in theology and canon law excepted, was to undertake the office of seneschal of the hall in weekly rotation.[2] A similar arrangement was in operation at New College,[3] and also at King's College, Cambridge.[4] The 'democratic' involvement of the fellows of the King's Hall in collegiate government might not have been so extensive as that which prevailed in the average type of English college, but a detailed study of the annually elected committees of seneschals[5] reveals that, although they were weighted towards relatively senior members of this royal society, there was, throughout the history of the College, a healthy turnover of personnel which prevented the growth of oligarchical government. Generally speaking, English colleges contrived to secure that the administrative burden in internal and external affairs would fall with distributive weight upon a broad section of the fellowship. English fellows were constitutionally involved in the governmental process from the start: the powers of the head of college were hedged around with effective checks and balances, and in the main the fellows seemed to acquiesce in this form of contractual division of authority worked out by the founder and developed and adjusted in the light of practical experience.[6] Even if mundane collegiate business was the

[1] See Cobban, op. cit., pp. 150–51.
[2] *Statutes*, i, ch. (4), p. 25.
[3] Ibid., i, ch. (5), p. 42.
[4] *Camb. Docs.*, ii, p. 533.
[5] See Cobban, op. cit., pp. 181–2.
[6] Ibid., p. 168.

preserve of small committees of fellows, the majority consent of the whole fellowship, registered through a college meeting, was normally required for items of high expenditure or matters of particular difficulty or delicacy which deeply affected the life of the society. The combination of the ultimate deterrent, the college meeting, and the operative principle of election to administrative office, ensured that a system of responsible government was firmly embedded in the constitutions of the majority of English medieval colleges.

The place occupied by the colleges in the English medieval universities in relation to the academic populations of Oxford and Cambridge can be gauged by considering detailed figures for the fourteenth century, the high point of the European collegiate endeavour.

In the fourteenth century the statutes of the eight Cambridge colleges furnished a total of 137 fellowships distributed as follows:[1] Peterhouse 14; Michaelhouse 6; the King's Hall 32; Clare 19; Pembroke 24; Gonville 20; Trinity Hall 20; and Corpus Christi 2. Except for the King's Hall, Michaelhouse, Corpus Christi and possibly Peterhouse, however, these statutory figures are misleading as to the actual number of fellows maintained. The number of fellows at Clare probably never exceeded thirteen; the usual number at Gonville appears to have been about four, and at Trinity Hall it was about the same, or occasionally even less; and in the mid-fourteenth century, Pembroke had only about six fellows, increasing to about nine at the beginning of the fifteenth century. When these actual numbers are added to the statutory figures for the King's Hall, Michaelhouse, Corpus Christi and Peterhouse, the more accurate total is recorded of about eighty fellowships provided by the Cambridge colleges in the fourteenth century. This is higher than the number of fellowships furnished by the Oxford colleges before 1379. It has been computed that prior to the doubling of the number of fellowships with the foundation of New College in that year, the six secular colleges supplied a total of only sixty-three fellows. While resident numbers in the English universities is a vexed problem to which there is no final solution, it is clear from these figures that college complements can have embraced only a fractionally small proportion of the overall academic population. As Oxford was the larger university in the fourteenth century, and since the Cambridge colleges provided a superior number of fellowships, it follows that the ratio of college fellows to university inhabitants must have been greater at Cambridge than at Oxford. Before 1379, therefore, the Cambridge colleges seem to have

[1] For this paragraph and the one following see ibid., pp. 44–6 and notes.

occupied a marginally more prominent position within the *studium* than did their Oxford counterparts.

On the basis of the revised figures, it would appear that the King's Hall provided about 40 per cent of fourteenth-century Cambridge college fellowships. This is a notable percentage output of fellows for an individual college, and is paralleled only by the performance of Merton College, Oxford. As Merton accounted for thirty or more from a total of about sixty-three fellowships before 1379, it is apparent that both the King's Hall and Merton each supplied just under half of the fellowships of their respective universities. Indeed, the King's Hall remained by far the largest and most prestigious of the Cambridge colleges until its position within the *studium* was emulated by King's College in the second half of the fifteenth century. It is not always appreciated that prior to the foundation of New College, Oxford, the King's Hall and Merton were the most successful large-scale realizations of the secular collegiate ideal in England. Merton's reputation derived from its status as the prototype of the 'graduate' college and from its sustained output of prominent schoolmen, and the King's Hall was marked out by its royal household origins and nature, its size, and by its particular and continuous relationship with the king and the court.

The foundation of New College, Oxford, by William of Wykeham in 1379 was something of a landmark in English collegiate history: in terms of scale, both in the number of its fellowships[1] and in the magnificence and layout of its buildings,[2] the college surpassed all previous foundations. In the past Wykeham has been often regarded as the first English founder to admit a sizeable undergraduate element as a permanent ingredient of a collegiate community.[3] But it is now known that the King's Hall, from the early part of the fourteenth century, made provision for the regular admission of undergraduates who were to form a wholly integral part of the college society.[4] By so doing, by bringing into being an association of university scholars engaged in study over the entire educational gamut

---

[1] New College was designed for a warden and seventy scholars: *Statutes*, i, ch. 5, p. 2.
[2] A. H. Smith, *New College, Oxford, and its Buildings* (Oxford, 1952).
[3] E.g. ibid., p. 16. Discussion of Wykeman as an educational innovator will be found in H. Rashdall and R. S. Rait, *New College* (London, 1901); A. F. Leach, *A History of Winchester College*, cit.; G. R. Potter, 'Education in the fourteenth and fifteenth centuries', *Cambridge Medieval History*, viii, ed. C. W. Previté-Orton and Z. N. Brooke (1936), pp. 688 ff.; C. P. McMahon, *Education in Fifteenth Century England*, reprinted from *The Johns Hopkins University Studies in Education*, no. 35, (Baltimore, 1947).
[4] See Cobban, *The King's Hall . . .*, pp. 53 ff.

from undergraduate to doctoral level, the King's Hall constituted itself the earliest prototype of the mixed collegiate society which has characterized the college scene in post-Reformation England. It has been stressed that a university society organized on Mertonian 'graduate' lines led to a divorce between the senior graduate members domiciled in the colleges and the mass of the undergraduate population living a separate existence in hostels, inns, or private lodgings.[1] The King's Hall and later New College importantly foreshadowed the general movement whereby the Mertonian collegiate tradition was deflected into those channels which produced the mixed or consciously balanced societies of the sixteenth century. But it would be unrealistic to attribute to one or two institutions what was effected over a long period of time and was, in any case, largely due to the operation of impersonal economic and social forces of change.

The piecemeal transference of the undergraduate population from the halls or hostels to the 'graduate' colleges was a movement which was largely completed by the Reformation.[2] The main disadvantage of the halls or hostels was that they were unendowed societies with no security of tenure beyond the period for which the premises had been leased. They were therefore unstable units, a situation exacerbated by an unedifying mercenary competition among their governing principals for the custom of the fee-paying undergraduates. In these circumstances, halls or hostels proved unequal to the task of maintaining discipline over the younger and more unruly members of the universities. It became clear that the long-term solution was to house the undergraduates in the colleges, but this could not be achieved overnight. Economic pressures acting upon the colleges, however, led them to adopt a course of action that ended in their absorption of the undergraduate population. Inflationary trends of the late fifteenth and early sixteenth centuries forced the colleges, whose revenues derived in the main from fixed rents, to find alternative ways of augmenting their finances. One such method was to open up their exclusive societies to undergraduates: the heart searchings and traumatic effects of this step can well be imagined. Nevertheless, considerations of finance prevailed over the insular feelings of the fellows, especially when they realized that they could supplement their incomes with tutorial fees. Although hall lec-

[1] E.g. Smith, op. cit., pp. 16 ff.; Cobban, op. cit., p. 48.
[2] For this paragraph I am indebted to H. E. Salter and A. B. Emden whose pioneering researches have thrown much light upon the reasons behind the gradual infiltration of undergraduates into the colleges. See, conveniently, Emden, *An Oxford Hall in Medieval Times*, cit., introductory.

tures – the *lectura aularis* – were delivered by principals or their graduate assistants at Oxford from at least the fourteenth century,[1] many of the halls did not possess tutorial facilities comparable to the colleges lacking, as they did, not only stability but also, one supposes, a sufficiently large and long-tenured graduate teaching element. As a result, the colleges were able to attract a steady stream of undergraduates on the strength of the tutorial advantages they could now offer.

One must not, however, antedate or exaggerate the dwindling rate of the halls or hostels. If we reckon with the detailed figures available for the Oxford halls, it is clear that the decline was of a gradual nature:[2] in 1444 there were about sixty-nine halls; in 1469 about fifty; in 1501 about thirty-one; in 1511 about twenty-five; in 1514 about twelve; and in 1552 about eight. The main period of decline would therefore seem to be the latter half of the fifteenth and early sixteenth centuries during which time teaching became more concentrated in the colleges, several of which annexed halls and took responsibility for their aularian inhabitants. But even when the halls were a minority constituent of university life, as they were by the mid-sixteenth century, the eight surviving Oxford halls could nevertheless *c.* 1550 accommodate more than 200 students compared with the total of just under 450 housed in the thirteen colleges.[3]

With the evolution of tutorial facilities in the colleges, the undergraduates would progressively feel less inclined to attend the ordinary lectures of the regent masters in the university schools, although at Oxford students were required to be present at public lectures until at least the mid-sixteenth century.[4] In these circumstances, the regency system of public instruction, which had been the mainstay of university teaching from the birth of the English *studia*, fell into gradual abeyance. The final blow to university teaching was dealt by the establishment of college lectureships[5] whereby fellows of a college, or others from outside, were appointed to deliver a definite course of lectures within a college at an agreed salary. These endowed college lectureships which were mostly,

[1] Pantin, *Oxford Life in Oxford Archives*, cit., p. 36.
[2] These figures derive from Dr Pantin's researches and are recently given in detail by J. K. McConica in his review of H. Kearney, *Scholars and Gentlemen: Universities and Society in Pre-Industrial Britain 1500–1700* (London, 1970), *E.H.R.*, lxxxvii (1972), p. 124 (Kearney is misleading on the history of halls and has an inadequate view of collegiate development): for more general treatment see Pantin, op. cit., p. 10.
[3] Pantin, op. cit., loc. cit.
[4] Ibid., p. 36.
[5] For college lectureships see ibid., pp. 36–7; Curtis, *Oxford and Cambridge in Transition 1558–1642*, cit., pp. 102–5; Cobban, *The King's Hall . . .*, pp. 80 ff.

though not always, of a public nature, and open to all comers in the university, became a permanent feature of the English collegiate scene after their inception at Magdalen College, Oxford, in 1479/80.[1] Thereafter, nearly every new college foundation made provision for lectures; and, at the same time, most of the older colleges revised their constitutions to keep pace with this new development.[2] Indeed, by the beginning of the reign of Elizabeth the colleges had become, to a lesser or greater extent, self-contained teaching units. Attempts by the universities to prop up the moribund system of university teaching proved ineffective.[3] The course of events in favour of the colleges had gone too far to be reversed and, by the third quarter of the sixteenth century, the colleges had emerged as the effective teaching organs within the universities.

Still comparatively little has been discovered about teaching organization in English colleges before 1500. In particular, it is difficult to chart the growth of tutorial arrangements and only widely-spaced glimpses are available prior to the general entrenchment of the tutorial system in the sixteenth century.

It is a natural development in academic societies that the senior members will aid, encourage and teach their younger companions: this was the procedure in the early English medieval colleges. For example, the Merton statutes of 1270 prescribe that teachers are to be chosen from the more advanced scholars to help the younger ones in their studies and to guide their moral welfare.[4] A similar enactment was in force at Peterhouse, Cambridge;[5] and, generally, the obligation by senior fellows to teach and influence morally the younger members of the society was one common to the majority of early English colleges. Clearly, there is here displayed the most basic type of tutorial organization, informal, unpaid and confined to foundation members. But with the institution of Wykeham's salaried tutorial system at New College a new dimension was realized: the system involved setting aside a sum of money from college funds as payment for

---

[1] *Statutes*, ii, ch. (8), pp. 47–9; N. Denholm-Young, 'Magdalen College', *V.C.H.* (Oxford), iii, p. 194.

[2] See Cobban, op. cit., p. 81 and n. 3; also Pantin, op. cit., pp. 36–7 and n. 16.

[3] For this largely abortive movement see Curtis, op. cit., p. 101 and Cobban, op. cit., pp. 81–2.

[4] *Statutes*, i, ch. (2), p. 12. For an instance of an early extra-collegiate tutorial arrangement at Oxford, *c.* 1220, see Pantin, op. cit., p. 37. A very brief view of the English tutorial system to the twentieth century is given by W. G. Moore, *The Tutorial System and its Future* (Oxford, 1968), ch. 1. The author, however, rarely extends his gaze to Cambridge.

[5] *Camb. Docs.*, ii, p. 12.

fellows or scholars who were to act as tutors (*informatores*) to the younger element in the society.[1] There is, however, no evidence that such tutorial facilities were extended to students who were not college members; moreover, there is nothing to show that the finances of Wykeham's undergraduates were vested in the fellows or senior scholars who acted as their tutors. The point is raised as the management of undergraduate finances came to be one of the principal duties of the college tutor and consequently one of the main ingredients of the mature English tutorial system.

It is not clear that the King's Hall ever possessed a salaried tutorial system in the Wykehamite sense, but there is sustained evidence from the 1430s onwards that the college received private pupils for tutorial instruction who were not members of the society;[2] and it is known that those fellows who served as tutors to pupils introduced into the college from outside were responsible to the college administration for the expenses incurred by their charges. There is here uncovered an arrangement whereby several of the fellows stood in the relation of *in loco parentis* to a company of pupils for whose finances they were answerable. This accords well with what little has been discovered of rudimentary tutorial organization in the unendowed halls of the period. In at least one Oxford hall of the early fifteenth century the finances of those undergraduates who looked upon the principal as their tutor (or creditor) were given over to his control and were accounted for term by term as money was expended on their behalf.[3] For the English colleges the King's Hall has furnished what is hitherto the earliest definite evidence concerning this form of tutorial organization in which the regulation of the pupil's finances is vested in a fellow, in his capacity as tutor, and which became a chief characteristic of the English collegiate arena of the post-Reformation period. But in the fifteenth century it is unlikely that the reception of private pupils for tuition at the King's Hall assumed the proportions of a regular college system:[4] for it is improbable that the college collectively was the motivating force behind this consequential but sporadic development. While the college presumably encouraged the movement, the intermittent nature of the

---

[1] *Statutes*, i, ch. (5), p. 54.
[2] For these private pupils (*pupilli*) see Cobban, *The King's Hall...*, pp. 67 ff.
[3] See the significance of master John Arundell's logic notebook discussed by A. B. Emden, *An Oxford Hall in Medieval Times*, cit., p. 193. It is probable that legists, who were of maturer years than the artists, would normally exercise a personal control over their expenditure. On this point see Salter, 'An Oxford Hall in 1424', *Essays in History presented to R. L. Poole,* ed. H. W. C. Davis (Oxford, 1927), pp. 421 ff. at p. 433.
[4] Cobban, op. cit., p. 70.

evidence indicates that the initiative in this direction lay with the individual fellow who desired to supplement his income with teaching fees. From later analogy, it may be supposed that the fellow-tutor would enter into a private arrangement with a parent or guardian who would then commit the pupil to his care and hand over a supply of money to be expended on the pupil's behalf over the stipulated period.[1] The situation just delineated denotes that every graduate fellow was a potential tutor needing only the ability or inclination to attract pupils. This presupposes that tutoring was geared to an open competitive market and that there was as yet no effort made to limit tutorial functions to a few fellows detailed by the college authorities for this purpose. Post-Reformation Cambridge parallels indicate that in the second half of the sixteenth century any fellow might become a tutor with one or more pupils in his charge;[2] and this is essentially the practice operating at the King's Hall from the 1430s. This flexible and rather amorphous tutorial organization gave way in the seventeenth century to the more centralized, collegiately-controlled system of tutorial teaching which is still one of the hallowed hallmarks of the 'Oxbridge' scene.

The admission of undergraduate commoners (strictly semi-commoners) at the King's Hall is a phenomenon of the first academic importance. As the college regularly admitted undergraduates from the early fourteenth century as fully incorporated foundation fellows, then its undergraduate element from the 1430s, augmented and diversified by the presence of private pupils, must have been very substantial. It is sometimes claimed that the admission of undergraduate commoners is an innovation associated with Bishop Waynflete's Magdalen College, Oxford, founded in 1448. In the founder's statutes of 1479/80 provision was made for the reception of not more than twenty commoners who were to be the sons of noble or worthy persons and were to be allowed to board in college at their own expense under the guidance of a tutor (*sub tutela et regimine creditorum vulgariter creancers nuncupatorum*).[3] On the basis of this, it has been concluded that 'from this new development Magadalen can claim to be not merely the last of the medieval colleges, but the first of the modern ones'.[4] But it is now apparent that however influential Waynflete's 'commoner' arrangements may have been for English collegiate life (which re-

[1] For such arrangements in Oxford colleges of the seventeenth century see G. H. Wakeling, *Brasenose Monographs*, ii, pt. i, Oxf. Hist. Soc., liii (1909), xi, p. 14.
[2] See Cobban, op. cit., p. 71 and n. 1.
[3] *Statutes*, ii, ch. (8), p. 60.
[4] Denholm-Young, 'Magdalen College' in op. cit., p. 195.

mains to be proven), they had been firmly anticipated earlier in the fifteenth century at the King's Hall, Cambridge.

Until the undergraduate commoners began to permeate the English colleges from the fifteenth century onwards, the normal type of academic commoner was of mature years and often of graduate status.[1] Most English colleges seem to have made provision for a number of residents who were not on the foundation. There were those who may be described conveniently as ex-fellow pensioners, comprising fellows who had vacated their fellowships but continued to reside in college as pensioners paying for their board and lodging. The second category consisted of residents who had never at any time been on the foundation and were admitted to the college either as commoners, taking full commons, or as semi-commoners, who paid only half of the commons rate for board of a lower standard. The division of the King's Hall commoner population into two distinct gradings, commoner and semi-commoner, affords proof of the fact that the origins of the stratified commoner system are to be placed at least as early as the first half of the fourteenth century.[2] The terminology for these academic *extranei*, as we may call them, is diverse to the point of confusion in the medieval era. At University College, Oxford, the terms *commensales* and *commorantes* are found;[3] at Oriel, lodgers were known as *commorantes* in the fifteenth and *commensales*, *communarii* or *batellarii* in the sixteenth century.[4] Rooms were let to *commorantes* at Canterbury College,[5] and at Exeter and Queen's *communarii* and *commensaes* are the terms employed.[6] At Merton *communarii* had a peculiar application[7] and at Eton College the *commensals* were privileged commoners who were given free tuition pro-

[1] See the remarks on medieval commoners by H. E. Salter, *Medieval Oxford*, cit., p. 100.
[2] Cobban, op. cit., p. 275.
[3] A. Oswald, 'University College', *V.C.H.* (Oxford), iii, p. 63.
[4] W. A. Pantin, 'Oriel College and St Mary Hall', ibid., iii, p. 120; see also specifically the references cited in the *Dean's Register of Oriel, 1446–1661* (ed. G. C. Richards and H. E. Salter, Oxf. Hist. Soc., lxxxiv, 1926), pp. 51, 56, 61–2; for *commorantes* see *Oriel College Records*, ed. C. L. Shadwell and H. E. Salter, Oxf. Hist. Soc., lxxxv (1926), pp. 52, 55–6.
[5] Rashdall, *Universities*, iii, p. 213, n. 1.
[6] Salter, *Medieval Oxford*, cit., p. 100. Among the *commensales* of Queen's in the late fourteenth century were John Wyclif, Nicholas Hereford and John Trevisa: see R. H. Hodgkin, *Six Centuries of an Oxford College* (Oxford, 1949), pp. 27–38.
[7] The Merton *communarii* appear to have been youths who were maintained for several years in return for the performance of specified duties. These *communarii* were therefore a charge upon the finances of Merton whereas elsewhere they were usually a source of revenue: *Registrum Annalium Collegii Mertonensis, 1483–1521*, ed. H. E. Salter, Oxf. Hist. Soc., lxxvi (1923), xv–xvii.

vided that they paid for their board and lodging.[1] At the King's Hall, commoners are referred to variously as *commensales, sojournants, commorantes, communarii* (and *semicommunarii*) and *perhendinantes*.[2] This last term, *per-(h)endinantes*, is the one most commonly used in Cambridge college statutes of the fourteenth and fifteenth centuries to denote lodgers,[3] and does not appear in the Oxford codes of the same period. *Pensionarius* is for the first time used in place of *perendinans* in the statutes of Christ's College, Cambridge, of 1506[4] and henceforth, in the sixteenth-century codes, *pensionarii* and *commensales* are the terms usually found.[5] It is probable that it was the prevalence of the designation *pensionarius* among the Cambridge colleges of the sixteenth century which led to its post-Reformation adoption to describe that class of undergraduate commoners who were not on the foundation.[6]

It is not always easy to be precise about the exact significance of the terminological usage in any given case. Our knowledge of these lodgers does not, in many instances, extend beyond surnames, periods of residence and rates charged for commons.[7] Of those that can be identified a fair number were beneficed clergy who had obtained episcopal leave to attend a university, often perhaps with ecclesiastical promotion in view. Commoners of this type would take either an advanced degree in arts or a degree in a superior faculty, but some, it seems, would simply attend a university for a 'refresher' régime of study in a congenial atmosphere. Relatives or friends of college fellows sometimes boarded for brief spells as commoners, but here the purpose would be social rather than academic.

[1] H. C. Maxwell Lyte, *A History of Eton College 1440–1910*, 4th ed. (London, 1911), p. 19; for an analysis of the statutory provisions regarding *commensales* see appendix A, p. 582.

[2] See Cobban, *The King's Hall . . .*, pp. 260–1.

[3] See e.g. the statutes of Peterhouse in *Camb. Docs.*, ii, p. 27, and the statutes of Queens' ibid., iii, p. 37.

[4] Ibid., iii, p. 208. The term *pensionarius* is recorded in the first quarter of the sixteenth century in the earliest extant Bursar's Book of Gonville Hall: see J. Venn, *Early Collegiate Life* (Cambridge, 1913), pp. 68–9, where a list of *pensionarii* is cited for the year 1513.

[5] From many examples see statutes of Clare of 1551 in *Camb. Docs.*, ii, p. 164; also the Edwardian statutes of Trinity College, Cambridge, of 1552, Trinity College Library, o. 6. 7., cap. xvi, pp. 20–1. However, *perendinant* is sometimes retained as a sectional heading in the statutes: see e.g. the early sixteenth-century statutes of Jesus College, *Camb. Docs.*, iii, pp. 120–1.

[6] The equivalent of the Oxford 'commoner'. On the post-Reformation pensioner at Cambridge see D. A. Winstanley, *Unreformed Cambridge* (Cambridge, 1935), pp. 200–1.

[7] An account of commoners and semi-commoners (not ex-fellows) at the King's Hall is given by Cobban, *The King's Hall . . .*, esp. pp. 273–9.

Commoners of noble lineage are occasionally found in colleges before 1500,[1] although as a grouping they were probably not significant until the sixteenth century.

An investigation of ex-fellow pensioners of the King's Hall in the fifteenth century[2] has yielded information which is of general interest for this elusive academic subject. Most of the ex-fellows had vacated their fellowships upon promotion to benefices and some of them were subsequently granted episcopal licence to study at university for a stipulated number of years. Ex-fellow pensioners of this study type were resident in the college for the greater part of each year when pursuing degree courses. Other ex-fellows, during the time that they were King's Hall pensioners, participated in diocesan administration in such capacities as episcopal chancellors or vicars general, and as archdeacons or their officials. Limited conclusions can be reached as to how ex-fellow pensioners who concurrently held benefices apportioned their time between the college and their charges. The inquiry found that beneficed ex-fellow pensioners did not neglect their livings through excessive residence in the King's Hall: time and energies were divided irregularly between college and living and, in some instances, the pensionership served the purpose of a base in the interim period between the tenure of successive benefices. For the majority of ex-fellows life as a pensioner was not an end in itself: it was regarded either as a means by which a former fellow might be conveniently housed while continuing his studies in the university or as affording an attractive lodging place, retained for intermittent use by those actively engaged in ecclesiastical administration.

In general, the colleges were wary about the admission of academic *extranei*. Most codes of college statutes place a cautionary emphasis upon the suitability and trustworthiness of potential commoners.[3] For college authorities had to guard against the entry of commoners who might prove to be a financial burden or who might introduce dissension into the college. It is sometimes asserted that the English colleges looked on pre-Reforma-

---

[1] For aristocratic commoners at the King's Hall see ibid., pp. 276–7. Other examples of aristocratic lodgers are Thomas Arundel at Oriel, Richard Courtenay at Queen's, William Gray and George Neville at Balliol, and John Tiptoft at University College.
[2] See Cobban, op. cit., pp. 266–8.
[3] E.g. the statutes of Michaelhouse in Stamp, *Michaelhouse*, cit., p. 44; the statutes of Peterhouse, Clare and King's in *Camb. Docs.*, ii, pp. 27, 136–7, 534–6; the statutes of Merton in *Statutes*, i, ch. (2), pp. 13 (1270), 26 (1274); the statutes of Balliol, Oriel, Queen's and New College, ibid., i, ch. (1), p. 20, ch. (3), p. 8, ch. (4), p. 18, ch. (5), p. 43.

tion commoners as a means of augmenting their revenues.[1] The profit motive behind the maintenance of commoners was doubtless a real one in the English universities, just as it was at Paris; but from what evidence we have (not very extensive) of the detailed workings of the commoner system at such colleges as the King's Hall and Queen's, Oxford, it is unlikely that much financial benefit was in fact realized.[2] The efficiency with which the commoner system was administered may have varied from college to college: on balance, however, it would appear that the admission of mature commoners was not a lucrative practice, yielding at most a marginal profit. It is probable that, in the course of time, considerations other than money came to prevail: and college founders came to see that good advantage was to be derived from a cautious diversification of the college complement. It was not altogether healthy for fellows to live in complete isolation. A moderate degree of intellectual and social contact with more mobile associates of like-minded interests could only have a broadening and salutary effect. For reasons of this kind, Robert Wodelarke, for example, intended that commoners should form, from the start, an integral part of his college of St Catharine's, Cambridge, in the 1470s.[3]

The study of the mature pensioner or commoner class in English and continental medieval colleges is an important area for extension. This was a class that formed one of the key bridges whereby the colleges interacted with the wider community. It is just one of the ways in which one can explore how far the medieval university dovetailed into the fabric of contemporary society. And it is probable that the sources for the investigation of this commoner grouping on the academic margins have been by no means exhausted.

The specific charitable functions of medieval colleges, as distinct from their quintessential charitable *raison d'être*, are not always given due historical publicity. It seems that in England the charitable aspect was not as extensive as that which permeated the Parisian collegiate movement. Several of the English college founders did indeed make a limited provision for the grammatical instruction of a handful of poor boys who were to live either within the college or were to be housed in the town. There was evidently a general idea current among college founders that some sort of

---

[1] See e.g. the remarks of W. Carr, *University College*, College Histories Series (London, 1902), p. 49 and for Paris colleges Gabriel, 'The College System . . .' in op. cit., p. 93.
[2] See Cobban, op. cit., pp. 272–3 and Hodgkin, *Six Centuries of an Oxford College*, cit., p. 28, n. 1.
[3] See Cobban, 'Origins: Robert Wodelarke and St Catharine's', *St Catharine's College 1473–1973*, ed. E. E. Rich (Leeds, 1973), pp. 18–20.

provision ought to be made for charitable grammar teaching in collegiate establishments. But this seems to have been a subsidiary aim, and if the various codes of statutes are compared one is left in no doubt as to where the priorities lay. The overall impression derived is that the provisions concerning the instruction of poor youths were often tagged on as a sort of afterthought or as a conventional sop to charity: for it is always stressed that these 'grammar' clauses were to apply only if and when the funds of the college would allow – that is to say, the grammar element, as we may loosely describe it, was to be sacrificed to the needs of the graduate members of the college. For example, the Peterhouse statutes enact that two or three grammar scholars are to be supported by the charity of the college but only if the finances of the foundation will permit. On evidence of good progress they might be made scholars; if not, they were to be removed from the college.[1] In much the same way, Walter de Merton arranged for the teaching of a group of *parvuli*, indigent and orphan children of the founder's kin (*de parentela*): provided that the revenues of the college were adequate, they were to be instructed in the rudiments of learning and the most promising of them were to be advanced to the status of scholar.[2] Similarly, the statutes of 1359 for Clare College, Cambridge, envisage the maintenance of ten poor boys from the parishes where the society held appropriated churches: they were to live in separate fashion from the members of the college and were to be instructed in singing, grammar and dialectic until the age of twenty when they were to be either ejected or promoted to scholarships.[3]

The general situation in English colleges seems to be that, even at an optimistic statutory level, grammatical teaching for poor boys was to be implemented only if the finances were judged healthy enough for this pointedly secondary purpose. It is also clear that, with the exception of the arrangements at Merton, these 'colonies' of grammar youths did not form an integral part of the college but remained apart from the society in the way of charitable appendages. As the majority of English medieval colleges could not afford to maintain even the full statutory complements of fellows, then, given the monetary priorities, these 'grammar schools' would have been insignificantly small and, in some cases, the statutory

---

[1] *Camb. Docs.*, ii, pp. 24–6.
[2] *Statutes*, i, ch. (2), pp. 6 (1264), 17 (1270), 36 (1274). For the endowments provided for near kindred and more distant relatives in English medieval colleges see G. D. Squibb, *Founders' Kin: Privilege and Pedigree* (Oxford, 1972), ch. 1.
[3] *Camb. Docs.*, ii, pp. 140–1.

provisions would have remained largely or wholly inoperative. The extreme instance is perhaps that of Queen's, Oxford, where the founder's statutes provided for the maintenance of poor boys up to the number of seventy:[1] in actual fact '. . . the poor boys rarely numbered more than one or two in the Middle Ages and three or four in the sixteenth century'.[2]

If the charitable teaching of grammar in English medieval colleges functioned on a negligible scale, at Paris the maintenance of poor students, or *beneficiarii*, was more widespread. No coordinated study of the *beneficiarii* has yet been made, but it seems that the practice was introduced by the College of the Sorbonne and subsequently adopted by many of the later Paris collegiate foundations.[3] Ave Maria College, for example, supported two *beneficiarii* in college and six in a separate house, the whole enterprise being buttressed by the fellows. But the charity of the Ave Maria College[4] extended beyond the support of *beneficiarii*. The founder, John of Hubant, established houses for ten poor aged women and for ten poor aged workmen, all maintained from the resources of the college. In addition, the fellows were required to distribute soup and bread daily to the Paris poor, to give away all clothing and shoes which were not absolutely necessary and to tour the Paris prisons each year to bestow money on the inmates. The theory behind these regulations was that there should be a constant humbling interaction between the academic population and the community. By means of this daily contact, students were to be made aware of the needs of the less fortunate members of society. The Ave Maria experiment is probably not altogether typical of the Parisian collegiate scene, but it may point to a more extensively developed concept of charity among the continental colleges than in England where for so long the charitable motive was arrested in the interests of preserving the quality of endowment for the graduate fellows. If the charitable aspect of collegiate studies can be expanded, it is to be encouraged. For amidst the utilitarian considerations which underlay the foundation of secular colleges, their position as charitable islands in the community must never be submerged.

Whereas the colleges were to exert a profound influence upon the universities of Paris, Oxford and Cambridge, they did not acquire a comparable constitutional or educational significance in the Italian or French

[1] *Statutes*, i, ch. (4), p. 30.
[2] R. H. Hodgkin, 'The Queen's College', *V.C.H.* (Oxford), iii, p. 132.
[3] See A. L. Gabriel, *Student Life in Ave Maria College, Mediaeval Paris*, Publications in mediaeval studies, xiv (Indiana, 1955), pp. 110–11.
[4] For details see ibid., passim; also Gabriel, 'The Practice of Charity at the University of Paris during the Middle Ages: Ave Maria College', *Traditio*, 5 (1947), pp. 335 ff.

provincial universities. In the main, the colleges in Italy and provincial France were primarily boarding houses for students and few emerged as educational units. Even the grandiose College of Spain at Bologna,[1] founded by Cardinal Gil Albornoz in *c.* 1367 and designed for thirty Spanish or Portuguese students of whom eight were to study theology, eighteen canon law, and four medicine, was not conceived as a teaching institution, although some lectures in theology were apparently given.[2] By the end of the fifteenth century Bologna had fewer than half a dozen colleges and of these only the College of Spain was of much long term consequence. Padua's first college was founded only in 1363 and before the sixteenth century collegiate establishments tended to be small; they assumed a far greater importance in Paduan life in the sixteenth and seventeenth centuries, and this appears to be the situation in several of the Italian *studia*. In the French provincial universities the early secular colleges of Toulouse, those of Vidal Gautier (1243), of Montlezun (1319) and of Verdale (1337) are of some constitutional eminence in the history of European collegiate development.[3] In particular, the college of Vidal Gautier may be cited as an example of a fairly advanced form of secular college founded fourteen years before that of Robert de Sorbon at Paris, about twenty years before the first colleges at Oxford and Bologna, and some forty years before the earliest Cambridge colleges. In Spain, apart from notable exceptions such as the Salamancan Colegio viejo de San Bartolomé, founded in 1401 and whose statutes reflect those of a student-university,[4] colleges did not figure prominently in the Spanish *studia* before the sixteenth century.

The relative unimportance of colleges in the universities of southern Europe before the sixteenth century is a phenomenon which is hard to explain. The generally wealthier and more mature character of the academic populations of Italy, southern France and Spain compared to that of northern Europe may have acted as a restraint on the collegiate movement in the early phase of university development. It is probable that the sophisticated student nation organization, with its high capacity for self-

---

[1] On the College of Spain see Rashdall, *Universities*, i, pp. 198–203 and B. M. Marti, *The Spanish College at Bologna in the Fourteenth Century* (Philadelphia, 1966); also C. H. Clough, 'Cardinal Gil Albornoz, the Spanish College in Bologna, and the Italian Renaissance', *Studia Albornotiana*, xii (1972), pp. 227 ff.
[2] Marti, op. cit., p. 32.
[3] See the instructive article by J. Faury, 'Les collèges à Toulouse au xiiie siècle' in E. Privat (ed.), *Les universités du Languedoc au xiiie siècle*, Cahiers de Fanjeaux, 5 (Toulouse, 1970), pp. 274 ff.
[4] Rashdall, *Universities*, ii, p. 89 and n. 4.

help, formed a more solid and permanent level of financial and fraternal support than was available in northern *studia*, thus lessening the need for a powerful collegiate enterprise. Moreover, the prevalence of student controls in all their various manifestations in southern Europe in the thirteenth and early fourteenth centuries may well have had a deterrent effect on prospective college founders. Investment in student régimes can hardly have been an exciting proposition, and it is noticeable that the modest collegiate growth experienced by the southern universities came with the reversion of authority to the teaching doctors.

As component parts of their universities any group of colleges will often reflect broad trends in university life, and for that reason they are potentially important study areas. The point may be illustrated with reference to the French provincial *studia*. Colleges were here numerous and the majority of them were founded by ecclesiastics, several being designed specifically for members of the religious orders.[1] Popes, cardinals and bishops figure profusely among the ranks of the founders and, in the event of a lay founder, the college was usually entrusted to the supervision of an ecclesiastic or to a mixed body of university and ecclesiastical officials. Even if we knew nothing of the attempts of the French episcopate to secure a stranglehold over the French provincial *studia*, we could derive a fair idea of the strength of ecclesiastical dominion from a study of the colleges. The most perfunctory appraisal of the French provincial collegiate system could leave no doubt about the intensity with which ecclesiastical control had manifested itself throughout the structure of the French provincial universities. The French colleges had no part to play in the fight for university autonomy from episcopal domination. They everywhere served to emphasize the omnipresence of the ecclesiastical arm and lingered on as its last main and perhaps stifling preserve long after university emancipation had been won. The French colleges tended to be passive reflectors of the ecclesiastical complexions of their universities; and in the English situation too, the colleges are indicators of the degree to which ecclesiastical authority had permeated the universities.

From one point of view, the Oxford colleges bore a closer affinity to the French provincial colleges than to those of Cambridge.[2] This stems from the consideration that the Oxford colleges were more exposed to

---

[1] On these French provincial colleges see A. B. Cobban, 'Episcopal Control in the Mediaeval Universities of Northern Europe', *Studies in Church History*, v (Leiden, 1969), pp. 1 ff. at p. 16 and notes.

[2] For this paragraph see ibid., pp. 18–19 and notes.

ecclesiastical influences than those of their Fenland counterparts. Of the ten secular colleges established in Oxford between the thirteenth and fifteenth centuries, no fewer than seven had ecclesiastical founders: five were founded by bishops, one by an archbishop, and another by an archbishop-elect. Of the thirteen Cambridge colleges for the same period, only three had episcopal founders, and two, Gonville and Godshouse, were founded by humble rectors. The remainder had as founders two kings, a queen, two rich lay patrons, a chancellor of the exchequer of Edward II, a provost of King's and a Cambridge guild. Moreover, following the French fashion, the majority of the Oxford founders placed their colleges under ecclesiastical supervision.[1] This presents a contrast to the Cambridge situation where the normal practice was to vest the power of visitation, not in an ecclesiastic but in the chancellor or vice-chancellor of the university, whose right of intervention was so hedged around with checks and balances as to render it largely inoperative in all but the most abnormal of circumstances.[2] From the start the Cambridge colleges were fiercely jealous of their independent status and, unlike the situation at Oxford, their attitude towards university and ecclesiastical authority was one of strict non-intervention.

From the collegiate situation one might argue that ecclesiastical influence would have been an ever-present reality to the fellows of the Oxford colleges; at Cambridge, on the other hand, the practical manifestation of ecclesiastical control can scarcely have made much impact on the daily lives of the college fellows. And this collegiate difference between Oxford and Cambridge may have some bearing on the differing intensities with which the contest for university autonomy was conducted at the English universities.[3] The slowness of the emancipation movement at Cambridge may not have been so much the result of lethargy on the part of the Cambridge masters. If the collegiate evidence is anything to go by, it seems that the question of ecclesiastical control assumed a more theoretical complexion at Cambridge than at Oxford. This being so, the Cambridge masters had no strong motive for combating a lenient and distant episcopal power which little affected the daily life of the university. It is, however, understandable that after Oxford had won ecclesiastical emancipation in the

---

[1] E.g. the bishop of Lincoln was visitor at Oriel and Lincoln, the bishop of Winchester at New College and Magdalen, the archbishop of York at Queen's and the archbishop of Canterbury at All Souls.

[2] See Cobban, *The King's Hall . . .*, p. 87.

[3] On this theme of Cambridge emancipation see Cobban, art. cit., pp. 20–1.

late fourteenth century, the Cambridge masters should desire a final definition with respect to Ely and Canterbury. Not only would this bring them into line with Oxford but with the mainstream of university development on the Continent. But throughout it seems that the issue of exemption from ecclesiastical jurisdiction was at Cambridge rather a matter of troublesome theoretical definition conducted without the heat and substance of the Oxford movement.

The general point illustrated by reference to the French provincial and English colleges is that one cannot afford to overlook the collegiate situation in any consideration of key university issues. The colleges may not serve as microcosms of university life because they may, in various ways, be untypical, but they can sometimes provide a deeper insight into university affairs than might otherwise be acquired from formal university records.

One of the salient features of the collegiate movement in the German and Scottish medieval universities was the emergence of the institutional form which may be labelled the college-university. This was the organizational permutation in which the colleges and university were virtually fused into a single entity. It was a constitutional development of some importance because it made a major contribution towards the evolution of a permanent professoriate in the *studia* of northern Europe.

Salaried lectureships were progressively adopted in the universities of southern Europe in the course of the thirteenth and fourteenth centuries, and this had the twofold effect of lessening the economic dependence of the lecturing staff on student finance and of encouraging a greater degree of residential stability on the part of a professoriate prone both to migrate from one university to another and to divide its energies between university and community employment.[1] The emergence of *nuclei* of salaried teachers in northern *studia* was a later development and their reliance upon the necessary regency system for the recruitment of teaching personnel was a weakness which promoted excessive academic mobility and a weighting towards the young and inexperienced teacher. The necessary regency system was an economical means of lecturer recruitment whereby every new master of arts or doctor of theology or law had to undertake to teach for about two years – that is, for the remainder of the year in which he had graduated and one year further. It would be wrong to think of the northern *studia* as entirely dependent on newly graduated masters or doctors for their teaching force: in addition to the 'necessary regents' there would be a

[1] See above, ch. 3.

group of lecturers who had remained in university teaching for several years supported by a college fellowship or an ecclesiastical benefice or by a religious order. Nonetheless, this pool of 'compulsory' regent masters formed the core of the teaching personnel in the northern universities until the later middle ages.

There may have been advantages in having a teaching force of youthful exuberance the members of which had to enter into competitive rivalry to attract a sufficiency of students on whose fees they relied for their livelihood. But the generally unremunerative nature of teaching in a university situation devoid of endowed lectureships impelled many young regent masters to seek alternative niches in society as soon as their compulsory lecturing stint was over. The departure of the more disgruntled regents who had little vocational interest in teaching and who resented imposed teaching duties, being impatient only to acquire lucrative employment, was doubtless no great loss to the academic community: but the drain of promising teachers driven by economic necessity and insecurity to exchange a university for an extra-university career was an intellectual haemorrhage of the most enervating kind. As the salaried lectureship became the norm in southern Europe the inadequacies of an unplanned teaching system at the mercy of the free flow of academic forces were more clearly perceived, and this moved the universities founded in northern Europe in the later medieval period to rationalize their teaching arrangements at an early stage of institutional growth.

There were different ways by which a more stable professoriate could be achieved. The municipal authority might pay salaries direct to professors on a temporary or more enduring basis or sponsor the annexation of prebends of local churches as a method of lecturer endowment, while the multiplication of colleges served to increase the number of lecturers enabled to teach in one centre for a substantial period.[1] In several places an amalgam of salaries, prebends and college fellowships, or of any two of these, provided the combined enticement for long-tenured teaching careers. These remunerative devices were widely disseminated among the later university foundations of northern Europe and are to be found, among others, in such centres as Vienna, Erfurt, Heidelberg, Cologne, Leipzig, Rostock, Louvain, Greifswald, Freiburg-im-Breisgau, Basel, Ingolstadt and Tübingen. In the German and Scottish universities the college was a

---

[1] A valuable article on the financing of lecturers in northern *studia* in the later medieval period is provided by J. Paquet, 'Salaires et prébendes des professeurs de l'université de Louvain au xve siècle' in *Studia Universitatis Lovanium*, 2 (Leopoldville, 1958).

main instrument through which the excessive mobility of teaching personnel was curbed. In the German *studia* of the late fourteenth and fifteenth centuries the colleges were designed primarily to supply the university with endowed lecturers.[1] Many of the colleges formed part of the founder's original plan; and, if not, they were added soon afterwards. For a time, in the German context, college and university teaching co-existed, but gradually the distinction blurred when both college and university teaching came to be performed by the same professors.[2] By this means, the German universities were furnished with a fixed professoriate which squeezed out the unendowed teachers from all influential spheres. This situation was paralleled in the three Scottish universities of the fifteenth century. At St Andrews and Glasgow there were originally no collegiate societies; and had it not been for the later colleges it is arguable that these small struggling universities would have foundered, wracked as they were by insufficient endowments and internal dissension between student-grabbing masters and the failure to retain a nucleus of teaching personnel of high calibre.[3] The foundation of colleges did much to stabilize the position and ultimately they were to supply most of the university teachers.[4] The fusion of college and university which became so close, but never quite complete, at St Andrews and Glasgow was, at Aberdeen, an integral part of the founder's plan from the beginning.[5] Between 1494 and the early years of the sixteenth century the founder, Bishop Elphinstone, made the identification of college and university the keystone of his Aberdeen enterprise in an effort to avoid the initial phase of confusion and weakness which had so beset the nascent universities of St Andrews and Glasgow. Following

[1] See, conveniently, Rashdall, *Universities*, ii, p. 283.
[2] Ibid., pp. 283–4.
[3] See e.g. R. K. Hannay, 'Early University Institutions at St Andrews and Glasgow: A Comparative Study', *Scottish Historical Revue*, xi (1914), pp. 266 ff.; R. G. Cant, *The University of St Andrews* (Edinburgh, 1946); A. I. Dunlop, *The Life and Times of James Kennedy, Bishop of St Andrews*, St Andrews University Publications, no. xvi (Edinburgh and London, 1950); J. D. Mackie, *The University of Glasgow 1451–1951* (Glasgow, 1954); J. B. Coissac, *Les universités d'Ecosse depuis la fondation de l'université de St Andrews jusqu'au triomphe de la réforme 1410–1560* (Paris, 1915), esp. chs. i–vi; J. Scotland, *The History of Scottish Education*, 2 vols. (London, 1969), i, ch. 4.
[4] For these early colleges, apart from the works cited in previous note, see e.g. J. Herkless and R. K. Hannay, *The College of St Leonard* (Edinburgh and London, 1905) and R. G. Cant, *The College of St Salvator*, St Andrews University Publications, no. xvii (Edinburgh and London, 1950).
[5] See the account of Aberdeen University in Rashdall, *Universities*, ii, pp. 318–20; R. Rait, 'The Place of Aberdeen in Scottish Academic History', *Aberdeen University Review*, xx (March 1933) and L. J. Macfarlane, 'William Elphinstone', ibid., xxxix (Spring, 1961) Scotland, op. cit., i, pp. 30–2; Coissac, op. cit., pp. 123–5.

the success of the Aberdeen experiment the fusion of college and university was later adopted at Glasgow and, to a somewhat lesser degree, at St Andrews.[1] The college-university, maturely realized at Aberdeen and seemingly also at Alcalá in Castile from 1499,[2] was a logical attempt, based on studied experience, to create a planned integrated university community with a more balanced and consistent staff/student ratio than would prevail in conditions of haphazard growth. The centripetal direction of the German and Scottish universities present a tidy contrast to the rambling centrifugal character of Oxford, Cambridge and Paris in the later medieval period. In the long term, the organizational response of the *studia generalia* in Germany and Scotland to their immense problems of internal instability and teaching shortcomings, resulting in the genesis of the college-university, proved a more generally formative influence on university development towards the close of the middle ages and beyond than the highly individualistic permutations in England and Paris.

The wealth of medieval collegiate material that has been made accessible this century from the sifting of muniment rooms and university archives has not been as productive as might be supposed: for it tends to be weighted heavily in one direction. Royal or episcopal foundation charters, papal bulls, title deeds, notarial instruments and the like are indispensable for filling out the external history of an institution. With material of this kind, the historian may particularize the stages in the acquisition and extension of the site, may trace the dealings of the college with neighbouring landowners, with institutions and with the university authorities. Only incidentally, however, does this type of material contribute to a knowledge and understanding of the inner workings of a collegiate society. Because of this, authors of college histories have, of necessity, drawn a good deal on the early codes of statutes for the medieval centuries. For some of the larger institutions, where the statutes are sufficiently lengthy and detailed, a considerable body of information may be gleaned.[3] But in the majority of cases the yield is poor, providing only the barest of outlines of institutional organization, and even this may not be entirely reliable. Early college statutes are notoriously misleading; in large measure, they remained statements of a founder's ideal rather than a working model for the present.

[1] See Rait, art. cit., p. 108; Scotland, op. cit., i, p. 32.
[2] Rashdall, op. cit., ii, p. 106.
[3] See the excellent use made of the lengthy detailed statutes of King's College, Cambridge, by J. Saltmarsh, 'King's College', *V.C.H.* (Cambridge) iii, pp. 382–5; also the utilization of the New College statutes by A. H. M. Jones, 'New College', *V.C.H.* (Oxford), iii, pp. 154–8.

This was so because lack of adequate endowments in the early years caused a marked divergence to develop between the statutory provisions and the actual everyday arrangements worked out in these financially embarrassed communities. As their wealth increased, these societies were better able to bring their organization into closer conformity with the founder's original aims: but this was often a late medieval or even a post-Reformation transformation.

It is only where the official, legal and statutory material relating to a college can be supplemented with a substantial corpus of internal records, such as accounts or bursarial rolls, that there exists the possibility of carrying out a study in depth of collegiate organization and life. Two generalizations can perhaps be made about European collegiate documents. Apart from the few lengthy and valuable series of records which survive, many early sets of college documents are so fragmentary that it is difficult to extract much data of general worth. Secondly, many sets of college records deal mainly with estate management and, self-evidently, it is not to be expected that these would provide much information on the internal life and economy of the academic societies to which they belong. In the English situation, we must rely for this on the type of accounts furnished by colleges such as Canterbury College, Oxford, and the King's Hall which deal principally with internal affairs.[1] Long sequence accounts of this nature are not abundant. But it is only by means of these that collegiate studies can advance along their most productive lines. What is required is a comparative examination of the constitutional, administrative, economic and business arrangements in medieval European colleges. This is the ideal and some progress towards it can be made; but as the materials for such an enterprise are limited, we may shortly reach a ceiling in the subject. Moreover, the fact that reliance has to be placed on a restricted sample of long sequence records raises all manner of problems of typicality which are not easily met. For example, to what extent are the detailed findings for the King's Hall, Cambridge, representative of the collegiate norm? In some respects, they are probably not. Given the royal household origins of the King's Hall and the fact that it always retained something of the flavour of the royal court from which it derived, it seems that it occupied a position midway between the average type of collegiate society of the fourteenth and fifteenth centuries and the more lucrative standards of the aristocratic households of the period towards which it gravitated. In these circumstances, it

[1] See *Canterbury College, Oxford*, 3 vols., ed. W. A. Pantin, Oxf. Hist. Soc., new series (1946–50) and Cobban, *The King's Hall* . . .

is difficult to arrive at a collegiate norm for such matters as a fellow's maintenance costs and habits of expenditure, the profitability of letting accommodation to non-foundation members, rates of payment to domestic staff, the incidence of private servants for fellows, teaching facilities in the form of tutorial arrangements and college lectureships and so on. One is often forced to compare findings from college accounts with those embedded in static college statutes. While these are not strictly comparable, it may be the only option available. Even where we have sets of parallel accounts for comparative purposes the exercise may be frustrated by the uneven distribution of data: that is to say, in each series of accounts information of a certain kind may be revealed for a limited period only to be withdrawn from view at an interesting point and superseded by data of a different category.[1] Hence, when comparing series of accounts, categories of data may be out of chronological phase. Given these difficulties, strict comparability between different series of accounts is an elusive quest, and one may have to settle for eclectic patterns.

It is not enough that collegiate history be firmly built into the context of the specific university: to be of greatest value it must be set within the framework of regional, national and even international academic history according to the scale of the enterprise and the availability of material. The main value of collegiate history is the contribution that it can make towards the elucidation of problems bearing on life in the medieval universities. This encourages the historian to regard the particular college under examination as a base for operations and not as an object of veneration. In other words, the investigation should transcend the institution. The college does not thereby surrender its identity but the emphasis of the research is upon features which, however large or small, are of general academic significance. Such an approach is wholly compatible with examining the minutiae of college history: indeed, only on the basis of the most exhaustive analysis of all the available college records can anything of worth emerge. But the selective process in the final presentation should separate out what, in the judgment of the author, is purely parochial from what is of wider import. As the colleges were among the leading influences shaping the social, moral and academic life of the universities in the later medieval period, they invite central rather than peripheral treatment.

[1] The problems in using the long sequence accounts of the King's Hall are discussed by Cobban, op. cit., ch. 4.

PART II

VII
Medieval student power[1]

The notion of student power is a crucial one for an understanding of university development in the pre-Reformation era. Organized student protest is virtually coeval with the emergence of universities in southern Europe where it became endemic for about two hundred years. In some respects, the motives that prompted medieval student revolt find an echo in the student movements of the second half of the twentieth century. But in other ways they are dissimilar and it would be misleading to press analogies too far. Medieval students had a highly utilitarian view of the function of the university in the community that is unlikely to command the respect of some of their modern counterparts. Revolutionary student activity in the medieval situation was rarely aimed against the established social order: it was either a defence mechanism or was channelled towards the winning of increased student participation within university structures. By 1500, however, student power movements had waned into insignificance and henceforth the masters' type of university has dominated in Europe. Only in very recent years has the ghost of the student-university been raised to challenge the magisterial concept of university organization.

It is difficult to discover what students themselves thought about the purpose of education at the medieval universities. There is a dearth of concretely informative educational treatises and sustained commentary before the mushroom growth of humanist tracts in the fifteenth century.

[1] Much of this chapter is adapted from my article 'Medieval Student Power', *Past and Present*, no. 53 (1971), pp. 28 ff.

Of the treatises that survive from the period 1200 to 1400 a goodly number are rather precious or fanciful or highly-wrought productions, lacking that mundane solidity that would be of the greatest value to the historian for an understanding of the educational process at the average student level.[1] But the cumulative evidence that we have, the evidence of university and college archives, of student letters, sermons and so forth, suggests that, at the ordinary student stage, there was not a great deal of scope for study as an end in itself. For the majority of students education was a severely practical business. A root cause of this is that medieval education in western Europe was often financed on a shoe-string budget: there simply was not the surplus wealth available for non-vocational courses on any scale. The average student, dependent as he was on a parent, guardian or patron for his finances, felt himself fortunate if he struggled through to a first degree.[2] This constant hardship and insecurity with which the student had to contend cannot but have conditioned his social attitudes. Doubtless the medieval student would speculate on the structure of society; he would debate the main theological and political issues of his day and he would have the opportunity to attend the magisterial disputations on matters of public concern;[3] he would criticize the established order of things; but, while at university, he would have little interest in changing the world in which

[1] For example, the educational ideas of Vincent of Beauvais and Pierre Dubois' scheme of education of 1309 are of great value and fascination in themselves but they give little insight into ordinary student attitudes of the thirteenth and early fourteenth centuries. See A. L. Gabriel, *The Educational Ideas of Vincent of Beauvais*, Texts and Studies in the History of Mediaeval Education, no. iv (Notre Dame, Indiana, 1956; repr. 1962) and A. Steiner (ed.), *The 'De eruditione filiorum nobilium' of Vincent de Beauvais*, Mediaeval Academy of America Publication 32 (Cambridge, Mass., 1938). See also Pierre Dubois' scheme trans. L. Thorndike, *University Records and Life in the Middle Ages*, Columbia University Records of Civilisation, no. xxxviii (New York, 1944), pp. 138 ff. and C. V. Langlois (ed.), *De recuperatione Terre Sancte: traité de politique générale par Pierre Dubois* (Paris, 1891), esp. pp. 49–53, 58–72. The *De disciplina scholarium*, written between 1230 and 1240 probably by the Englishman, Elias of Trikingham, and falsely attributed to Boethius, provides a more practical guide to student conduct and values and was widely read in the medieval universities: see *De disciplina scholarium*, *Petrologia Latina*, ed. J. P. Migne, lxiv (Paris, 1860), pp. 1223–38 and the remarks of A. L. Gabriel, *Garlandia: Studies in the History of the Mediaeval University*, cit., p. 147. The *De commendatione cleri* (between 1347 and 1365), perhaps written by a German student at Paris University, is somewhat disappointing because it does not inspire confidence in its reliability: see trans. Thorndike, op. cit., pp. 201 ff. with Latin text, appendix i, pp. 409 ff.
[2] On the conditions and aspects of life of medieval students see C. H. Haskins, *Studies in Mediaeval Culture*, cit., chs. 1–3.
[3] For a list of late thirteenth-century *quaestiones* see A. G. Little and F. Pelster, *Oxford Theology and Theologians c. 1282–1302*, Oxf. Hist. Soc. (1934), pp. 104 ff.

he lived. The overriding student consideration was to become part of the established social pattern. In his later career, the graduate's skills might be employed, for example, in the propagandist warfare of ideological conflict in the papal, imperial or royal service.[1] To this extent, the university student might eventually be involved in movements which promoted adjustments within the social order. But, at the university phase, the student's world was geared to conservative modes of thought.

The medieval universities were largely vocational schools.[2] They trained students in the mastery of areas of knowledge that could be utilized in one of the secular professions of law, medicine or teaching, or in the service of the Church. Theology, 'Madame la Haute Science', was very much a minority discipline, the pursuit of some of the ablest spirits in the universities, but too rarefied and time-consuming for the student mass. Most students seem to have gone to a university to qualify for one of the well-paid, secure jobs on the market for which there was often the fiercest competition. With the laws of supply and demand uncertain for the student and, bereft as he was of a state system of financial aid, the normal student ambition was to gain lucrative employment within the safety of the established order. Career analyses of medieval students seem to bear this out,[3] and there is a lot of support for this view in contemporary literary sources. For example, in the sermon literature of the thirteenth century the utilitarian outlook of students is a recurring theme.[4] Making allowances for propagandist bias, it is difficult to disregard the ferocity and consistency of these sermon attacks. The worldliness of the student body highlighted in John of Garland's *Morale Scolarium* of 1241 has already been instanced.[5] John of Garland's censure is typical of the many condemnations of medieval students by a minority of enlightened critics who sought to keep alive

[1] On the close relations between the Italian law schools and secular and papal government see W. Ullmann, *Principles of Government and Politics in the Middle Ages*, cit., p. 290.
[2] See e.g. G. Leff, *Paris and Oxford Universities in the Thirteenth and Fourteenth Centuries*, cit., esp. pp. 1–11, 116–18.
[3] For the English situation see A. B. Emden, *A Biographical Register of the University of Oxford to A.D. 1500*, 3 vols. (Oxford, 1957–9) and *A Biographical Register of the University of Cambridge to 1500* (Cambridge, 1963). Details of careers of Swiss students at Bologna are given by S. Stelling-Michaud, 'L'Université de Bologne et la suisse, à l'époque de la première réception du droit romain', *Studi e memorie*, new ser., i (Bologna, 1956), pp. 547 ff. Further references to analyses of foreign students at Bologna are cited in the notes to p. 547.
[4] See the evidence assembled by Haskins, op. cit., ch. 2. Haskins relied a lot on A. Lecoy de la Marche, *La chaire française au moyen âge, spécialement au xiiie siècle*, 2nd ed. (Paris, 1886) which is a mine of information on this subject.
[5] See above ch. 1, p. 18.

educational notions that transcended the short term and the immediately consummable.

It might be argued that there were students who did not fit into the establishment mould and who led a wandering life of protest against the basic canons of society. Much prominence has been given to the alleged 'Order of the Wandering Scholars', to the 'Goliards', the followers of Golias, the symbol of vice, ribald materialism, lawlessness and anti-authoritarian attitudes.[1] The problem of itinerant loose-living clerks was a permanent feature of medieval society and the ecclesiastical authorities made repeated legislative efforts to bring them to heel.[2] But there is no evidence that these *clerici vagantes* constituted an Order.[3] They may have embraced students in their ranks, but, from the thirteenth century onwards, these were probably not recognized as *bona fide* members of their universities.[4] They seem to have lived a shadowy existence on the periphery of the academic community and, certainly, their attitudes cannot be taken as representative of the student norm. The important movements of student protest in the medieval period were directed towards specific ends; they were not the explosive outgrowths of pent-up anti-establishment feelings. Nowhere does it appear that direct action within the universities was channelled towards the ultimate reformation of the wider community. To think in such terms, to imagine that medieval students formulated the idea of a university as a microcosm of society would be anachronistic. Medieval student power did not embody this degree of self-conscious awareness.

Nor were student protest movements concerned with the content of university courses if by this is meant the selection of the ingredients of the syllabus or curriculum. The medieval student was not faced with the bewildering range of options that confronts his modern counterpart. There was an agreed hard core of studies in the medieval universities derived

---

[1] H. Waddell, *Wandering Scholars* (London, 1954), passim; J. H. Hanford, 'The Progenitors of Golias', *Speculum*, i (1926), pp. 38 ff.

[2] F. J. E. Raby, *A History of Secular Latin Poetry in the Middle Ages* (Oxford, 1934), ii, p. 339.

[3] Loc. cit.

[4] From an early stage the universities framed legislation to exclude from their societies students who were unattached to a definite master or who did not follow a set course of study. It therefore became increasingly difficult for those who led a wandering life, with no serious educational purpose, to capitalize upon the privileges of scholarity of the bona fide student body. Evidently, the schools of Erfurt in the thirteenth century had faced the problem of distinguishing between the genuine and the false scholar: see G. C. Boyce, 'Erfurt Schools and Scholars in the Thirteenth Century', *Speculum*, xxiv (1949), esp. pp. 11–12.

from a series of time-honoured texts. Study took the form of the critical evaluation and discussion of a prescribed corpus of writings by means of the commentary, the disputation and the question.[1] As ultimate truth lay beyond the reach of human understanding, study and dialectical inquiry could serve only to elucidate within an *a priori* thought system. The mastery of a difficult discipline, the sharpening of the critical faculties, the ability to expound logically, the careful digestion of approved knowledge, these were the features of the average university education. Teaching and learning were innately conservative processes and, at the ordinary student stage, questioning was conducted as a form of training within an accepted intellectual framework. Only at the most advanced university levels do we find anything approximating to the broadly-based educational ideal which theoretically underpinned medieval education. For the most part, the universities provided an undergraduate training designed rather to perpetuate a body of doctrine than to promote independent lines of thought. Students went to university to absorb the material set before them and, to a large extent, this was based on memory work and rote learning. Robert de Sorbon's advice to students on how to be successful at a thirteenth-century university illustrates this passive function. The founder of the celebrated College of the Sorbonne at Paris urged students to apportion their time wisely, listen attentively to all they are told, make copious notes, memorize the essential facts, discuss their problems with fellow students, and finally, to pray for success.[2] It would appear that medieval students broadly acquiesced in current educational assumptions and none of their rebellions had, as its aim, what could be called the widening or modernization of the syllabus. It was not until the traumatic influx of members of the aristocracy into the universities in the fifteenth and sixteenth centuries, combined with the impact of humanist learning, that pressures for this kind of reform became a reality.[3]

The social origins of medieval students are but partially known. Both the geographical scale of the problem and a chronology of some three hundred years make it extremely hard to evolve reliable patterns. Not that

---

[1] See e.g. Leff, *Paris and Oxford Universities in the Thirteenth and Fourteenth Centuries*, p. 5.
[2] Lecoy de la Marche, op. cit., pp. 453–4; Haskins, *Studies in Mediaeval Culture*, p. 56, quoting from Robert de Sorbon's *De Conscientia et de tribus dietis*, ed. F. Chambon (Paris, 1903).
[3] For the impact of the aristocracy on the English universities see e.g. M. H. Curtis, *Oxford and Cambridge in transition 1558–1642*, cit., esp. ch. 4 and the different conclusions of K. Charlton, *Education in Renaissance England*, Studies in Social History (London and Toronto, 1965), ch. 5.

there has been any shortage of studies on the figure of the medieval student. For example, in the past thirty years or so, a crop of works has appeared on the theme of student provenance.[1] These are valuable contributions, but there is no coordinated view of the findings and there are still vast areas of this 'human geography' to be examined. Where one has to delve without the benefit of even matriculation registers the task becomes doubly difficult and serious gaps are inevitable. Besides matters of provenance, knowledge of medieval student life has been enriched in recent years by a galaxy of monographs and articles on manifold aspects of the student condition in different countries.[2] In spite of these advances, however, it is still not possible to be precise about student recruitment to the medieval universities and one can only hazard a series of general observations.

It is clear that the universities of the thirteenth and fourteenth centuries were not aristocratic institutions. As the universities were, *par excellence*, centres for vocational training, gateways to lucrative careers, those who attended them did so primarily from a sense of social urgency, from a need to realize professional amibition. There were minority groups of nobility to be found in the universities of southern Europe from their inception, and these *studia* were perhaps more closely interwoven with the aristocratic framework of society than in the north; nevertheless, in no wise could they be labelled aristocratic preserves until the later medieval period. From the late fourteenth century, members of the aristocracy began to permeate the universities in accelerating numbers. The motivation is imperfectly understood, although the gradual adoption of humanist studies by the universities presumably made them more attractive venues to a class which was not over-concerned with education as a training for a professional career.[3] By 1500, the aristocratic intake was a consistent and important area of recruitment to European universities, but this development lay beyond the effective lifespan of the student power movement. The evidence collected so far suggests that in the thirteenth and fourteenth centuries the majority of undergraduates were recruited from the middling to lower orders in society, from the sons of knights and professional men, merchants, burgesses, artisans, yeomen and so forth.[4] Some were drawn from the humblest of circumstances and went to university as protégés of local patrons. By the fifteenth century many of the newer universities had a definite legislative category

[1] See Stelling-Michaud, 'L'Histoire des universités au moyen âge et à la renaissance au cours des vingt-cinq dernières années', cit., p. 121 and notes.
[2] Ibid., p. 123 and notes.   [3] E.g. ibid., p. 120.
[4] E.g. ibid., p. 119; Rashdall, *Universities*, iii, p. 408.

for the scholar who could prove his poverty which guaranteed his exemption from all manner of financial dues. Students of this status were fairly numerous in the arts faculties of the German universities.[1] At the other end of the social spectrum, the wealthier student with high or noble connections was more commonly concentrated in the south, at least until the fifteenth and sixteenth centuries when the distribution of this species of student between northern and southern Europe probably became more evenly balanced. Typically, the southern student was more mature than the northern undergraduate, was a student of law or medicine, and would perhaps have experience of community employment before starting his university career. It was from this sector of the academic commonwealth that student power was born.

Medieval students meet us more often in the mass than as individuals,[2] and this limitation extends to the students who engineered and participated in rebellions at the universities and who served as representatives in university government. We know little of their social existence outside the university context beyond what can be inferred from general considerations. The rebellions themselves are documented only in the baldest relief which defies attempts at detailed reconstruction. The names of the leaders are undisclosed and the numbers of students who took part in the revolts cannot be easily gauged. Whether or not members of the lecturing staffs are ever to be found in the ranks of rebellious students is another elusive matter. Nor can we follow in detail the fortunes of the student representatives who tried to make student participation a permanent feature of university life. These difficulties apart, the theme of medieval student power is of such interest that it deserves to be analysed as far as the evidence will allow.

The spontaneously generated universities which emerged in twelfth-century Bologna and Paris became the archetypes which determined the twofold pattern of university organization in the middle ages: the former gave birth to the concept of a student-controlled university, the latter to that of a masters' university. It has already been averred that the first student movement in European history had crystallized at the University of Bologna by the early thirteenth century. The idea of guilds of students directing the affairs of a university and keeping the teaching staff in a state of subservience has been alien to European thinking for over five hundred

[1] Stelling-Michaud, art. cit., pp. 119–20; also J. M. Fletcher, 'Wealth and Poverty in the Medieval German Universities' in *Europe in the Later Middle Ages*, cit., ch. 14.
[2] See the remarks of Haskins, op. cit., p. 72.

years. But one of the two original universities was, for more than a century, a student-dominated institution and the prototype for a large European family of universities either partially or mainly controlled by students.

The reasons for the evolution of this phenomenon of student power at Bologna have been discussed and the extensive system of student controls has been described.[1] From the end of the twelfth to the first half of the fourteenth century the Bolognese *studium* shone forth as a living example of a university wherein the students, through their elected representatives, controlled all that was vital to the direction of the academic community and held the teaching doctors in a state of legislative subservience. It is possible that the statutes of the student guilds give too highly coloured a view and that there was a measure of divergence between statutory provisions, embodying declarations of intent, and actual everyday arrangements. After all, the students had a vested interest in attracting and retaining the ablest teachers on the academic circuit, and perhaps the rigours of the régime were not quite as severe as the testimony of the statutes implies. But making every allowance for this, the strength of the student domination at thirteenth-century Bologna is an impressive and marmoreal feature in the history of west European education.

The Bologna students, at the dawn of the university movement, acted from the dictates of necessity and not according to an ideological view of the student rôle in university affairs. This came later, as a rationalization of an achieved position of power. The student-university emerged as an attempt to solve empirical problems: it was not advanced as a visionary thesis of European university organization. Only when it was seen that the loose informal magisterial arrangements at Bologna would afford ill protection to the foreign student community was the student alternative called into being. The maturity of the Bologna law students and the prior involvement of many of them in positions of responsibility in society gave them a groundwork of valuable experience from which to draw when devising a workable university constitution which mirrored features of their republican environment.

The consignment of the doctors to a satellite existence within the *studium* was an expression of the strength and confidence of the self-appointed student republic which exercised the right to hire and dismiss teaching staff at will. The constitutional subordination of the doctors, however, did not detract from the high regard in which their professional expertise and

[1] See ch. 3.

learning were held. The majority of Italian teaching doctors would have been conditioned to detailed accountability from their experience, direct or indirect, of public offices: and this ethos of restraint and control that pervaded the civic sector would have mitigated somewhat the unpalatability of the student régime without in any way condoning it. Probably the only way in which student power could have been neutralized at Bologna would have been by the operation of a widespread boycott of the Bolognese *studium* by European lecturers. But the fact that many of the Bologna teachers were Bolognese citizens possibly prevented such boycotting action from getting off the ground. Moreover, there was apparently a shortage of teaching doctors possessed of sufficiently large private incomes to present an adequate counter-economic challenge to the students whose economic bargaining strength was the basis of their power position within the university structure. It seems that some of the lecturers were not unduly concerned about their economic dependence on the students. Indeed, there may have been some resistance by teaching doctors to the transition from the system of payment by student fees to that of salaried lectureships on the grounds that this would lead to a fall in incomes; and in some universities, including Bologna, student fees and salaries ran concurrently in the late thirteenth and early fourteenth centuries.

The detailed nature of the student controls at Bologna, the attention to the minutiae of human affairs, the attempt to legislate for every conceivable situation, these are all reflective of the legalistic cast of mind of the student jurists who were the architects of the concept of the student-university. But the legislative severity of the student machine was impartially administered in that it fell with an equal weight on student officers and doctors alike. The student guilds demanded of the doctors the same degree of professional integrity and punctilious statutory observance that they imposed on their own members. When elected to a lectureship, a doctor became the holder of an academic trust, which had to be discharged solely in the interests of the student community. The piecemeal character of student fees, in conjunction with the boycotting system, acted as a financial regulator which could be used to give a sharp reminder to teachers of the full extent of their responsibilities. Although the methods were sometimes unsavoury, the student régime was at least highly principled in intent; and the history of the later universities demonstrates that corrupt behaviour was far from unknown among the ranks of lecturers in magisterial universities.

Of the medieval Italian universities Padua came closest to the Bologna model. Padua, as a *studium generale*, seems to date from a migration of students from Bologna in 1222.[1] A considerable migration of Paduan students to Vercelli occurred in 1228, but the university's fortunes revived after 1260. Fresh migrations from Bologna in the early fourteenth century further boosted the *studium*; and the earliest surviving code of statutes, those of the jurists of 1331,[2] reveal a university shaped in all essential respects according to the Bolognese pattern. The whole gamut of student controls was reproduced at Padua with one or two additional refinements.[3] As at Bologna, the teaching doctors were at first elected by the students.[4] By the fourteenth century some of the doctors were in receipt of salaries from the commune but the students, it seems, still retained a strong bargaining voice in determining the rates of payment. Student direction of the lecturing system was similar to that of Bologna, and the doctors were required to make monetary deposits as guarantee for their proper academic conduct as defined by the dictates of rectorial jurisdiction.[5] The punishments to be meted out to doctors in contravention of the statutes are set out in greater detail than at Bologna. They ranged from simple fines and deprivation of salary to suspension from lecturing duties and complete expulsion from the university. The machinery of secret denunciation of lecturers for statutory offences was a vital part of the Paduan student university.[6] As in the case of Bologna, the statutory model is perhaps more reflective of thirteenth-century conditions than those of the later medieval period. A point of difference between Bologna and Padua which is worth recording is that the latter, from its early life, was subject to a greater measure of communal supervision. This was exercised by means of four citizens, the *trattatores* or *sollecitatores*, who co-operated with the student rectors over a range of affairs relating to the *studium* and who formed a kind of advisory board intermediary between the students and the citizenry.[7]

---

[1] For the early history of the Paduan *studium* see Rashdall, *Universities*, ii, pp. 9 ff.

[2] Printed in *Archiv für Literatur- und Kirchengeschichte*, vi, ed. H. Denifle and F. Ehrle (Freiburg im Breisgau, 1892), pp. 379 ff.

[3] E.g. *Archiv*, vi, bk. 2, rubs. iv, viii, pp. 423–4, 428; bk. 4, rub. ii, pp. 469–71.

[4] Ibid., vi, bk. 2, rubs. i, ii, pp. 416–18, 519–20.

[5] As in n. 3.

[6] Ibid., vi, bk. 1, rub. xxii, p. 409. In northern Europe a 'spy' system was sometimes adopted by the masters in the German universities to report on students who spoke in the vernacular, instead of Latin, in the classrooms or in their lodgings: see *The Manuale Scholarium*, trans. and ed. R. F. Seybolt (Cambridge, Mass., 1921), pp. 66, n. 4, 72, n. 2.

[7] On *trattatores* or *sollecitatores* at Padua see Kibre, *Scholarly Privileges in the Middle Ages*, cit., pp. 59, 61, 71, 79–80, 329.

As far as one may judge, this degree of communal participation through selected citizens proved beneficial to the student cause and did not, in the thirteenth century, hamper the working of the student machine.

Student power at Bologna had emerged as a by-product of the struggle for survival in a hostile environment. Student power at Padua bore the stamp of a conscious imitation which embodied the assumptions on which the Bolognese system was based. The Paduan model was the expression of a belief that the form of university that had evolved at Bologna should serve as a prototype for university organization in southern Europe. The planned adoption of the Bolognese structure helped to promote the idea that the core and essence of a university was the student guild. Teaching doctors were necessary adjuncts who were to be selected, continuously assessed, supervised and disciplined by the students. Eminent scholars might bring high distinction to a university and every effort should be made to attract the ablest teachers. Respect was to be paid to their scholarship and professional standards. Within the university organization, however, they were to be in the nature of academic consultants who have a specialized commodity to sell but who were to be denied the exercise of power; this, at any rate, is the statutory ideal, the epitome of the sovereign student republic embodying the fundamental principle of direct accountability of teaching staff to the student mass.

Reasons for the acquiescence of the teaching staff in the exercise of student power have already been advanced.[1] In face of the stark reality of dependence on student fees, underpinned by the perennial threat of boycott, the lecturers were the economic prisoners of the student community until the salaried lectureship was established as the liberating method of remuneration. But even the phase of student fees had its qualified attraction: for in a populous Italian university, with large student audiences, it was possible for a successful lecturer to realize a substantial income. Moreover, the migratory tendencies of university teachers moving from university to university or alternating between university and community employment may have gone some way towards lessening the full impact of student power on individual teachers who were prepared to submit for a limited duration. This cannot, however, have been more than a contributory factor. Short tenures and a rapid turnover of personnel were not peculiar to southern *studia*. By the operation of the necessary regency system they were common in northern Europe until the later medieval period: and these did not generate student power. Nevertheless, allied to more

[1] See above, pp. 65-6, 170-71.

crucial issues, an unstable teaching force does presumably provide a pliable framework within which student power can put down roots. In addition, detailed accountability for the administration of public offices was deeply ingrained in civic Italian life; and the transference of this principle to the academic arena in the form of lecturer responsibility to a mature student fraternity was at least logically defensible in that environment. Although the student universities were clouded in a murky legalism they won a grudging *de facto* recognition by both communal governments and the teaching doctors.

In the event, the model of the student-university which evolved at Bologna and was perpetuated at Padua proved too extreme for general adoption in this unadulterated form. Almost everywhere in Italy it was accepted that students might participate to some appropriate degree in university government: to that extent, student aspirations were widely met.[1] But the fully-fledged concept of the student-university was quickly overtaken by compromise and replaced by the mixed constitution whereby power was shared between students, teaching doctors and the communes: this became the normal state of affairs in medieval Italy. Universities such as Perugia, Pisa, Florence, Pavia and Ferrara all exhibited this tripartite division of power in varying permutations. The Florentine statutes of 1387, together with supplementary documentary material extending from 1320 to 1472, give an especially good illustration of the mixture of student controls and doctoral and communal powers.[2] And the jurist statutes of Pavia of 1395 are noticeable because, while they retain the outward form of student controls, the provisions are couched in general and sometimes vague terms reflective of the much-diluted degree of participation which

[1] For the nations in the Italian *studia*, other than Bologna and Padua, see Kibre, *The Nations in the Mediaeval Universities*, pp. 123–9: the author, however, does not analyse the situation in terms of student power. The Italian universities, apart from Bologna, are described by Rashdall, *Universities*, ii, pp. 1–62; and much of value will be found in Denifle, *Die Entstehung der Universitäten des Mittelalters bis 1400*, passim.

[2] *Statuti della Università e Studio Fiorentino dell'anno MCCCLXXXVII*, with appendix of documents from 1320 to 1472, ed. A. Gherardi (Florence, 1881). For student controls see e.g. rubs. xxv (pp. 34–5), xlv (pp. 54–5), xlix (pp. 60–3), l (pp. 63–4), lix (pp.7 2–3). The election of most of the teaching doctors was entrusted to a body of officials and governors appointed by the commune, but the students were permitted to elect to four specified chairs, salaried by the commune: rub. xli (pp. 50–2). The rector and students were encouraged to denounce unsatisfactory doctors to the commune, and if the charges were proven, the doctors had fines deducted from their salaries (appendix of documents, no. xxxvi, 20 April 1366, pp. 145–6). At least three times a month the officials of the commune were bound to consult the students secretly about the conduct of the doctors (appendix, no. xli, 28 Sept. 1366, pp. 149–51).

students had come to accept in the fourteenth century.[1] Even the more ephemeral Italian universities of Vicenza, Vercelli and Piacenza appear to conform to this 'mixed' classification. On the other hand, the universities of Naples and of the Roman Court were institutions *sui generis* which did not fit into any recognizable mould: they were authoritarian establishments which were incompatible with student power.[2]

The whittling away of student power in Italy was due, in large measure, to two interrelated circumstances: the increasing control of the communes over the universities and the establishment of a salaried professoriate. Most of the Italian *studia*, with the exception of Bologna, owed their existence to civic action taken either unilaterally or in association with groups of seceders from another university. Arising from this primary rôle, the municipal authorities were anxious to have a permanent controlling influence in university affairs. In practical terms, this meant that both professors and students had to be made dependent on the communes. The most effective way of achieving these objectives was by the provision of municipal salaries for university teachers.

Salaries probably made their European début at the Castilian university of Palencia in the first quarter of the thirteenth century: here the salaries were derived from the diocesan tithes and were the outcome of a royal initiative backed up by the papacy.[3] In 1224 Frederick II tried to entice scholars to his new University of Naples by offering privileges and what may well be salaries (*donaria*).[4] Salaries at Toulouse seem to date from a treaty of 1229 whereby Count Raymond VII of Toulouse agreed to pay the stipends of a number of professors for ten years. The professors were to find that the count did not really have their financial interests at heart

---

[1] *Statuti e Ordinamenti della Università di Pavia, 1361–1859*, ed. L. Franchi (Pavia, 1925). For examples of student controls see rubs. xxviii, pp. 32–4, xxxvi, pp. 37–8, lxviii, pp. 58–9, lxxv, p. 62.

[2] For the authoritarian character of the Naples *studium* see e.g. C. G. Mor, 'Il "Miracolo" Bolognese', *Studi e memorie*, new ser., i, pp. 170–1; Kibre, op. cit., pp. 128–9. On the University of the Roman Court see Rashdall, *Universities*, ii, pp. 28–31.

[3] J. San Martín, *La Antigua Universidad de Palencia* (Madrid, 1942), pp. 27, 31–2. Quotes from the Spanish chroniclers who recorded the institution of salaries are given p. 17, n. 2. The bull of Honorius III of 30 Oct. 1220 confirming the use of diocesan tithes for salary purposes is printed, appendix i, pp. 77–8. For the primary chronicle evidence see Jiménez de Rada (Rodrigo), archbishop of Toledo, *Opera Praecipua* in *PP. Toletanorum quotquot extant opera*, iii (Matriti, 1793), *cap.* xxxiv at p. 174; also Lucas Tudensis (Don Lucas de Tuy), *Chronicon Mundi* in A. Schottus, *Hispaniae Illustratae*, iv (Frankfurt, 1608), p. 109. See also Rashdall, *Universities*, ii, pp. 66–7; Post, 'Masters' Salaries and Student-Fees . . .' art. cit., p. 187.

[4] J. L. A. Huillard-Bréholles, *Historia Diplomatica Friderici II*, cit., ii, p. 451.

and the papacy had to put pressure on the unwilling benefactor to honour his undertaking.[1] The Italian universities, then, cannot be reckoned the pioneers of a salaried professoriate. But they were the first to promote the idea of municipal academic salaries with a view to attracting and retaining the most celebrated teachers, and in the hope of lessening the economic power of the students. Salaries were offered by the communes of Vercelli in 1228, by Siena in 1250 and 1262, by Modena between 1250 and 1260, by Padua between 1260 and 1262 and by Vicenza in 1261.[2] Bologna was one of the last of the Italian communes to provide salaried lectureships (dating from c. 1280), and this is perhaps a sign of the strength of the student movement in the city.[3]

The financial independence of the lecturing staff vis-à-vis the students was dearly bought. The price that was exacted was the surrender of university autonomy in Italy to the communes. During the fourteenth and fifteenth centuries communal powers and paternalistic supervision in academic matters were significantly increased and many of the Italian *studia* were placed under the control of officials (*officiales* or *reformatores*) appointed by the communes.[4] Student power, bereft of its economic teeth, fell a victim to communal politics. It lingered on in Italy as a movement without much substance: by 1500, it had been reduced to nullity.

The Italian student power movement had not primarily been the outcome of a conceptual difference of opinion as to how a university ought to be organized, although this inevitably became an issue in the course of the thirteenth and fourteenth centuries. The central dilemma of student power in medieval Italy seems to have been that it was either too strong or too weak to be perpetuated as a constant force in university politics. The excesses of student power at *studia* such as Bologna and Padua made the notion of the fully-extended university unacceptable as a general model; and the more diluted forms of student participation in the majority of Italian universities rendered the students vulnerable to communal powers.

---

[1] Denifle, *Die Entstehung der Universitäten* . . ., pp. 326 ff.; C. E. S. Smith, *The University of Toulouse in the Middle Ages*, cit., esp. pp. 32, 57 ff.

[2] See conveniently Post, art. cit., pp. 193–4.

[3] Ibid., pp. 194–5 and p. 194, n. 7; Rossi, art. cit., p. 239. But see also above ch. 3. n. 88. For examples of salaries paid in medieval universities see G. M. Monti, 'L'Età Angioina' in *Storia della Università di Napoli* (Naples, 1924), pp. 78–87; J. Paquet, 'Salaires et prébendes des professeurs de l'université de Louvain au xvᵉ siècle' in *Studia Universitatis Lovanium*, 2 (Leopoldville, 1958), p. 9 (this article is a most valuable study); Brucker, 'Florence and its University, 1348–1434' in op. cit., pp. 230–2 and notes; Denifle, op. cit., passim.

[4] E.g. Rashdall, *Universities*, ii, p. 60.

In the long term the communes could not allow the autonomous student republics to take permanent root in the Italian cities and they determined to eliminate this embarrassing form of competing jurisdictional power. A satisfactory *modus vivendi* with both doctoral and communal authority eluded the Italian students in the medieval universities. In retrospect, the Italian brand of student power does not appear to have proved a very helpful contribution to corporate university development. But, as an inspirational idea for student aspirations in western Europe, the pioneer advances of the students in Italy can scarcely be overrated.

It would, however, be wrong to deny the existence of a medieval student power movement in some respects echoing that of the present, a movement characterized by differing views of university government and involving the drive for student participation on a partnership basis with university teachers. We seem to find evidence for this in the French provincial universities of the late thirteenth and fourteenth centuries. These student movements are inseparably bound up with the evolution of university independence from ecclesiastical authority.[1]

By the fifteenth century the episcopate of northern Europe had come to an acceptance of the principle that the life blood of a university was its autonomy: while the university might be tenuously supervised by an external authority, this supervision must be made compatible with the *de facto* autonomous position of the academic guild. Earlier assumptions had been different. As previously mentioned, the initial phase of university life in northern Europe had been marked by an episcopal outlook which tended to categorize the university guilds almost as ecclesiastical 'colonies'. The universities were viewed as static organisms to be incorporated within the existing ecclesiastical framework and subjected to a more or less permanent tutelage, a notion totally at odds with the ideology of the masters' guilds.[2]

One of the perplexing problems in this field of university-episcopal relations is to discover why episcopal power lasted for so long in some of the universities of northern Europe but was relatively quickly reduced elsewhere. Investigation of this problem with regard to medieval France

---

[1] For the following discussion of the French provincial universities and the issue of freedom from ecclesiastical control, involving student power movements, see the more detailed treatment and references in my article, 'Episcopal Control in the Mediaeval Universities of Northern Europe', *Studies in Church History*, v (Leiden, 1969), pp. 1 ff.

[2] See A. B. Cobban, art. cit., pp. 1–2.

suggests that the student power movement is often the key to the autonomy situation in some of the French provincial universities.

The medieval French provincial universities offer a rich kaleidoscope of organizational patterns that would be hard to surpass in any other university grouping. By the early fifteenth century the majority of the French *studia* had produced hybrid constitutions based on a fusion of the archetypal forms of Paris and Bologna. The nature of the constitutional compromise varied widely from university to university. For example, Caen in the north was powerfully influenced by the Parisian mould and was basically a masters' university;[1] whereas Aix-en-Provence in the south was cast in the shape of a qualified student-university.[2] The typical French *studium*, however, evolved a form of constitution which held a more even balance between the competing claims of masters and students in university government: sometimes the evolutionary process was accompanied by violent conflict. Several of the older French *studia* such as Montpellier, Orléans and Angers experienced a measure of violence in the fourteenth century which caused them to modify their pronouncedly magisterial structures. As in the Italian universities, legal studies predominated in the *studia* of provincial France, with medicine at one or two centres a close second.[3] Arts faculties were dwarfed by the prominence of law and students commonly received their arts training in extra-university schools before enrolment at the university.[4] A consequence of this is that, as in Italy, the average age of the French provincial student body was higher than in those universities with large faculties of arts. If the municipalities exercised much less authority over the French *studia* than in Italy the same cannot be said of the ecclesiastical powers. For what especially distinguishes the earlier French *studia* is the extent to which they were subject to episcopal control.[5] In the thirteenth century the bishop's authority was all-pervasive; it gradually relaxed with the passage of time and in several places it was effectively challenged and diluted. Elsewhere, however, a substantial episcopal authority over the university was perpetuated well into the fifteenth century.

It is puzzling to find that the powers of the bishops endured for such a lengthy period in the early French provincial *studia*. One would have

---

[1] For the constitutional arrangements at Caen see Rashdall, *Universities*, ii, pp. 197.
[2] Ibid., ii, p. 189. The statutes of 1420–40 are printed by Fournier, *Statuts*, iii, no. 1582.
[3] Rashdall, op. cit., ii, p. 209.
[4] Loc. cit.
[5] See the remarks of Rashdall, op. cit., ii, p. 208; see also Cobban, art. cit., p. 4.

thought that the masters and doctors of provincial France would have followed the lead provided by Paris University in this matter of the winning of independence from episcopal control. But the provincial teachers were seemingly not very willing to stage the counter-offensives that had so distinguished their Parisian comrades. This does not mean that they were unconcerned about the extensive jurisdictional powers of the local diocesans or their representatives. They were much perturbed by the omnipresence of the ecclesiastical arm. And throughout France minor inroads were made upon aspects of episcopal jurisdiction, for example in matters such as the granting of the teaching licence and the drafting of university statutes. It is undeniable, however, that advancement was painfully slow and this decided conservatism of the masters and doctors in the face of the ecclesiastical powers is one of the most arresting features of French provincial university history.[1]

How are we to explain this degree of submission to episcopal domination? It may be assumed that the French masters and doctors were just as concerned about university freedom as their colleagues at Paris, Oxford or Cambridge. The trouble was that they were caught in a cleft stick: they resented encroachments of episcopal power but they feared the strength of the student movement even more. The Bologna pattern of student nations had made rapid inroads in the provincial French universities,[2] and this had given rise to the demand for more student participation in university administration. It was over this delicate affair that relations between the law students and their teachers were sometimes strained to breaking point in the early French *studia*. This is hardly surprising because the students and teaching staff harboured diametrically opposed views on the nature of university government.

The French law students were not aiming to secure a monopoly control over university government.[3] They exhibited none of the excesses that are found in the Italian student scene. Whether at Montpellier, Orléans, Angers, or Avignon, the students were seeking nothing more than a partnership with the doctors and masters in university administration. From the standpoint of the lecturing staff, however, any organized bid for student governmental power was a development to be totally resisted. The French doctors and masters interpreted the student victories in Italy as aberrations which must not be allowed to become established features of the university

---

[1] Cobban, art. cit., pp. 4–5.
[2] Kibre, *The Nations in the Mediaeval Universities*, pp. 129 ff.
[3] For the next three paragraphs see Cobban, art. cit., pp. 5–8.

world. Against the students were marshalled all the legal arguments that the Italian teachers had used to prove that students were devoid of professional standing. The French lecturers were determined to stem the tide of the student advance and attitudes hardened on both sides. It was perhaps this widespread prevalence of antipathy between the students and their lecturers which more than any other single cause impeded the progress towards university autonomy in the French situation.

By the fourteenth century the French provincial *studia* were in a state of ferment: there were tensions between the ecclesiastical authorities and the senior members of the guild, tensions between the latter and the students, and tensions between the students and the other two combined. In the midst of this unstable situation the doctors and masters were forced to choose between unpalatable alternatives. If they had ranged themselves with the students against the ecclesiastical powers university autonomy might have been achieved in provincial France at an earlier date. A cohesive front by the doctors, masters and students, allied with the potential threat of the academic migration, which had been used to such effect at Paris and in the Italian *studia*, would have proved a formidable weapon in the drive for university independence. In the event, however, the masters and doctors chose the conservative path, made common cause with the ecclesiastical authorities and thereby evinced a preference for a university system of magisterial oligarchy under episcopal supervision to one of autonomous university government shared with the students.

Despite the ultra-conservative attitudes of the doctors and masters, episcopal control was successfully contested and reduced in several of the French universities in the fourteenth century. The students seem to have been anti-episcopal only in the sense that they were opposed to any authoritarian source that resisted the student participation movement in the universities. And in those universities where episcopal control was challenged and broken the initiative came, not from the lecturing staff, but from the law students. The point is best demonstrated by a brief consideration of individual cases.[1]

The jurist university of Montpellier (*c.* 1230) was from the outset subject to the all-embracing supervision of the bishop of Maguelone. This oppressive régime failed to incite the masters and doctors to a state of organized resistance. But in the early fourteenth century the law students were roused to a rebellious pitch because both the bishop and their lecturers were intent

[1] For more detailed coverage of these cases with references see Cobban, art. cit., pp. 8–13.

on stifling the growth of student nations which were partially designed to promote student participation in the affairs of the *studium*. The tide of student revolt gathered momentum and reached such an intensity that in 1339 the internal university situation was reviewed by the papacy. The result was the new constitution of 1339 which must be regarded as a qualified victory for the students insofar as it gave them a considerable stake in university government. Although the authority of the bishop was not immediately phased out the main force of episcopal strength had been irrevocably sapped: and this had been due, above all, to the initiative of the organized student movement.

A similar pattern of events was staged at the University of Angers (early thirteenth century). The breaking of the episcopal monopoly occurred later than at Montpellier but here also the chief impetus came from the rebellious students. As at Montpellier, the bishop had supreme power over the university and exercised control through his representative, the *scholasticus*, who served as the *de facto* head of the *studium* and who governed with the support of the masters and doctors. Student nations probably emerged in the thirteenth century, but as late as 1373 the law doctors refused to allow the nations to participate in university business. Late in the fourteenth century the law students rebelled against the authoritarian government of the *scholasticus* and the doctors. The dispute was settled in 1398 by the framing of a new constitution whereby the students were conceded a share in university administration. The authority of the bishop and the *scholasticus* was not extinguished overnight but, in retrospect, it seems that the student rebellion marked the decisive point in the university's advance towards freedom from ecclesiastical domination which became a reality in the course of the fifteenth century.

Orléans (early thirteenth century) experienced a like sequence of events. The organized strength of the student movement was instrumental in emasculating the ecclesiastical power in the early fourteenth century. The evidence suggests that the law doctors assumed a more positive stance in the struggle for guild autonomy than was usual in the early French *studia*. And at Orléans there may even have been a temporary alliance between the students and the doctors against the bishop, a rare occurrence in the French situation.

But the student movement was not everywhere successful in provincial France. For example it met with signal failure at Avignon where, in the second half of the fourteenth century, the students twice rebelled against a reactionary ecclesiastical system of government from which even the doctors were virtually excluded. In this special papal enclave, however, the entrenched resources of ecclesiastical authority, supported by the doctors, easily crushed the student revolts and it was not until 1459 that the law students acquired a voice in the councils of the university.

The association between student power and the fight for university emancipation from ecclesiastical tutelage was not a continuing phenomenon of the French *studia* newly founded in the fifteenth century. Generally speaking, the fifteenth-century episcopate had come to accept that the essence of a university was its autonomy and that there was a duty to promote university maturity and independence. Consequently, the later French *studia* were relatively free of the university-episcopal tensions which had so embittered the lives of their predecessors. It seems probable, however, that the democratic student movements of the fourteenth century had some bearing on later university development. Certainly, a modest vein of student democracy is a feature of the university scene in fifteenth-century France. For example, universities such as Aix (1409), Dôle (1422), Poitiers (1431/2), Valence (1452-9), Nantes (1460) and Bourges (1464) accommodated varying amounts of student involvement although it is not always possible to say whether participatory rights were more nominal than real.[1] Whatever the case, one might tentatively suggest that the student victories of the fourteenth century had prepared a climate of opinion favourable to a cautious acceptance of the principle of limited student participation.

The general situation in the French universities relative to student power can now be briefly summarized. In several of the French provincial *studia* student rebellions occurred in the fourteenth century against the combined forces of the university teachers and the ecclesiastical authorities: at Orléans and Angers, at any rate, student activists seem to have embraced largely those of about twenty years or over, especially bachelors or licentiates of law or masters in arts.[2] The revolts were not everywhere successful: but where the rebellions were effective, as at Montpellier, Orléans or Angers, they led to the extortion of new constitutions by which students were given participating powers in university government. At the same time, the successful student rebellions dealt the death-blow to ecclesiastical controls in

[1] The constitutions of these *studia* are described by Rashdall, *Universities*, ii, 186 ff.; see also Kibre, op. cit., pp. 152-6. Pearl Kibre's remarks on Dôle and Nantes (p. 156) are slightly misleading. It is true that the division into nations is lacking but these universities did have mixed constitutions and should not be regarded as purely magisterial foundations.

[2] Information supplied by my research student A. J. Scarth who is currently engaged on a thesis on medieval French provincial universities.

university affairs. Doubtless university independence would have evolved in the fullness of time even if there had been no student rebellions but, by hastening the process, the law students have some claim to be regarded as the architects of autonomy in several of the *studia* of provincial France.

It is not easy to be precise about the form that student participation assumed in the medieval French universities. According to the revised constitutions[1] that followed in the wake of the student rebellions participation seems to have been extensive and, in some places, may well have amounted to a kind of partnership with the university teachers. Whether or not student involvement was directed towards what are today called 'appropriate areas' is difficult to say. On balance, the revised constitutions do not suggest that representation was confined to selected fields because there are no statutory provisions for reserved items of business, although this alone is by no means conclusive. In the French universities founded in the fifteenth century the degree of student involvement was modest but eludes close definition. Whatever the measure of student participation, in France, as in Italy, it had virtually collapsed by the sixteenth century. Where student nations survived, they remained as units of administrative convenience, not as organs of student power.

Of the remaining European *studia* the Spanish universities hold some interest for this subject of student power. Most of the universities of Spain were royal creations designed to bring prestige to the various kingdoms in which they were established.[2] In this respect, their function was similar to that of Frederick II's University of Naples (1224) which was doubtless an inspirational model for the Spanish rulers. The royal connection was stressed in some instances by the introduction into the *studium* of a chancellor who was a crown nominee. Moreover, several of the Spanish universities had close links with cathedrals or other churches which found expression in the authority exercised over the *studium* by the local bishop or capitular master of the schools. Given this apparatus of royal-ecclesiastical control which permeated the university structure in Spain it is an intriguing paradox to find that several *studia* harboured internal constitutional arrangements prompted by the Bolognese example.

Little is known of the constitution of Salamanca (*c.* 1227–8) before the

---

[1] See e.g. the constitutions of the universities of Montpellier, Angers and Orléans in Fournier, op. cit., ii, no. 947; i, nos. 430–7; i, no. 22; also Cobban, art. cit., pp. 9, 10, 11.
[2] The main features of the Spanish universities are summarized by Rashdall, op. cit., ii, pp. 64–5; see also Kibre, op. cit., pp. 156–8 and H. Wieruszowski, *The Medieval University: Masters, Students, Learning*, cit., pp. 91–4.

promulgation of Benedict XIII's statutes in 1411.[1] By this code a considerable degree of student participation was sanctioned. Power was apparently shared between the students, represented by an elected rector and council, and the cathedral *scholasticus*, sometimes styled the university chancellor. The doctors, however, were far from being cyphers and they were never reduced to anything like the state of subjection of their counterparts at Bologna or Padua in the heyday of student power. Moreover, Martin V's new constitution of 1422 severely curtailed student democracy and increased the stake in university government of the *scholasticus* and the salaried doctors.[2] Valladolid (*a.* 1250) was a form of modified student university at least from the early fifteenth century when it acquired statutes based on those of Salamanca.[3] The university was given new statutes in the sixteenth century, and what is particularly interesting about these is that they perpetuate student democratic arrangements at a time when they had faded in the *studia* of Italy and provincial France. By this constitution[4] the governing council of the university comprised the rector (not a student), the chancellor, half of the salaried doctors and eight student councillors. But the most arresting feature was that the election to the salaried chairs was to be left in the hands of the students who made their choices after hearing trial lectures delivered by the candidates.[5] If these statutes embody a real situation then Valladolid occupies a position of some note among the European universities of the sixteenth century. Lérida,[6] founded by James II of Aragon in 1300, likewise made concessions to student controls, although there was also a chancellor appointed by the king. A dispute resolved at Lérida in 1354 throws some light on the participating rôle of the students there in the election of their professors.[7] The wrangle had arisen several years before: it broke out between the city and the rector and students over the question of whether the mace-bearers (*clavarii*), appointed by the city to elect the salaried professors, were obliged to consult

---

[1] For Salamanca see Rashdall, op. cit., ii, pp. 74 ff.; Kibre, op. cit., pp. 156–7. The earliest extant statutes of 1411 are printed in Denifle, *Archiv*, v (1889), pp. 167 ff. They form a fascinating code: they owe much to the Bolognese model but also contain some important modifications, e.g. the authority vested in the cathedral *scholasticus*.

[2] Rashdall, op. cit., pp. 87–8.

[3] For Valladolid see ibid., ii, pp. 69 ff.

[4] Details are given ibid., ii, pp. 72–3.

[5] Ibid., ii, p. 73.

[6] For Lérida see ibid., ii, pp. 91 ff.; Kibre, op. cit., pp. 157–8. Documents relating to Lérida are published by Denifle, *Archiv*, iv (1888), pp. 253 ff.

[7] For this case see R. Gaya Massot, 'Provisión de Cátedras en el Estudio General de Lérida', *Analecta Sacra Tarraconensia*, xxx (1957).

with the rector and selected students before making their choices. Ramón Bas, a lector of the Franciscan house at Lérida and highly regarded by both parties, was made arbiter of the quarrel after the matter had been referred to the king. In his arbitration, Ramón Bas confirmed the student claim to associated consultation with the city representatives in professorial elections. The *studium generale* at Lérida had a chequered history and seems to have been in grave decline by the early fifteenth century. Nevertheless, many of the statutory provisions were reproduced in the universities of Perpignan (1350) and Huesca (1354).

The oldest Spanish university, Palencia (1208-9), belonged to the magisterial Parisian type and Saragossa (1474) was partially of this kind. The fifteenth-century universities of Barcelona (1450), Palma (1483), Sigüenza (1489), Alcalá (1499) and Valencia (1500) are not easily classifiable but do not seem to be preserves of student power.

With the exception of the great European university of Salamanca, the Spanish universities were national rather than large cosmopolitan centres. They tended to be conservative authoritarian structures and, although several apparently tolerated a measure of student democratic involvement, they do not appear to have been areas of pronounced student radicalism. There is little to indicate that student powers were wrested after the kind of upheavals that occurred in Italian or French provincial *studia*. The extent to which student power was a reality and not merely a constitutional form in the Spanish universities is a tangled matter which cannot be resolved in the light of present knowledge. But the authoritarian environment in which the Spanish *studia* had their being and their lack of a turbulent international character suggest that they would not be major vehicles of student democracy.

The restoration of the magisterial concept of university organization in west European *studia* is associated with the mounting disquiet that was generated about the efficacy of student power. In the fourteenth century there was widespread unease about the wisdom of granting official status to student associations. And secular and ecclesiastical authorities showed a common interest in deflating student militancy by attacking its organizational strength. For example, in 1312 Philip IV of France forbade the student nations at Orléans to hold assemblies because they were a divisive influence in the university and often led to injury or even death.[1] Eight years later the bishop of Maguelone tried to suppress student organizations

---

[1] Fournier, op. cit., i, no. 36; Kibre, op. cit., p. 133.

at Montpellier for the same kind of reason.[1] Apart from the belief that student power was an actual or potential menace to both academic and urban peace there was the general complaint that the students had a bad to indifferent record in university administration. There are numerous allegations that student rectors were often men without the necessary capacity to uphold the university statutes or to maintain discipline over the student body.[2] There was undoubtedly some degree of rectorial corruption: there are instances of rectors trying to rig their re-elections or ruling in arbitrary fashion with cliques of drinking companions.[3] Although the more responsible student element tried here and there to depose these charlatans, the outcome was not always successful.

But it was not only the student leaders who caused misgivings. The conduct of ordinary student representatives came under attack. It is claimed that they sometimes came armed to assemblies and disrupted the proceedings by boisterous and unseemly acrobatic behaviour.[4] That legislation was required to be passed to curb such ongoings might indicate that there was substance in the repeated charges of student irresponsibility. At Toulouse University in the fifteenth century there was a concerted attempt by the lecturers to deprive the student councillors of their statutory rights of participation. The *parlement* at Toulouse, to which university cases were regularly referred, had to keep reminding the lecturers in no uncertain terms of their legal obligation to accept student representatives in university assemblies.[5] Whether the action of the lecturers was provoked directly by student misconduct or was part of a general policy to wind down the machinery of student participation is not clear. At Toulouse it seems that student representatives played some general part in elections to vacant chairs, but they were not allowed to pass judgment on the academic credentials of the candidates.[6] Presumably this kind of intermittent feuding between students and lecturers was a common feature of those French uni-

---

[1] Fournier, op. cit., ii, no. 923; Kibre, op. cit., loc. cit.
[2] On the shortcomings of the student rectorship see e.g. V. Laval, *Cartulaire de l'Université d'Avignon* (Avignon, 1884), i, p. 25n.; evidence for the 'evils' of the rectorship is cited by Abbé Nadal throughout his *Histoire de l'Université de Valence*, ed. M. Aurel (Valence, 1861).
[3] For striking examples at Florence University see Brucker, 'Florence and its University, 1348–1434' in op. cit., p. 227.
[4] Cobban, art. cit., p. 7 and n. 2.
[5] Fournier, op. cit., i, nos. 858, 860, 868; Smith, *The University of Toulouse in the Middle Ages*, pp. 188, 189, 192; J. Puget, 'L'Université de Toulouse au xive et au xve siècles', *Annales du Midi*, xlii (1930), pp. 362–3, 365–6.
[6] Fournier, op. cit., i, no. 858.

versities with mixed constitutions in the later medieval period. It was a war of academic attrition in which student participating powers were gradually reduced to an empty form.

It cannot be supposed that irresponsibility was confined to the student body. There was apparently a good deal of it among the university teachers. We hear complaints of academic simony in the sense that chairs were being disposed of to the highest bidder, who might be totally unsuitable for a teaching post.[1] In the second half of the thirteenth century there were attempts by the Bologna doctors to secure the majority of the teaching positions for members of their own families: in other words, to establish an hereditary professoriate. Fortunately, this object was frustrated.[2] Students frequently alleged that there were lecturers who neglected their academic duties by failing to cover the courses,[3] by omitting to give the requisite number of disputations which the less able teachers found a great trouble, and by the excessive use of substitutes to lecture in their places.[4] In 1486 the *parlement* at Toulouse deprived two law lecturers of their positions because they had not lectured for two or three years and had not even provided substitutes.[5] There was also much student resentment at the absence of teaching doctors who were involved in business affairs in the university town or in neighbouring cities: for example, in *c.* 1280 the Bologna students were concerned that too many of their teachers were engrossed in communal business to the detriment of their academic duties.[6] In the mid-fifteenth century the Paduan doctors came under criticism for a range of offences. In 1457 the Venetian Senate (Padua was then subject to Venice) alleged that declining student numbers at Padua were due primarily to the negligence of the teaching doctors. It was claimed that the doctors were careless about the content of their lectures and that they were not giving the required quota because they were absent on business in other cities; and the lecturing substitutes provided did not meet with student approval[7].

---

[1] E.g. at Toulouse: Fournier, op. cit., i, nos. 858, 860, 868; Smith, op. cit., pp. 188, 189, 192; Puget, art. cit., p. 364.
[2] See Rashdall, *Universities*, i, pp. 214–15.
[3] Colourful evidence is supplied for Florence by Brucker, 'Florence and its University, 1348–1434' in op. cit., p. 233. For Toulouse see Fournier, op. cit., i, no. 858; Smith, op. cit., p. 188; Puget, art. cit., pp. 363–4, 375.
[4] For Toulouse: Fournier, op. cit., i, nos. 860, 866; Smith, op. cit., pp. 189, 190; Puget, art. cit., p. 364. See the provision of 1430 against the use of substitutes at Pavia, *Statuti e Ordinamenti della Università di Pavia*, p. 149.
[5] Puget, art. cit., p. 375.
[6] Sarti and Fattorini, *De Claris . . .*, i, p. 245.
[7] Kibre, *Scholarly Privileges in the Middle Ages*, pp. 76–7.

The extent of academic irresponsibility and corruption and how it was apportioned between the students and their teachers cannot be assessed by any quantitative means. It is often impossible to separate out fact from allegation and counter-allegation. In those university situations where students and teachers were rivals in the bid for university power there must have been propagandist distortion from either side. Nevertheless, west European society, or at least its establishment element, ultimately concluded that university government was to be the preserve of university teachers, with or without the aid of external bodies, and that the students were to be reduced to the ranks of the listeners and the learners. It may have been thought that the problem of corruption among lecturers was one that was remediable by eternal vigilance and corrective action. The institutionalization of student power, however, was a more intractable matter. As a system, it had been tested for a respectable length of time and it had been found wanting. It had come to be regarded as a more or less permanently disruptive force in university and urban society. Instability and quixotic idealism may have signalized the early phase of university development, but this kind of ethos was antithetical to the ordered, authoritarian canons of society in the later middle ages. From the establishment point of view there seemed to be only one solution: the suppression of significant forms of student participation and the full reinstatement of the magisterial type of university. The university structures of southern Europe had to be brought into alignment with the governmental systems of the universities in the north, even if this curtailed some of the rich diversity in the higher educational life of western Europe. Rightly or wrongly, the collective European experience had judged that professional maturity was a more hopeful directing force of stable university evolution than the erratic uncertainties of youth.

In reflecting on the demise of student power it is vital to distinguish between the fully-extended student-university and university systems which embraced a degree of student participation. The autonomous student-university was a remarkable experimental form, but it is unlikely that it ever commanded a willing acceptance in medieval Europe beyond a committed section of the student population. Contemporaries regarded the academic situation at Bologna and Padua as an aberration, an anomaly contrary to the natural order which would be set to rights in the fullness of time. Doubtless the extremist models of Bologna and Padua served as a permanent student ideal, the quintessence of the medieval student commonwealth, but in terms of practical politics they had little chance of long survival in their unadulterated shape. They offered too much violence to the professional sensibilities of university teachers and were a constant jurisdictional challenge to state authority. Few would have viewed these student republics as permanent alternatives to magisterial organization; and few would have regretted their passing when their epitaph was written by the ubiquitous appearance of the salaried lectureship. The compromise phoenix that arose from the moribund excesses of the student-university was a student participation movement. This seemed to acquire a measure of tolerance on the part of teachers and external authorities alike, even if that tolerance sometimes followed in the path of bitter conflict. So widespread did qualified student involvement become in southern Europe that it might have established itself as a permanently acceptable principle of university organization. Limited student democracy had a prospect of longevity which the fully-fledged student-university never had. In the event, however, this too fragmented and dissolved before the hierarchical pressures of society. Where is one to lay the emphasis for the collapse of student involvement? Was student incapacity for government so great that the students themselves dug the grave of the movement? Or is this just a propagandist convenience designed to buttress the reversion of power to oligarchical assemblies? Was magisterial government so patently superior to student administration? Would student power in any case, whatever its record, have fallen prey to the combined forces of the salaried lectureship, the growing state control of the universities, and the hardening hierarchical social and political climate of the later middle ages? These are the ingredients of the student power problem. But their relative weightings are imponderables because of the scattered and random nature of the evidence which enables us to perceive the many facets of medieval student power but does not often allow us to follow through a given situation with the desired amount of detail. In these circumstances, it does not seem possible to analyze further the features which appear to have contributed to the waning of student power or to assign to any one of them an overriding emphasis. We are left with an eclectic view, a mosaic in which the parts are clearly delineated but which quickly merges into the realm of speculation.

Medieval student power was chiefly a phenomenon of southern Europe having its roots in Italy, parts of provincial France and, to some extent, in Spain. It was shaped and directed mainly by the relatively mature law students. In the northern universities of England, Scotland, Germany, Bohemia, the Low Countries and Scandinavia student power did not materialize as a serious challenge to the dominance of the masters. In this connection one or two general points may be offered by way of tentative explanation, although only the most minute researches into each university's development within the context of its regional environment can bring the overall pattern into anything approaching a definite focus.

It is reasonably clear that in the northern universities the arts faculties occupied a larger and more important position within the *studium* than in southern Europe where they were sometimes mere adjuncts to legal studies or to medicine. Much of the university effort in the north went into the training of young men for the majority of whom the B.A. degree would be an academic ceiling.[1] In terms of maturity and worldly experience these adolescents were ill-equipped to organize and spearhead movements of student protest. The average northern student was less politically and legally sophisticated and less highly motivated than his southern fellows. The product of a fairly humble background, he was likely to regard the university as one of the few or even sole means of modest social advancement. These circumstances, allied to his tender years,[2] would make him predisposed to accept the hierarchical assumptions upon which the university was built and to acquiesce, albeit with the reluctance of youth, in the disciplinary codes imposed by the magisterial guilds on their undergraduate populations. By contrast, many of the southern students were recruited from wealthy backgrounds and some were of noble origin. A sizeable proportion of them were in their twenties or even older, and some came straight to university from holding positions of responsibility in society. For students of this type the disciplinary provisions of the northern *studia* were inappropriate. The mature students in the south had a more legalistic, contractual view of university life than was prevalent in the north. In the southern environment, where the universities were closely integrated with the needs of organized professional life, the students were encouraged to think of the universities and lecturing staffs as agencies to be used and hired to best serve their own conveniences and future professional interests. In a society saturated with notions of independent guild organization it is not too surprising that the students should seek to transplant the idea of the autonomous corporation to the university

---

[1] F. Eulenberg (in the late nineteenth century) estimated that the majority of German students of the late fourteenth and fifteenth centuries took no degree (figures quoted by editors of Rashdall, *Universities*, iii, p. 334).

[2] On the age of northern medieval students see Rashdall, op. cit., iii, pp. 352–3. See also the cautionary discussion by E. F. Jacob, 'English university clerks in the later Middle Ages: the Problem of Maintenance', *B.J.R.L.*, xxix (1946), pp. 308–9.

arena as the mechanism most suited to fulfil their needs. The much contested claim that students by themselves had full professional status on a
par with extra-university professional activity was an aspiration that probably struck few chords in the average northern student who was not so
attuned to this kind of self-conscious legalism and whose immediate legal
problems were not likely to be so pressing. For in the northern *studia* the
protectionist functions of the magisterial guilds were extended to embrace
the associated student bodies and this, along with the fact that the masters
often took an effective lead in the struggles against hostile external parties,[1]
sheltered the students from many of the dangers to which their counterparts were exposed in southern Europe, thereby lessening the motivation
for student power enterprise. Mixed nations of masters and students and,
occasionally, purely student nations arose here and there in northern
Europe, but they were of little consequence as power units.[2]

The sustained nature of royal or municipal support given to the northern
universities may well have a bearing on the insignificance of student power
in the north. It is well known that the old-established universities of Paris,
Oxford and Cambridge owed a great deal to monarchy for their healthy
independent growth. The aid of the Capetian kings was vital to the winning
of autonomous status by the masters' guild at Paris in the crucial years of
the thirteenth century; and in the fourteenth and fifteenth centuries the
university fell increasingly within the tutelary orbit of royal authority.[3]
Oxford and Cambridge too benefited from a royal protection that extended
from the thirteenth century to the Tudor age. Like considerations apply
to the universities founded in northern Europe in the late fourteenth and
fifteenth centuries.[4] Many of these such as Prague (1347–8), Vienna (1365),

---

[1] E.g. the Parisian masters of the arts faculty assumed the lead against the efforts of
the bishop of Paris and the chancellor of Notre Dame to stifle the independence of the
university, and the masters' guilds of Oxford and Cambridge fought the issue of
emancipation from episcopal jurisdiction. All three magisterial guilds, as in most north
European *studia*, secured for their students a strongly privileged position vis-à-vis the
town.

[2] E.g. mixed nations appeared at Prague and Vienna (Kibre, *The Nations in the Mediaeval
Universities*, pp. 169, 175): the Leipzig nations were for masters only. At Heidelberg,
the nations quickly disappeared and they did not develop at Erfurt or Cologne (Kibre,
op. cit., p. 177). In fifteenth-century Scotland the nations at St Andrews at first included
no students: at Glasgow and Aberdeen the nations were student organizations, but
they do not appear to have exercised much power (Kibre, op. cit., pp. 182, 183).

[3] See Leff, *Paris and Oxford Universities in the Thirteenth and Fourteenth Centuries*, esp. pp.
27–51.

[4] The late medieval universities of Germany, Bohemia and the Low Countries are
described by Rashdall, *Universities*, ii, ch. 9.

Heidelberg (1385) and Leipzig (1409) owed their origins and continuing well-being to the initiative of kings and local rulers. Others such as Cologne (1388) and Rostock (1419) were the outcome of municipal enterprise. And, generally speaking, the north European *studia* of the later middle ages had, from the start, the protection of royal or city authorities intent on bolstering up the universities as symbols of national, provincial or civic prestige while, at the same time, securing the maximum economic advantage from them. It is extremely difficult to assess the possible impact of this complex situation of controls for the issue of student power. What one can perhaps say is that the visible presence of a benign authority which guaranteed a relative security would engender conditions within which the separate groupings of the university could more easily cohere to form a tightly-knit society. When this measure of security was absent, as it often was in southern Europe, the effect might be to exacerbate the potentially divisive forces in the *studium* as students and lecturers sought unilaterally to create for themselves a means of insurance which could lead to organized student power. If king or emperor were remote figures and the local municipality hostile, the students would have to fall back on their own resources to an extent that was not usually necessary in the north. The immediacy or remoteness of a benign authority as a possible barometer of student power can be no more than an unconfirmed hypothesis but study of the medieval university situation suggests that it may have at least a general application in terms of northern and southern Europe.

The extent to which a university was a cosmopolitan centre has probably to be taken into account when considering the incidence of student power. As a result of the striking expansion of northern universities in Germany, the Low Countries, Scotland and elsewhere in the latter half of the fourteenth and fifteenth centuries students were given the opportunity to attend a university in their home region. The removal of the necessity for students to make long journeys to Europe's earliest universities meant that these inevitably lost a lot of their international character.[1] And the newer *studia*, deeply rooted in their regions, to a greater or lesser degree served national or provincial rather than broad cosmopolitan needs. Paris was the supreme focus of northern cosmopolitanism until its intake was clipped by the proliferation of the new universities in the later medieval period.[2] The English universities, on the other hand, had never been re-

---

[1] See the remarks of Kibre, op. cit., pp. 185–6.
[2] For estimates of changing numbers at Paris see Rashdall, op. cit., iii, pp. 330–1. Although Paris undoubtedly became less international in the later medieval period, the

markable for their international nature, recruitment being mainly from the British Isles.[1] With the grand exception of Paris, it would be generally true to say that the northern *studia* were somewhat less cosmopolitan than the southern universities outside Spain. Although student power did not take root in the international environment of Paris, there may still be substance in the idea that the more indigenous academic communities of the northern *studia* were, by their nature, less conducive to the genesis and growth of student power than the turbulent, multi-national assemblies of the south. One must not forget that student power at Bologna had been the creation of the foreign students: for some considerable time the native Bolognese were excluded from the guilds. And the concentrations of indigenous students in northern universities may well have acted as a brake on the student power movement.

Finally, in conjecturing why student power failed to emerge in northern Europe it may be relevant to draw attention to a development of major constitutional importance, namely, the evolution of a permanent professoriate. This breakthrough in north European *studia* was pioneered, above all, by the German and Scottish universities.[2] It is particularly associated with the policy of founding colleges to serve as lasting endowments for university teachers. In some instances, for example at Aberdeen, the university was fused with a college from the beginning as an integral part of the founder's plan.[3] The annexation of prebends of local churches proved a successful alternative method of endowment for teachers and, in several places, both systems are found.[4] It is true that Paris and the English universities had laboured under the handicap of rapidly fluctuating lecturing staffs and yet had escaped the growth of student controls: nevertheless, the establishment of long-tenured teaching *nuclei* in north European *studia* was a development that firmly reinforced the magisterial nature of university organization just as the spread of municipal chairs militated against student strength in southern Europe.

---

contraction in the areas of recruitment must not be exaggerated. This is well illustrated by a recent geographical analysis of 1535 bachelors of the English-German nation at Paris between 1425 and 1494 which reveals a wide recruitment basis: see Gabriel, 'The English-German Nation at the University of Paris from 1425–1494' in *Garlandia*, pp 169–70.

[1] See Rashdall, op. cit., iii, p. 336; Kibre, op. cit., pp. 160–1, 166–7.

[2] Rashdall, op. cit., ii, pp. 221, 283–4, 320, 323.

[3] See above ch. 6, pp. 156–7.

[4] Paquet, 'Salaires et prébendes des professeurs de l'université de Louvain au xve siècle', art. cit., passim has much useful information on this subject.

Although student power did not germinate in northern Europe it was apparently an embryonic issue in the Paris schools of the twelfth century. Thierry of Chartres complained that there were masters who, to win popularity, ingratiated themselves with their students and prostituted their professional capacity.[1] But the magisterial concept of academic freedom prevailed at Paris and is neatly etched in the words of William of Conches: he tells us that the Paris schools refused to allow their students to be the judges of their masters with the power to impose upon them the rules of speech and silence ('. . . *discipulos magistrorum iudices, legemque loquendi et tacendi imponentes*').[2] This is an interesting vignette which presumably conceals more than it reveals; but it does presage the future distribution of academic power in northern *studia*. For the stand taken in twelfth-century Paris provided the canon of professional conduct that was to serve as a model for university teachers in northern Europe throughout the medieval period.

The ideology of student power had its birth pangs in the legal soil of thirteenth-century Italy. Here was forged the vision of the autonomous student republic, free from the trammels of external control and served by a lecturing force, elected by and responsible to the student body. As an idea, this was a magnetic source of inspiration for the student commonwealth of southern Europe in its drive for participating rights in university structures. The nearest approximations to the notion in practice were realized at the universities of Bologna and Padua, but there only for a limited duration. The excesses of the Bolognese and Paduan movements were not typical of the university scene in medieval Italy which was characterized by more modest degrees of student democratic involvement. Everywhere in Italy in the fourteenth and fifteenth centuries student power succumbed to the onslaught of communal shackles and to the concomitant growth of the salaried lectureship. It would be misleading, however, if medieval student power were to be equated solely with the Italian situation. At least an equal emphasis should be given to the student achievements of provincial France. Medieval student power ultimately failed. The universities, overwhelmingly orientated towards the professional needs of society, became increasingly reflective of the establishment which they served. The unsettling nature of student power, with its weapons of the

---

[1] See E. Lesne, 'Les écoles de la fin du viiie siècle à la fin du xiie' in *Histoire de la propriété ecclésiastique en France* (Lille, 1940), v, p. 163; also Gabriel, 'The Cathedral Schools of Notre-Dame and the Beginning of the University of Paris', *Garlandia*, p. 57.
[2] Lesne, op. cit., p. 501; Gabriel, op. cit., loc. cit.

boycott and the migration, posed too great a threat to the more ordered, sedentary character that the universities were acquiring in the fourteenth and fifteenth centuries. Society expected an adequate return for the investments sunk in the universities, investments in the form of endowed lectureships, colleges, permanent university buildings and so forth. That return was deemed to be put in jeopardy by the machinations of student politics. The indifferent student record in university administration, perhaps exaggerated by propaganda, provided the establishment with a more immediate reason for the phasing out of student participation as a vital force in west European universities. The lessons of medieval student power are not necessarily of direct relevance to the twentieth century. But those who are concerned with university management could do worse than look over their shoulders at the aspirations and actions of students in the medieval past.

VIII

The academic community

Considering the academic population as a whole, one can make a first division into endowed and unendowed elements. Generally speaking, far more is known about the endowed personnel than about the unendowed members of the community: this is so because stabilized living in fixed institutions is usually more productive of documentary material than is the case with unattached migratory existence. For this reason, one of the most difficult of the problems arising from a study of the academic population is that of the social status and living conditions of the great mass of unendowed students domiciled in the hostels or lodging houses of the university town.

Was the typical medieval undergraduate a poor student in any real sense of the term? Did the average student have to beg, borrow or steal his way through university? Were there provisions to ensure that poverty would be no ultimate barrier to ability? One of the principal sources which might be expected to supply some insight into these basic problems is the substantial corpus of model student letters contained in the formularies and writing manuals of the professional *dictatores*.[1] Even if the majority of student letters are not original but models composed by the practitioners of *dictamen*, the very fact that they are stereotypes presupposes that the contents will be generally representative of the everyday problems confronting the average student. From these letter collections, it is clear that the most persistent theme is lack of money[2] from which circumstance stem

[1] See the seminal study of C. H. Haskins, *Studies in Mediaeval Culture*, cit., ch. 1, pp. 1 ff.
[2] See ibid., esp. pp. 7–14 and notes.

most of the related hardships. Making allowance for the rhetorical em-
bellishments of the *ars dictandi*, we learn that students might suffer from
shortage of food, clothes, bedding, books, parchment and so on. They
complained bitterly of the cold, often fell ill, were sometimes robbed of
what little they had, were exposed to the extortion of avaricious lodging-
house keepers, and might even be imprisoned following a brawl with
citizens of the town.[1] Admitting that the medieval student was subject to
a degree of privation and insecurity which would be crippling by twentieth-century levels of academic endurance, one must be hesitant about
accepting all of this letter evidence at face value. And this consideration
has a direct bearing upon the concept of student poverty. Confusion has
arisen because poverty has too often been assumed without taking sufficient
cognisance of mitigating circumstances. If a student complains in a letter
to a relative or patron about money shortage, this does not necessarily
mean that he is poverty-stricken or anything like it. Here one must remember that the medieval period was subject to repeated shortages of coin;[2]
and if a deficiency in the availability of coin coincided with years of bad
harvest and sharply rising prices the student might find himself severely
embarrassed for a time, but in no wise reduced to a state of grinding
poverty. Apart from the need to set student cash shortages within the context of the general monetary movements of the period, there are other factors
which might partially explain temporary lack of resources. It might be due
to the unwillingness of parents or guardians to supply further instalments
until a later date to encourage the student to curb personal extravagance and
to cultivate sounder budgeting; or bad reports of the student's conduct and
lack of progress in the schools may have reached relatives or patrons causing
them to delay in sending further monetary assistance; or perhaps economic
difficulties at home may have led to an interruption of financial supplies;[3]
or if the students lived in a university hostel shortage of ready cash might

---

[1] On the frequency with which students might be lawfully or unlawfully detained in
prison see e.g. the detailed situation at Paris in the thirteenth, fourteenth and fifteenth
centuries in Kibre, *Scholarly Privileges in the Middle Ages*, cit., chs. iv, v, vi.
[2] See e.g. E. F. Jacob, 'English University Clerks in the later Middle Ages: the Problem
of Maintenance', *B.J.R.L.*, xxix (1946), pp. 304 ff. at p. 306.
[3] For examples of diverse reasons for monetary delay see Haskins, op. cit., pp. 14 ff.;
Jacob, art. cit., p. 307 prints a letter in which finances are refused because of ill-conduct;
also in *Formularies which bear on the History of Oxford c. 1204–1420*, ed. H. E. Salter, W. A.
Pantin and H. G. Richardson, 2 vols., Oxf. Hist. Soc., new series, iv, v (1942), ii, pp.
360–1.

be due to the guarded monetary policy of the principal, to whom arts students' revenues were often entrusted, and who deliberately kept his charges on a tight pecuniary rein.[1] Thus, while the chief characteristic of student letters may be the cry for money, the recurring deficiency of ready cash does not necessarily imply real poverty for the student majority, but may mean no more than temporary embarrassment. And the view that the typical medieval student lived his life on the bare margins of subsistence is not one that is now generally accepted. The majority of students were of intermediate social status,[2] and their financial state presumably reflected this middling community position.

Detailed figures are available for a number of universities which tend to corroborate this point. Of the 1535 bachelors promoted in the English-German nation at Paris between 1425 and 1494, on the basis of the *bursa*, the amount each student could afford for weekly living expenses,[3] only 270 (17.58 per cent) paid no *bursa* and were classified as poor students (*pauperes*); 719 (46.84 per cent) paid *bursae* of a minimum nature; 413 (26.91 per cent) paid *bursae* of a medium kind; and 133 (8.67 per cent) paid *bursae* befitting those of a richer class.[4] Thus, the *pauperes* and the rich students accounted for only 26.25 per cent of the total, leaving 73.75 per cent of the students who paid *bursae* ranging from a minimum to a comfortable level. There were similar proportions at other universities. For example, of 6579 students who matriculated at the university of Vienna between 1377 and 1413, only 1629 (25 per cent) were treated as poor scholars; at Leipzig University between 1409 and 1430 the figure was 19 per cent;[5] at Freiburg between 1508 and 1514 about 17 per cent were classified as 'poor'.[6] Sample figures of this nature for the medieval universities are fairly consistent in indicating that a majority of the students could afford to pay a reasonable rate for their weekly expenses or commons and were by no means hovering on the poverty line: they doubtless had

---

[1] Jacob, art. cit., pp. 306–7: also in H. E. Salter, 'An Oxford Hall in 1424', *Essays in History presented to R. L. Poole*, cit., p. 422. The more mature students of law probably managed their own finances.

[2] See the remarks of Rashdall, *Universities*, iii, p. 408.

[3] A. L. Gabriel, 'The English-German Nation at the University of Paris from 1425–1494' in *Garlandia*, cit., p. 176. Examples of degree fees based on weekly maintenance costs are found for Oxford in *The Register of Congregation 1448–1463*, cit.; see W. A. Pantin's comments, p. xxiii.

[4] Ibid., pp. 186–7.

[5] Figures quoted ibid., p. 187.

[6] J. M. Fletcher, 'Wealth and Poverty in the Medieval German Universities' in op. cit., p. 433.

to economize stringently and often ran into periods of acute need. But many of them had potential reserves at a distance from which they could draw to alleviate a temporary monetary crisis.

There were, however, in medieval universities a significant proportion of genuinely poor scholars to be found mainly among the younger members of the arts faculties. The poorest of them could not afford to live in a hostel or to pay lecture fees or graduation expenses or to meet the strict requirements of academic dress. Poor scholars seem to have been more numerous in the universities of northern Europe, and especially in the German *studia*, than in southern Europe where the arts faculties were smaller and the students more affluent.[1] Matriculation records of Avignon in the fifteenth century show that the incidence of poor scholars was slight;[2] and the infrequency of colleges in the Italian universities is an indication of the fact that most of the students could afford to make their own accommodation arrangements. The older universities eventually came to terms with the problem of poverty by evolving methods to enable ability to cross the series of hurdles from matriculation to graduation. The records of the English-German nation at Paris, for example, reveal that in the later medieval period, at any rate, it was customary to grant dispensations to students who could attest to their poverty. As previously mentioned, between 1425 and 1494 17.58 per cent of bachelors promoted by the English-German nation were categorized as *pauperes*.[3] There were similar financial dispensations for poor students at late medieval Orléans.[4] In addition, the custom whereby poorer students could determine as bachelors or incept as masters under the aegis of a richer scholar who could bear the burden of the collective expenses seems to have been widely practised in Europe's universities.[5] Moreover, poor students could often hope to augment their incomes by acting as individual or communal servants[6] reminiscent of 'working one's way through college'. In general, the

---

[1] See Verger, *Les universités au moyen âge,* cit., pp. 173–4.

[2] Ibid., p. 174.

[3] Gabriel, art. cit. in op. cit., p. 186. On the dispensation of poor scholars at Paris see G. C. Boyce, *The English-German Nation in the University of Paris,* cit., pp. 164–7. It was quite common at Paris for scholars who were not 'poor' but temporarily short of funds to receive their degrees without paying degree fees which were delayed until financial matters improved: ibid., pp. 90–94.

[4] See *Les livres des procurateurs de la nation germanique de l'ancienne université d'Orléans 1444–1602,* i, pt. i, ed. C. M. Ridderikhoff (Leiden, 1971), pp. xix, 2, 7, 11.

[5] See Rashdall, op. cit., iii, pp. 144–5 and p. 144, n. 2; on sub-determination at Paris see Boyce, op. cit., pp. 96–100 and appendix ii, pp. 184–5.

[6] See e.g. Rashdall, op. cit., iii, pp. 408–9 and notes.

older universities seem to have met the problems of poverty at first by a series of palliatives and later by a combination of *ad hoc* measures and a more regular system of dispensations.

The later medieval universities, learning from the cumulative experience of the past, were more prone to adopt a systematic approach from the start. In Germany, the problem was accentuated by the large number of young arts students who could not afford to travel to *studia* elsewhere. And the German universities made deliberate efforts to deal understandingly and generously with all students who could plead genuine poverty: they were treated as a class apart worthy of special consideration at every stage in their academic career.[1] Towards this end, the arts faculties made statutory exemptions in their favour, for example, dispensations from fees for matriculation, lectures and official exercises, from the regulations governing academic dress, and from the rule enjoining residence in a hostel.[2] Payments for official university exercises were normally dispensed, but difficulties arose over the private exercises held by regent masters to supplement their incomes, and who were not always willing to teach poor scholars free of charge: in most cases, however, a compromise position was formulated.[3] As far as degree fees were concerned, universities might require of exempted scholars an undertaking that they would reimburse the faculty when their incomes would allow: a few instances of repayment have been recorded.[4] Some of the German universities, for example, Freiburg, Erfurt and Vienna, provided low-rate hostels or burses for poor scholars,[5] and in others they lived as servants in houses of the wealthier masters.[6] This latter practice became so common that at Ingolstadt in 1507 it was decreed that no scholar could be treated as 'poor' unless he was in employment as a servant.[7] The criterion of poverty, usually a defined low income ceiling, varied from university to university and at Ingolstadt the student was required to furnish testimonial letters from his

---

[1] J. M. Fletcher, art. cit. in op. cit., pp. 410, 423 ff. and Fletcher, *The Liber Taxatorum of Poor Students at the University of Freiburg im Breisgau*, Texts and Studies in the History of Mediaeval Education, no. xii (Notre Dame, Indiana, 1969), p. 5. This valuable document reveals how the statutory provisions relating to poor scholars were implemented at Freiburg.

[2] Fletcher, art. cit. in op. cit., pp. 423 ff.

[3] Ibid., pp. 427-9.

[4] For the situation at Freiburg see ibid., pp. 431, 434-5 and *The Liber Taxatorum*, cit., pp. 6-7.

[5] Ibid., pp. 425-6; Rashdall, op. cit., iii, pp. 405-6.

[6] Ibid., p. 425.

[7] Loc. cit.

home town to certify to his poverty.[1] A scholar's 'poverty' was kept under periodic review, and his financial obligations would be altered according to his changing circumstances.[2]

Thus, in one group of universities in the fifteenth century, there is definite proof of an extensive legislative system designed to ensure that ability would not be penalized through lack of finance. The extent to which these enlightened attitudes permeated the older *studia* in their earliest phase is uncertain, but it is clear that they made belated attempts to come to terms with the problem.

At the other end of the social scale to the struggling undergraduate was the rich nobleman. In general, members of the aristocracy did not infiltrate the universities on any scale until the latter half of the fifteenth century, although there were from an early date small colonies in the universities of southern Europe which were seemingly more closely identified with the fabric of aristocratic life than *studia* in the northern latitudes. The southern *studia*, however, could not be classified as aristocratic centres until the later medieval period. The reasons for the aristocratic adoption in the late fifteenth and sixteenth centuries are not entirely clear; but, as previously stated, the piecemeal incorporation of humanist studies probably rendered the universities more enticing *foci* to a class which was not overtly preoccupied with education as a training for professional life.[3] In the fifteenth century aristocratic students formed small but significant groupings in most of Europe's universities. The German universities, for example, came to be very dependent for their financial and political support on rich members of the lay nobility;[4] and they made conscious efforts to attract students of this nature on what was tantamount to a contractual basis. In return for extra financial contributions members of the nobility who studied at the universities were accorded a series of academic privileges and exemptions. The noble element did not always constitute a central part of the university community insofar as aristocrats often lived apart in private houses with their suites and private tutors. As a social grouping, the advent of the lay nobility is indicative of a more intense

[1] Ibid., pp. 424–5; Stelling-Michaud, 'L'histoire des universités au moyen âge et à la renaissance au cours des vingt-cinq dernières années', art. cit., pp. 119–20.
[2] For procedure at Freiburg see Fletcher, art. cit. in op. cit., pp. 433–4 and *The Liber Taxatorum*, p. 6. At Paris also poor scholars were expected to repay dispensed fees if future circumstances would allow: Boyce, op. cit., pp. 166–7.
[3] See e.g. Stelling-Michaud, art. cit., p. 120.
[4] On the position of lay nobility in German universities see Fletcher, 'Wealth and Poverty in German Universities' in op. cit., pp. 410–13.

stratification of academic society, of the deeper cleavage between rich and poor which is so marked a feature of university history towards the close of the middle ages.

This socio-economic division is also found among the ranks of the regent masters in the later medieval period. A study of the situation at fifteenth-century Pavia,[1] for example, shows that 30 to 50 per cent of the masters had an annual salary of less than fifty florins, which was not much above that of an unskilled workman of the region. Doubtless masters could supplement this income in a number of ways, and they were exempt from a variety of taxes imposed on other members of the urban society. Nevertheless, this salary level, which was especially applicable to regents in the arts faculty, was an insubstantial form of remuneration compared with the rewards available in the civic arena. Above these low-salaried arts masters a fair number of regents could command between fifty and two hundred florins a year, the equivalent perhaps to the kind of income realized by a middling communal official; and about 20 per cent of the regents had salaries of between 200 and 600 florins, bringing them within the range of high-ranking functionaries of the commune. Only about 5 per cent of the masters, mainly eminent jurists and medical doctors, could earn between 600 and 2000 florins, which enabled them to live in luxurious style. Clearly for the majority of lecturers at this sample university the rewards were modest and seemingly a good deal lower than the lecturer incomes which could be realized in the Italian *studia* at an earlier period. The expansion in Europe's lecturing force consequent upon the growth of the university movement in the late middle ages had reduced the earning power of many lecturers on the academic circuit. But if the remunerations were small, there were compensations in terms of social prestige which some would value as highly as the monetary aspect. At fifteenth-century Louvain the average salary was at first between 150 and 200 florins falling later to between 100 and 150 florins, which indicates that the mean scale of remuneration was only of a mediocre nature.[2] Where a proportion of incomes were derived from ecclesiastical benefices, as at Paris, it is more difficult to estimate average earnings, but one must suppose that differentiation would have been considerable, ranging from masters who held

---

[1] For this valuable study see D. Zanetti, 'A l'Université de Pavie au xve siècle: les salaires des professeurs', *Annales: Economies, Sociétés, Civilisations*, 17 (1962), pp. 421 ff.: the period examined extends from 1387 to 1499. A currency explanation is given on p. 424; see also Verger, op. cit., pp. 174–5.

[2] See J. Paquet, 'Salaires et prébendes des professeurs de l'université de Louvain au xve siècle', art. cit., pp. 1 ff.

benefices of minimal value to those who held a plurality of livings and were of an affluent condition.[1] In the German universities a deep division developed between rich salaried lecturers and non-salaried regent masters, and this had an important constitutional effect.[2] Because of the need to establish a permanent teaching force, salaried positions were created in all faculties; the money for this purpose was often donated by local aristocrats or by municipal authorities which gave these secular powers an interventionist stake in university affairs. The privileged standing of the salaried lecturers found expression in the governmental machine of many of the German *studia*. This led to a transference of power from the numerous unsalaried masters of arts to the doctors in the superior faculties which had a majority of salaried positions. Gradually, the unsalaried masters were squeezed out of areas of responsibility, and they had difficulty in making a livelihood on the basis of the traditional regency system reproduced from the Paris model. By contrast, the salaried regents evolved higher living standards, and some of them married into the bourgeois society of the university town; they co-operated closely with local ruling families and thereby helped to promote secular control over the German *studia*. By the end of the fifteenth century, the German universities were heavily stratified, not only with regard to the student population, but also in terms of the teaching contingent. The hardening social and economic differentiation destroyed a capacity for corporate action and rendered the German universities weak in the face of external domination.

As a general trend, it would therefore appear that social and economic contrasts were accentuated in the universities in the later middle ages. They became victims of an increasing commercialism, a mercenary spirit which manifested itself in the razor competition for the better salaried positions and in the material involvements of élitist groups of highly salaried lecturers in the social and business maelstrom of urban life. The earlier community cohesion, born of battles fought in common and cemented by a less pronounced economic division, was gradually eroded and the universities tended to sectionalize, which lowered their ability for effective united action.

Of the endowed personnel at the universities college fellows came to occupy an important category in the fourteenth and fifteenth centuries. The diversity of the collegiate scene in Europe has been discussed in

---

[1] See the remarks of Verger, op. cit., p. 175.
[2] For what follows on the German universities see Fletcher, art. cit. in op. cit., pp. 413–23.

chapter six and generalizations are clearly difficult to draw. But college fellows who, in the main, were engaged in advanced courses of study, were well-appointed members of the academic population, although by wider community standards they were not high in the economic hierarchy. A fellowship would satisfy basic needs at an acceptable level and provide extra communal comforts which added a savour to the austere régime of daily life.

Fellows were given a weekly allowance from college funds to cover the cost of their board or commons. Most colleges geared this allowance system to a sliding scale with stipulated minimum and maximum limits, and this was regulated by fluctuations in current grain prices.[1] This meant that the allowance system was designed to ensure a constant relationship between the cost of a fellow's commons and varying price levels. The standard maintenance rate for commons in most fourteenth-century English colleges was about 1s per fellow per week, but provision was normally made for this rate to increase proportional to the rising price of grain.[2] At Oriel College, Oxford, for example, the maximum limit was 1s 3d, to come into force when the quarter of wheat was selling at 10s or more in Oxford or in the surrounding district; and at New College, Oxford, the commons rate might increase to 1s 4d in times of scarcity, and, in the event of the bushel of wheat fetching more than 2s in Oxford or in neighbouring markets, the commons limit was to be advanced to 1s 6d.[3] The rates specified in Paris colleges are more diverse, but the sliding scale principle seems to have been, in essence, the same as in England.[4] Collegiate maintenance was organized to relieve the fellow of the necessity of drawing overmuch upon his private financial resources in order to meet the costs of his basic living requirements. In this connection, one must assume that a medieval fellow would have some independent source of income: he would need this to defray the expenses of the luxury items of food and drink ordered over and above his allowable commons. In some colleges, in times of severe scarcity when the college funds would not stretch to cover the exceptionally high commons rate entailed, the fellow would be expected to make some contribution from his private income

[1] See Cobban, The King's Hall . . ., cit., pp. 139–41.
[2] Ibid., p. 140.
[3] Loc. cit.: Statutes, i, ch. (3), 15; ch. (5), 38–9.
[4] See e.g. the arrangements at the Ave Maria College where the founder, John of Hubant, stipulated that, during times of scarcity, the master and chaplain, with the consent of the governors, were to defray the additional expenses out of the funds of the society: A. L. Gabriel, Ave Maria College, cit., p. 223.

during the period of crisis. This arrangement was given statutory expression, for example, at the fourteenth-century Ave Maria College, Paris.[1]

In the absence of much concrete data, one can only speculate on possible sources of private revenue. Fellows who were regent masters would derive an income from teaching in the university schools. A number of fellows would realize an income from benefices held concurrently with fellowships whose value was less than the prescribed statutory maximum;[2] and, as in the case of students, some fellows would be able to draw upon financial aid from relatives or patrons. Although fellows of medieval colleges might not have much in the way of private income, and an 'income ceiling' of £5 (made up in different ways) was prescribed by several English college statutes of the fourteenth and fifteenth centuries,[3] it is likely that the majority were not entirely dependent upon the bounty of the founder. In some of the wealthier colleges, however, a larger reserve of private income was probably required.

This was certainly true of the King's Hall, Cambridge. In this royal foundation the allowance system was not geared to a sliding scale: instead, the fellows were given a flat rate of 1s 2d per week by direct exchequer grant, and the fellows had to find the remainder from their own resources.[4] Between 1382–3 and 1443–4 the average charge levied on the King's Hall fellows for their weekly commons ranged from 1s 2½d to 2s 3½d giving an average of 1s 8¼d per week over the whole period,[5] which is a high maintenance rate equivalent to a luxury level in the generality of colleges. The King's Hall fellows had to find each week from their own means the difference between the flat rate commons allowance of 1s 2d and the actual amount charged for commons. Over the fifty-four year period investigated the average King's Hall fellow had to pay sums ranging from about 7¾d to 1s 1¾d per week, that is from about £1 14s to £3 per annum;[6] these figures, which include an allowance for luxury items or sizings, have been 'corrected' by means of a price index.[7] It is therefore clear that in this *collège de luxe* it was necessary for a fellow to possess a source of substantial

---

[1] Ibid., pp. 361–2.
[2] For 'income ceilings' considered compatible with the retention of fellowships in English and Parisian colleges see Cobban, *The King's Hall*, p. 146, n. 1.
[3] Loc. cit. Whereas English college founders prescribed fairly uniform allowable rates of income applicable to all fellows, French founders, on the other hand, generally stipulated a scale of statutory rates graded according to academic standing: A. L. Gabriel, *The College System in the Fourteenth-Century*, cit., p. 90.
[4] Cobban, op. cit., pp. 129 ff.
[5] Ibid., p. 139 and table 5 (pullout), column 16 (opposite p. 126).
[6] Ibid., pp. 135, 137.   [7] Ibid., pp. 134 ff.

income to enable him to defray even his basic bills and certainly if he were to participate to the full in communal collegiate life. The King's Hall probably offered a level of material comfort midway between that of the average type of college of the fourteenth and fifteenth centuries and the more luxurious standards of the rich aristocratic households of the period towards which it undoubtedly gravitated.

Dr Emden has produced evidence to show that in 1424 the average charge for commons per week in an Oxford hall was about $6\frac{1}{2}d$, that is, just under a penny a day.[1] In the same year, the average sum charged to each King's Hall fellow was $1s\ 9\frac{3}{4}d$, just under $3d$ a day.[2] This year is fairly representative since over the whole period 1382-3 to 1443-4 the average charge for commons was $1s\ 8\frac{1}{4}d$ per week. If the figures furnished for one Oxford hall in 1424 are typical, we may conclude that the average commons rate in the King's Hall was approximately three times that normally levied in halls or hostels of the period. This conclusion would doubtless have to be amended in the case of the halls of the legists where boarding rates were significantly higher than in establishments designed for the majority of the less mature students. It has been reckoned that in 1450 the total expenditure of an economically-minded undergraduate living in hall need be no more than about $50s$ a year.[3] But the evidence for hall economy is at present very slight and no firm conclusions can be drawn.

The mature commoner population of the colleges has been partially described in chapter six and that material need not be repeated here. Maintenance costs of commoners and semi-commoners living in colleges seem to have been considerable. For in addition to the full rate of unsubsidized commons, or semi-commons as the case may be, and expenditure on luxuries, the commoner had to pay a room rent or *pensio*. At the King's Hall, the customary rental for a single room was $6s\ 8d$ per annum and $13s\ 4d$ for a set consisting of two chambers, one of which probably served the function of a study.[4] A third rating of $10s$ a year for a single room is occasionally found.[5] These rentals, assessed on the basis of the number, size and quality of the rooms, were not excessive judging from the rates charged in other colleges. When John Wyclif and Nicholas Hereford lived as *commensales* at Queen's College, Oxford, in the latter half of the four-

---

[1] A. B. Emden, *An Oxford Hall in Medieval Times*, cit., p. 194.
[2] Cobban, op. cit., table 5 (pullout), column 16 (opposite p. 126).
[3] See Jacob, art. cit., p. 312.
[4] Cobban, op. cit., pp. 268-9.
[5] Ibid., p. 269.

teenth century, they were charged 20*s* for their rooms;[1] at Oriel, until
Thomas Gascoigne was granted a rent free room for life in 1449, he had
apparently been paying an annual rent of 20*s* for more than twenty years;[2]
the bursars' roll of University College of 1392 records that room rentals
in that year varied from 6*s* 8*d* to 20*s*;[3] and in a general survey of Oxford
commensales H. E. Salter cites typical room rents fixed at 10*s*, 13*s* 4*d*, 16*s*
and 20*s*.[4] In addition to the substantial expense of rentals, many commoners employed servants who had to be maintained at the rate of at
least half commons.[5] The detailed figures for the King's Hall show that
the maintenance costs of commoners were approximately three or four
times as great as those of the average fellow.[6] While the King's Hall expenditure levels are not typical, the 3 or 4:1 ratio of commoner:fellow
expenditure may be reflective of a more general pattern. Instances are
found of the promotion of commoners and semi-commoners to the ranks
of the fellows,[7] but how widespread this practice was has not been determined. On present findings, however, it seems that while a degree of
academic mobility existed for members of the commoner class, they were
occasional happenings, making sporadic breaches in the rather solid wall
dividing foundation members from the motley assembly of tolerated
lodgers.

The average age at which students entered medieval universities has probably been assessed at too low a level. It is true that numerous young boys
of eight to fifteen are found in university towns; but not all of them were
necessarily engaged upon the arts course. A proportion of these boys came
up to the university town to master the rudiments of grammar in order
to equip themselves for the arts course proper;[8] they were instructed either

---

[1] Wyclif paid 40*s* for two rooms in 1365–6; in 1374–5 and 1380–1 he paid 20*s*. Nicholas
of Hereford paid 20*s* for a room in 1380–1: see J. R. Magrath, *The Queen's College*, 2
vols. (Oxford, 1921), i, p. 122 and notes; also R. H. Hodgkin, 'The Queen's College',
V.C.H. (Oxford), iii, p. 133.

[2] See the *Dean's Register of Oriel 1446–1661*, cit., p. 370.

[3] W. Carr, *University College*, cit., p. 49.

[4] Salter, *Medieval Oxford*, cit., p. 100.

[5] On commoners' servants at the King's Hall see Cobban, op. cit., pp. 270, 271, 273,
279 and n. 4.

[6] Ibid., p. 271.

[7] Ibid., pp. 263–4; and Cobban, 'Origins: Robert Wodelarke and St Catharine's' in
op. cit., p. 20.

[8] See Jacob, art. cit., p. 308; also A. L. Gabriel, 'Preparatory Teaching in the Parisian
Colleges during the Fourteenth Century' in *Garlandia*, cit., pp. 97 ff.: grammar students

in grammar schools established in the town or, as at Paris in the fourteenth
and fifteenth centuries, in some of the colleges,[1] but not in the universities
per se, although the latter came to exercise a measure of supervision over
this grammatical instruction.[2] Those amongst them who evinced little
aptitude for study would be weeded out and would not embark upon a
university discipline. If soundly based in arts, however, youths of thirteen
or fourteen might be enrolled in the arts faculties. The statutes of 1215
granted to Paris by Robert de Courçon state that no one was to begin
lecturing in arts before his twenty-first year and before studying in arts
for at least six years.[3] This would give a possible starting age of thirteen
or fourteen. The statutes of the English-German nation at Paris of 1252
require those determining in arts (i.e. equivalent of taking the B.A. degree)
should be at least nineteen years of age and have studied arts for four or
five years,[4] which presupposes a minimum commencing age of fourteen.
But these are only static glimpses and the duration of courses varied considerably from university to university and also within the same university
at different times. At Paris, for example, the minimum age for determination as a bachelor was, in the fourteenth century, reduced to the completion
of the fourteenth year.[5] There was a general tendency in the later medieval
period for a reduction in the years needed for the arts course[6] and, in these
variable circumstances, it is not easy to arrive at binding conclusions about
the ages of students in arts faculties. Slight information can sometimes be
derived from college statutes which may prescribe a minimum entry age.
In the English situation, the statutes of 1380 of the King's Hall, which
admitted undergraduate fellows from the early fourteenth century, fixed
the minimum age of admission at fourteen;[7] and at New College, the
youngest undergraduates were not admitted until they had completed their
fifteenth year.[8] But these are minima and the average would have been
somewhat higher. It is probable that the entry age of medieval undergraduates varied a good deal more than those of the twentieth century,
but fifteen to seventeen was perhaps the commencing age in arts for a

---

were received at the Ave Maria College, Paris, in their eighth or ninth year (ibid., p.
98).
[1] Gabriel, art. cit., esp. pp. 97–101.
[2] Ibid., pp. 99–100; see also the Oxford regulations for grammar teaching (early
fourteenth century) in *Statuta Antiqua*, cit., pp. 20–3, 169–74.
[3] *Chartularium Universitatis Parisiensis*, cit., i, no. 20.
[4] Ibid., i, no. 202.   [5] Gabriel, art. cit., p. 100.
[6] See Rashdall, *Universities*, i, pp. 462–4 and notes.
[7] Cobban, *The King's Hall*, p. 59.   [8] *Statutes*, i, ch. (5), 7.

majority of students in northern *studia*: as formerly mentioned,[1] the law students of southern Europe were more mature, many of them being in their twenties, and some of them in their thirties, upon entry to university.

There were no formal entrance qualifications to medieval universities, although some colleges would carry out their own oral examination.[2] All the student required was a proficiency in Latin sufficient to cope with the exigencies of university instruction where lectures and academic exercises were conducted in Latin. He would also be expected to converse in Latin within the university precinct; and in the later medieval period, Latin speaking was often enforced by statute in halls and colleges. Assuming that the average student was capable of following and benefiting from his course and had the requisite amount of financial support for survival, his chances of realizing a degree were fair. A lot of the student wastage, and the rate was incomparably higher than would be tolerated in a modern university, probably occurred in the early stages when undergraduate numbers were inflated by students and idlers unfitted for the stringencies of the academic life. As there was no artificial cushioning in medieval universities to gloss over lack of aptitude or ability the dead wood was naturally excised to the benefit of the whole academic community. Medieval universities felt no collective guilt responsibility to shepherd the weaker brethern along the road to a dubious degree. The régime was hard, the standards exacting, and the students were expected to display a dedication equal to the precious endeavour on which they were engaged. Although the student was not obliged to sit written examinations for the attainment of a degree, he was nevertheless severely taxed at every point in his undergraduate career. One could say that the degree was awarded on the basis of a total and continuous assessment of the student's performance. In accordance with the mileage principle, the undergraduate had to attend the prescribed number of lectures in each course, and had to show a detailed knowledge and understanding of the stipulated texts. Moreover, the student had to prove himself an academic practitioner by the mastery of a series of complex exercises specified for different stages in the course. Finally, he was subject to lengthy probing oral examinations. The tangled web of statutory requirements governing degrees in the universities was so diversified that it is not easy to relate medieval to twentieth-century degree criteria.

---

[1] See above p. 61. On the various aspects of Bolognese academic life see Zaccagnini, *La vita dei maestri e degli scolari nello Studio di Bologna nei secoli xiii e xiv*, cit., passim and appendix of important documents, pp. 141 ff.

[2] See Gabriel, art. cit., p. 100; Rashdall, op. cit., i, p. 342; Cobban, op. cit., p. 59.

In addition, one must reckon with the extensive practice of dispensations or graces which was a convenient instrument whereby the statutes could be rendered flexible and students might proceed to a degree without fulfilling the statutory letter in every respect.[1] And the fact that students might interrupt their studies because of pressures in private life and linger over a degree course beyond the minimum prescribed duration makes comparison with most modern procedures even more troublesome. Nevertheless, the impression gained is that a degree system designed to produce graduates versed in logical analysis and capable of fine intellectual distinctions and rigorous precision of mind and examined by prolonged practical and oral assessment was one of innate difficulty by any educational criteria.

The lectures which the undergraduate had to attend were divided into ordinary and extraordinary or cursory lectures.[2] The twofold distinction between the ordinary and extraordinary lectures in arts was based on the method of teaching and on the standing of the lecturer. Ordinary lectures, which were the official lectures prescribed by university statute, were delivered by the regent masters on every *dies legibilis* at the most favoured hours of the day, usually in the morning. No competing lectures, for example by bachelors, were permitted during the hours reserved for these magisterial ordinary lectures thereby ensuring that the *bona fide* student population would not be detracted from attendance upon the university's staple diet of official instruction. In the domain of the ordinary lecture the master was supreme: as a member of the teaching guild he was a wholly independent functionary who lectured *ex officio* without supervisionary restraint. His task was not merely to provide a detailed exposition of a text but to give magisterial rulings on related problems arising from the text. In arts faculties, at any rate, students attending ordinary lectures were expected to repeat the substance of the master's lecture each day and to give a weekly repetition of the central points discussed during the week. Masters were generally limited to one course of ordinary lectures at a time: and if, by any chance, the regent master was unable to complete the course and another master could not be found as substitute, then exceptionally, a bachelor might be assigned the task. By contrast, the extra-

[1] See e.g. W. A. Pantin's discussion in *The Register of Congregation 1448–1463*, cit., pp. xxi–xxii.

[2] On ordinary and extraordinary lectures in arts see e.g. J. A. Weisheipl, 'Curriculum of the Faculty of Arts at Oxford in the early fourteenth century', *Mediaeval Studies*, xxvi (1964), pp. 143 ff. at pp. 150 ff.; for law faculties see recently H. Coing, *Handbuch der Quellen und Literatur der neueren europäischen Privatrechtsgeschichte*, i (Munich, 1973), pp. 71–2.

ordinary or cursory lectures were normally delivered by bachelors acting under the supervision of a master, though occasionally a master himself might opt to lecture cursorily on a text. The extraordinary lecture was conducted at a lower level of expertise than that required for the ordinary lecture in arts: it usually consisted of a straightforward reading, paraphrase and summary of an official text. Cursory lectures were of value to the student as they helped to familiarize him with the text without involving him in the complexities arising in the course of the ordinary lectures. In law faculties there was considerable variation in the distribution of texts as between ordinary and extraordinary lectures. In civil law, according to the Bologna statutes of 1317, the *Codex* and *Digestum Vetus* were to be read *ordinarie* and the *Infortiatum* and the *Digestum Novum* were to be read *extraordinarie*. In canon law, the *Decretum* and the Decretals of Gregory IX were to be treated in ordinary lectures and the Clementines and *Liber Sextus* were to be dealt with in extraordinary lectures. A similar type of division is found at Orléans and at other *studia* although the variations on the basic Bologna division were legion. In the Montpellier statutes of 1339 it is enacted that fees were to be exacted only for ordinary lectures, and this monetary consideration was doubtless a factor in the assignment of texts for ordinary or cursory treatment.

Apart from hearing lectures the student was also required to attend the public disputations which each master was supposed to stage once a week on an afternoon of a *dies disputabilis*.[1] Although *quaestiones*, arising from the text, were discussed by the masters at the morning ordinary lectures, these were not *quaestiones disputatae* or *quaestiones determinatae* in the full sense of the term, but merely speculative extensions of the master's *lectio:* the formal, solemn magisterial disputations, the *disputationes ordinariae* or *solemnes*, were those separately and publicly mounted. Among the artists these disputations were often of two major types: *de sophismatibus* or *de problemate*, which comprised logical matters, and those *de quaestione*, which related to mathematics, natural science, metaphysics and other areas of *quadrivium* study. Advanced arts students had to participate in the magisterial disputations as a preparation for obtaining the grade of bachelor.

In arts faculties, the bachelor was in the nature of a magisterial apprentice who was in the process of learning his teaching craft. He could not teach independently but only under the direction of a master. As he was not yet a member of the masters' guild he did not have the capacity to determine questions (that is, to provide final solutions to problems

1 For these magisterial disputations see e.g. Weisheipl, art. cit., pp. 153–6.

debated) in public disputations by himself: the right of determination belonged to the office of master, and a bachelor could only share in this determining function. But in northern *studia* especially, the contribution of the bachelors in the realms of cursory lectures, disputations and in the various academic exercises which formed part of the teaching régime, was of considerable importance in a situation where the pool of regent masters was so uncertainly maintained from year to year. Although each new master in arts was obliged to teach for about two years (the necessary regency system) those who had the requisite ability and financial resources would normally undertake study in one of the superior faculties after completion of their imposed teaching period. While there was no objection to a master continuing to lecture in arts when studying in a higher faculty, the commitments of time made this conjunction difficult. The study of theology, law or medicine, involving the full round of ordinary and extra-ordinary lectures, disputations and other academic exercises, would not afford much leisure for the master in arts to continue ordinary lectures in the arts faculty on any regular basis: and it seems that relatively few masters in arts were able to combine these lecturing and study functions in different faculties. At Oxford, in the fourteenth century, the common practice was for masters in arts to enrol in a superior faculty after the necessary regency period and to sever teaching connections with the arts faculty.[1] In these circumstances, the supplementary teaching rôle of the bachelors in arts was indispensable.

The medieval undergraduate's life proceeded without the therapeutic aid of many licensed recreations.[2] For the universities, perhaps mirroring the negative ecclesiastical denial of the body, attempted to suppress organized levity; the poverty of mind here displayed was a reaction to the enormous disciplinary problems universities had to meet, but it was an over-reaction in areas which were not central to the matter of serious disorder. Most forms of gambling, games of chance, including even chess,[3] dancing, and many outside sporting activities were deemed likely to prove a grave distraction from study and a possible source of disturbance and were therefore prohibited.[4] Some musical diversions were given a restricted tolerance, as long as neighbouring students were not inconvenienced. The keeping of pets such as dogs, ferrets, hawks and other birds was dis-

[1] Ibid., p. 166.
[2] On this subject see Rashdall, op. cit., iii, pp. 419 ff.
[3] See *Statutes*, i, ch. (5), 48.
[4] This is a very general statement and the situation differed a good deal from university to university and from college to college.

allowed in most colleges and halls. Sober relief might be afforded to students on ecclesiastical festivals or on the feast days of patrons of nations or faculties; but even here their movements tended to be kept on a tight rein. For students who lived in colleges minstrel entertainments were occasionally permitted,[1] and in the later fifteenth and sixteenth centuries Latin plays were sometimes performed.[2] But if communal recreation was generally discouraged, there were some who recognized the value, indeed the necessity, of private exercise as a counter to the sedentary life. A letter of 1315 from a physician of Valencia to his two sons studying at Toulouse, which prescribes a detailed physical, hygienic and dietary régime, demonstrates the care which students might be expected to pay to their physical as well as intellectual education.[3]

The repressive nature of the university and college statutes towards non-academic activities produced, in a section of the student body, a violent libertarian response and the worst excesses of drunkenness, gambling, immorality, disorder and crime were found in all medieval universities.[4] Students were frequently embroiled in feuds with the citizenry, sometimes resulting in serious injury or death. The spread of colleges and university-controlled hostels did something to curb the level of student indiscipline, but right throughout the medieval period the student population continued to reflect the violence and volatile unrestraint of contemporary urban societies. By striving to suppress student *joie de vivre* and *camaraderie* instead of channelling into a constructive and relaxing form, medieval university and college authorities made a collective error of judgment which had an injuriously divisive effect on the student populations they directed.

As formerly mentioned,[5] the syllabus followed by the medieval student centred, in each discipline, upon a related group of agreed texts. Teaching was conducted by means of the two basic instruments of the *lectio* or *lectura*, the reading and commenting on the prescribed text, and the *disputatio*, the formal debate of several types (and the less formal debating exercises) governed by strict procedural rules and devoted to a problem normally arising from a point in an authoritative source.[6] Disputations

[1] See e.g. Cobban, *The King's Hall*, pp. 222 ff. and notes.
[2] Ibid., pp. 227–9.
[3] The letter is printed by L. Thorndike, *University Records and Life in the Middle Ages*, cit., pp. 154–160.
[4] For selected cases see Rashdall, op. cit., iii, pp. 427 ff.
[5] See above pp. 166–7.
[6] For a detailed discussion of the curriculum and teaching methods at Paris and Oxford

were of value both for the teacher and the students: they permitted the former to explore more deeply difficult questions which could not conveniently be discussed within the ambit of the *lectio*, and to the latter they gave the opportunity to test developing dialectical skill. For the most part, the student was expected to master a corpus of approved doctrine and was assigned a passive rôle in the educational process which placed an emphasis on memory work and rote learning. But within the context of the disputation and the less formal exercises held in halls or colleges there was greater scope for the expression of independent lines of inquiry. Although the central problem to be discussed, the *quaestio*, would usually be geared to an authoritative reference, the cut and thrust, the *pro* and *contra* of logical debate, might well lead the participants into avenues of thought which departed from the given orthodoxy. And the final summing up of a formal debate, the *determinatio*, would, on occasion, embody something akin to creative inquiry. Even if many of the students were too young to take an active part in the formal disputations, as spectators they were witnesses to an intellectual voyage of discovery which might transcend the rigid canons of their authority-dominated educational framework. These liberating opportunities were maximized during the staging of disputations *de quolibet*. These were occasions when any proposition, regardless of respect for authority, could be debated, embracing matters of current ecclesiastical and political concern. Such disputations were celebrated happenings, and they were open to all comers: they were not bound by a fixed agenda and anyone might raise any issue for debate. Disputations *de quolibet* provided a much-needed release for some of the intellectual frustrations generated by an educational system so orientated towards reverence for authority. An impressive diversity of subjects were debated, which, at Paris, covered important doctrinal and political matters such as the suppression of the Templars.[1] Although disputations *de quolibet* were particularly prominent in theological faculties, they are also found in law, medicine and arts. Disputations *de quolibet* in arts, for example, are well authenticated at Oxford in the fourteenth century.[2]

In medieval, as in modern universities, studies were divided into what were considered to be rational segments which could be digested in a

---

see Leff, *Paris and Oxford Universities in the Thirteenth and Fourteenth Centuries*, cit., pp. 116 ff.; and for the different categories of disputation see ibid., pp. 167–74. See also Verger, *Les universités au moyen âge*, pp. 60–3. Rashdall, *Universities*, i–iii, has copious information on curricular and teaching matters.

[1] Leff, op. cit., p. 172.   [2] Weisheipl, art. cit., pp. 182–5.

prescribed minimum number of years; and the intellectual energies of both teachers and students were mainly concerned with the imparting and reception of given data and not with research as now understood. Medieval students were just as concerned with a predictive rotational academic regimen of obligatory lectures and exercises as are twentieth-century students in the more traditional type of university. The popular conception that medieval students were free to seek enlightenment as the spirit moved is not borne out by the weighty volume of statutory controls which regulated minutely each stage in the academic obstacle race. It is true that the medieval student was at liberty to interrupt or prolong his studies, but economic pressures were such that it was incumbent upon him to comply with the academic regulations and endeavour to complete the course as rapidly as possible: if a degree is viewed as a passport to security the average student will not be concerned with dissipating his energies in the elusive quest for an ever-widening comprehension.

In the thirteenth century, the majority of students could not afford to buy copies of the texts studied, at least without great sacrifice, because of the high manuscript price levels: consequently, the student was very dependent on the reading and expounding of the texts in the university schools. The situation was ameliorated from the later thirteenth century by the growth of cheaper, utilitarian methods of manuscript production encouraged and then rigorously controlled by the universities.[1] The system was based on the multiple copying of *exemplars*, which were accurate copies of the texts and commentaries used in teaching. Each *exemplar* was divided into separate pieces or *peciae*, usually of four folios each (eight pages), and relating to different portions of the text. Several copyists could therefore engage on the same *exemplar*, each reproducing a different *pecia*. The system enabled students to hire or buy relatively cheap copies of the particular section of the text under review. The freer circulation of texts relieved the student of some of his claustrophobic dependence on the lecturer's every word, lessened the strain on his memory, and permitted study in a more relaxed and private environment. But the *pecia* system was only a palliative, albeit a good one, and there were still many students who could not afford to take full advantage of it: the problem

[1] See Verger, op. cit., pp. 63–4. For the *pecia* system see J. Destrez, *La Pecia dans les manuscrits universitaires du xiiie et du xive siècle* (Paris, 1935). For the Oxford book trade see G. Pollard, 'The University and the Book Trade in Medieval Oxford', *Beiträge zum Berufsbewusstsein des mittelalterlichen Menschen* (Miscellanea Mediaevalia, 3, 1964), pp. 336 ff.

was solved only with the advent of printing and the faster growth of university and college libraries.

If the average student desired to study beyond a first degree and had few resources, he had either to acquire a college fellowship or secure a supporting benefice and a subsequent episcopal dispensation for further study at a *studium generale*. As the colleges could only absorb a small proportion of graduates, and many universities were without numerous colleges, there was extremely fierce competition among university personnel for benefices. Indeed, provision became the driving objective of armies of European students, some of whom would begin to negotiate ecclesiastical livings during their undergraduate careers. A young university bachelor submitting an individual petition to the papal curia for a benefice would stand little chance of favourable response. His chances would be greatly enhanced, however, if he could place his request on a collective petition sanctioned by the university authorities.

As far as is known, the earliest university rolls of petitions were sent from Paris and Oxford in the first quarter of the fourteenth century.[1] Between 1340 and 1440 Paris prepared rolls on thirty-five occasions (although not all were sent), and a fair number were compiled for Oxford and Cambridge between 1340 and 1400. Rolls were also sent from the French provincial universities, from the Spanish *studia* of Salamanca, Lérida and Perpignan, and from the German universities during and after the Great Schism. Rolls were not, however, sent as a matter of routine: they were sent irregularly,[2] often on a special occasion such as the accession of a new pope. Moreover, the form of the rolls varied considerably. At Paris, the officially sponsored rolls were magisterial in character, sometimes supplemented by semi-official particular rolls representing other sectional interests, for example, bachelors of theology, decrees and arts. Oxford and Cambridge combined masters, bachelors and advanced students in one roll, usually set out in order of seniority from the doctors of theology downwards. In the German universities the rolls were more democratically organized, and in those of the French provincial *studia* bachelors

---

[1] See D. E. R. Watt, 'University Clerks and Rolls of Petitions for Benefices', *Speculum*, xxxiv (1959), pp. 213 ff. at p. 214: this paragraph owes much to this article. On university rolls see also E. F. Jacob, 'Petitions for Benefices from English Universities during the Great Schism', *T.R.H.S.*, 4th ser., xxvii (1945), pp. 41 ff. and 'On the Promotion of English University Clerks during the later Middle Ages', *J. Eccles. Hist.*, i (1950), pp. 172 ff.

[2] Rashdall, *Universities*, i, p. 555 was mistaken in thinking of the Paris rolls as annual affairs.

and undergraduates are much in evidence. After the Council of Constance, however, there was a decline in the number of rolls sent to the papal curia, which was a manifestation of the wider reaction against papal provisioning seen as increasingly incompatible with the high claims of the sovereign secular state; and the pontificate of Eugenius IV saw the virtual end of university collective petitioning.

The university rolls had to contend with competing rolls of powerful lay and ecclesiastical personages and, in England, the universities had to take account of the Statute of Provisors which made the sending of rolls a difficult matter.[1] It is probable that a goodly proportion of university scholars received some concrete return from these collective petitions, even if the benefice or position of first preference was not secured. Certainly, the disquiet felt by the universities in the early fifteenth century about the running down of the system of university petitioning would suggest that the returns had been worth the candle.

[1] See Jacob, 'English University Clerks in the later Middle Ages: the Problem of Maintenance', art. cit., pp. 319–20.

IX

The universities and society

The relationship between the medieval universities and contemporary society has not been adequately explored on any scale. The magnitude of the task is self-evident. Where the materials for such an undertaking are so diversified and so widely dispersed, synthesis can only be partial and tentative. And as the universities were the products of a broad spectrum of regional differentiation, any attempt to place them within a socio-political context involves the study of a multiplicity of societies. The markedly legal and utilitarian environmental ethos of Italy, southern France and the Iberian peninsula contrasted sharply with the more speculative intellectual atmosphere current in advanced educated circles in northern France and in England; and, in turn, these latter relatively sophisticated societies were rather different from the potentially anarchical and semi-barbarous conditions prevalent in pre-Reformation Scotland. Even the most cautious of answers to the problems posed by the interaction of society upon the universities can be evolved only on the basis of detailed regional investigations. Moreover, one cannot estimate statistically the extent to which the medieval universities were service agencies for different areas of secular and ecclesiastical employment until the careers of a sufficiently large and representative number of university graduates have been analysed and grouped into meaningful categories. Only then shall we be in a position to judge how far the universities were the 'technological institutes' of an earlier age, although there seems little doubt that the universities were primarily vocational schools for the professions, affording only a minimal expression for the concept of study *per se*.

One of the most common criticisms levelled against the medieval universities is that the kind of academic training they offered was divorced from the practical needs of society. A popular view in the past has been that the universities turned out hordes of dialecticians who were without immediate professional or social value: in other words, graduates who would require a reorientation in outlook and a basic retraining to fit them for the world of secular or ecclesiastical employment. But it is not really plausible that western medieval society would have continued to give of its limited surplus wealth for so long to support social parasites living a fantasy existence in ivory towers. Medieval university education, at all but the most rarefied levels, was considered to be socially useful, providing a range of intellectual skills germane to community functioning.[1] The fundamental disputational training of the medieval scholar is sometimes viewed as an arid form of mental gymnastics which served as a barrier to academic progress and was at best a social irrelevance. It may well be that in the later medieval period the Aristotelian-based logical disputation had a place of excessive veneration in the schools and tended to discourage forms of inquiry along new and invigorating lines.[2] But if latterly the disputation helped to create a kind of constipation in Europe's intellectual development relieved only by the salutary impact of humanism, for the greater part of the medieval period a sound training in logic and the art of the disputation was a valuable preparation for most areas of professional activity. In a legally-orientated society of competing rights and privileges, conferred by a hierarchy of authorities and jealously guarded, there was endless scope for the utilization of the dialectical and disputational expertise of the graduate in law. In this morass of conflicting legal positions, material success could be gained and preserved only with the aid of that rigorous exactitude of mind fashioned by the academic machine. For this reason, university graduates were much sought after for positions in lay and ecclesiastical households where their dialectical apprenticeship could be applied to the complexities of administration and the snares of litigation. The same type of dialectical subtlety was required in the diplomatic service, and university graduates, especially those in civil law and theology, were preferred for the delicate business of negotiation and the drafting of treaty

[1] A general but deeply reflective article on this theme is that by F. M. Powicke, 'The Medieval University in Church and Society' in *Ways of Medieval Life and Thought*, cit., pp. 198 ff.
[2] See e.g. the remarks of Rashdall, *Universities*, iii, pp. 453–4.

arrangements. There were also good opportunities for the harnessing of dialectic and rhetoric to the service of propaganda, and the European universities supplied their share of literary distortionists for the manufacture of polemical material for the lay and ecclesiastical powers.[1] The products of Europe's law universities, and especially those of Italy and provincial France, were readily absorbed into royal, imperial or papal service as counsellors, as judges, and as promoters of an ideological standpoint.[2] By means of this graduate recruitment, the principles of Roman and canon law permeated the governmental structures of Europe. In this sense, the law universities were agencies of cardinal importance in shaping the very texture of, and juristic principles underlying, European political organization in its manifold forms. Universities which specialized in theology and philosophy made an equally, though less tangible, contribution to community life.[3] Their concern with the analysis of abstract concepts, their preoccupation with the eternal and the universal, provided the moving backcloth of ideas so necessary for a continuing review of human and ethical values and for the investigation of principles of political science, of the nature of justice, and of other moral and juristic constants fundamental to social development. Whereas the law universities were concerned with the ordering of contemporary society in accordance with conservative legal canons, an essentially static outlook rooted in the immediate present, the theological and philosophical *studia* were more absorbed in the direction in which society was or ought to be progressing. This combination of the empirical and the abstract, of the concretely rational and the metaphysical, was the complementary face of medieval university life, and as such it bore a direct relevance for the ordering and creative forces in society.

That the universities were susceptible to changing social and professional needs to the extent that they were prepared to sanction curricular adaptations to meet new responses thrown up by society may be illustrated from the particular examples of the Italian *studia* and the English situation as represented by Oxford.

In the centuries following the break-up of the Roman Empire in the west there was no significant demand for rhetoric.[4] It is true that rhetoric

[1] See e.g. N. Rubenstein, 'Political Rhetoric in the Imperial Chancery', *Medium Aevum*, xiv (1945), pp. 21 ff.
[2] W. Ullmann, *Principles of Government and Politics in the Middle Ages*, ed. cit., pp. 199–200, 280, 290.
[3] See ibid., pp. 290 ff.
[4] On medieval rhetoric see C. S. Baldwin, *Medieval Rhetoric and Poetic* (New York, 1928) and J. J. Murphy, 'Rhetoric in Fourteenth-Century Oxford', *Medium Aevum*,

enjoyed a temporary revival during the Carolingian period, but this was soon eclipsed by the revolutionary impact of logic. In Italy, however, rhetoric had always been kept alive owing to the primacy there of legal studies and, in the thirteenth and early fourteenth centuries, the Italian universities were the centre of a remarkable revival in the study and teaching of rhetoric which found a low-level and highly utilitarian expression in England.

In the thirteenth century rhetoric was a collective term for different branches of related study. Oratory, which had constituted the classical art of rhetoric, re-emerged in thirteenth-century Italy as an important feature of civic, papal and imperial affairs. Italian social and political organization in the twelfth and thirteenth centuries was especially conducive to a renaissance of the spoken word. The quasi-independent position of the Italian communes, their defiant republicanism and involvement in imperial and papal politics, led to a substantial extension of the need for platform oratory. Special handbooks containing model speeches for communal functionaries and even for university lecturers testify to the rhetorical explosion which pervaded Italian society in the early phase of university life. Italian universities may well have catered for this need for spoken rhetoric, but it was in the area of written rhetoric or *dictamen* that the universities assumed special responsibilities.

Dictamen (*ars dictaminis, ars dictandi*), the science of letter-writing and, by extension, of other forms of literary composition governed by rigorous procedural rules, dates as an art from at least the writings of Alberic of Monte Cassino in the second half of the eleventh century.[1] But it was not until the *ars dictandi* became an indispensable training for clerks in papal, imperial, royal and episcopal service that it was raised to a position of primacy in the arts faculties of the Italian universities.[2]

The rôle of the papal chancery in the development of the *ars dictandi* must be stressed. The supranational character of papal affairs demanded the services of a far-flung network of highly-trained notaries and the formulation of the most exacting business methods. It was essential that extreme care should be taken in the drafting of official documentation, as error or exploitable loophole might have the most serious repercussions

---

xxxiv (1965), pp. 1 ff. where a good summary of the development of rhetoric to the fourteenth century is supplied.

[1] See C. H. Haskins, *Studies in Mediaeval Culture*, cit., pp. 171–3.

[2] For the teaching of the *ars dictandi* and the *ars notaria* in Italy and France see L. J. Paetow, *The Arts Course at Medieval Universities*, cit., pp. 67 ff.

in a society whose rights derived from the written word. The instrument at hand was *dictamen* and its specialized offshoot relating to the craft of the notary, the *ars notaria* (*ars notarie*). The demand created by the papal curia for graduates trained in *dictamen* and/or the *ars notaria* was paralleled by that of the imperial chancery and by royal administrations all over Europe wherever the civil law prevailed. There is no evidence to prove that the *ars dictandi* as such achieved separate faculty status in the Italian *studia*: despite the promotion of the discipline by *dictatores* of the calibre of Buoncompagno and Guido Faba, *dictamen* was never wholly divorced from its association with the arts course. But it is strong witness to the close relationship between the Italian universities and the professional needs of society that the *ars notaria* seems to have acquired a quasi-separate faculty standing, first at Bologna by 1250, and at other *studia* later in the century.[1]

Notarial courses in the Italian universities were conducted within the ethos of the arts faculties and not under the direct aegis of law.[2] Nevertheless, notarial instruction had a much stronger practical legal emphasis in Italy than in northern Europe. And in several of the Italian *studia* one could acquire a combined theoretical and practical training in the *ars notaria* of near professional thoroughness;[3] this would be completed by a period of apprenticeship with an established notary, a stage of at least two years duration.[4] Many of the teachers of the *ars notaria* in the universities were themselves notaries in the town and members of the notarial guild.[5] Degrees, as such, were not awarded: the licence to practice as a notary was the end-product of the university course. Poised between the purely academic sector of university life and the professional community, the *ars notaria* occupied a transitional position in the university-community nexus.

The *ars notaria* was not taught in England in any formal sense: neither the *ars dictandi* nor the *ars notaria* developed separate faculty organization. Nevertheless, something akin to these disciplines was taught in an adulterated and semi-official form at Oxford. English society did not create a demand for notaries in any way comparable to the Continent. Civil law, regarded as antithetical to the common law, was not much in evidence in thirteenth-century England and did not experience a revival until the early

[1] Loc. cit.
[2] See I. Hajnal, *L'Enseignement de l'écriture aux universités médiévales,* 2nd ed., L. Mezey (Budapest, 1959), p. 154.
[3] Loc. cit.
[4] Ibid., pp. 154–5.
[5] Ibid., p. 155; see also Hajnal, 'A propos de l'enseignement de l'écriture dans les universités médiévales', *Scriptorium,* xi (1957), pp. 3 ff. at pp. 15–16.

fourteenth century. The opportunities for notaries were therefore limited, but they are found in the thirteenth century and in some numbers in the fourteenth century:[1] they were employed in ecclesiastical courts, in private mercantile business and, to some extent, in departments of secular government. The available evidence suggests that from a fairly early date Oxford provided a training in subjects closely associated with the work of the professional notary.

The earliest reference to *dictamen* at Oxford occurs in the university statute, *a*. 1313, concerning grammar, which shows that a knowledge of *dictamen* was a necessary qualification for a teacher of grammar.[2] In a statute of 1432 a revealing insight is given into the teaching of the 'useful subjects' at Oxford.[3] The purpose of the statute was disciplinary and was designed to enforce a more rigorous control over students learning the art of writing, the *ars dictandi*, French, the composition of deeds and procedural routine in the English courts.[4] It is highly improbable that these students were engaged upon the regular arts course since they are described as *scolares competenter in gramatica solummodo*. This implies that Oxford made provision for a type of student who went to university to receive a quick cram course of study in order to fit him for a business career. The subjects listed in this statute of 1432 indicate that he would be given a course of practical study related to that embraced by *dictamen* and the *ars notaria* but at a more simplified and less integrated level. One cannot suppose that such instruction was concerned with the requirements of the notary public as such, but it would have given the student some grounding in legal principles and familiarized him with some of the procedures of notarial practice.[5] From what fragmentary data there are, it seems that subjects of this nature were taught in some rudimentary form at Oxford from the early part of the thirteenth century: for from the reign of John there survives a legal formulary pertaining to the drafting of letters and other documents. And it seems probable that practical subjects of this kind were

[1] See the recent study by C. R. Cheney, *Notaries Public in England in the Thirteenth and Fourteenth Centuries* (Oxford, 1972), passim.
[2] See *Statuta Antiqua*, p. 20.
[3] Ibid., p. 240.
[4] Loc. cit. See H. G. Richardson, 'Business Training in Medieval Oxford', *A.H.R.*, xlvi (1940–1), pp. 259 ff. at p. 259; see also Richardson, 'An Oxford Teacher of the Fifteenth Century', *B.J.R.L.*, xxiii (1939), pp. 436 ff.
[5] See Cheney, op. cit., p. 78. On similarities between Italian notarial manuals and the subject matter taught at Oxford see Murphy, art. cit., pp. 15–17. On vocational training of this nature see generally Hajnal, op. cit., ed. cit., ch. v, pp. 154 ff.

sustained at Oxford until they progressively faded in the course of the fifteenth century for reasons which are not altogether clear.

From the beginning of the reign of Henry III there were at Oxford a number of teachers who specialized in the 'useful subjects' which had a direct application to the practical problems of business administration.[1] The teachers of these courses, which included instruction in the drafting of charters, wills and letters, conveyancing, the keeping of accounts, court practice and heraldry, did not necessarily have a degree:[2] nevertheless, they set up their schools in the town of Oxford and were subject to the control of the university authorities who thereby gave explicit recognition to the system of university extension. Among the foremost of these teachers of the practical subjects was Thomas Sampson who taught in Oxford from c. 1350–1409. Judging from the survival of some of his formularies of model letters and deeds, Sampson seems to have been primarily a practitioner of *dictamen*, although accountancy and conveyancing were among his specialisms. A certain Simon O. and William Kingsmill achieved a degree of prominence as teachers in the Sampson mould in Oxford in the early fifteenth century. Probably many of the youthful students who attended these practical courses had never at any time intended a university degree, but had come to take a rapid course in business administration to qualify for a modest post in lay or ecclesiastical households. Some of the students may have been refugees from the arts course who had come to grief, cut their losses, and settled for a less exacting but 'useful' qualification. One of Sampson's letters mentions a boy who transferred from the arts course to learn these practical subjects preparatory to entering aristocratic service.[3] The object of this type of utilitarian study at Oxford was not to turn out a finished product, but to lay a necessary academic foundation for the many-sided work of business administration, a training which might occupy no more than six months.[4]

Here, in medieval Oxford, there is in operation the ingredients of university extension courses designed to form a meeting ground between the more strictly academic concerns of the university and the practical world

[1] Richardson, 'Business Training in Medieval Oxford', p. 275; see also W. A. Pantin, 'A Medieval Treatise on Letter-Writing, with examples, from the Rylands Latin MS. 394', *B.J.R.L.*, xiii (1929), pp. 326 ff.
[2] Richardson, art. cit., p. 261; *Statuta Antiqua*, pp. 169, 172.
[3] See *Formularies which bear on the History of Oxford c. 1204–1420*, ed. H. E. Salter, W. A. Pantin and H. G. Richardson, 2 vols., Oxf. Hist. Soc., new series, iv–v (1942), ii, 407.
[4] Ibid., ii, 372. On the Oxford grammar schools and business instruction see N. Orme, *English Schools in the Middle Ages* (London, 1973), pp. 75–7, 190.

of community affairs. The Oxford situation represents England's particular response (nothing comparable is known for Cambridge) to its indigenous social needs, and this can be usefully set alongside the parallel, if more spectacular and high-powered developments in the Italian *studia*. It seems probable that similar forms of university extension occurred elsewhere in northern Europe,[1] but much remains to be discovered about these fringe areas of medieval university life.

University response to professional pressures either by internal reorganization as in Italy or by the university extension of Oxford underlines the essential rôle of the medieval universities as service agencies catering for a hierarchy of social need. In theory, the medieval university was open to all comers: it was a place of general resort, and the sending of a student to a university was a financial investment from which a tangible return was expected. The incorporation of community skills was a visible realization for those who cast the university in this utilitarian mould. At the other end of the intellectual scale, there were, in every generation, scholars who attempted to endow education with a higher purpose and who laboured to provide a theoretical corrective to the specialized competitive forces which pervaded society around them. By their writings, they sought to keep alive educational breadth, to promote the idea that education was a life-long process and a means of perfecting human qualities. Whether one is talking of a John of Salisbury, or a Hugh of St Victor, or a Vincent of Beauvais, or of a galaxy of humanist writers, their common stance was to make an educational gesture against the materialism of society in which academic life was so obviously implicated. Their detailed, over-elaborate educational programmes[2] went beyond what could be fulfilled by any but the most extraordinary of men: the scale was idealistic and called for a universality of knowledge and comprehension which transcended the reasonable objective of any educational system. But the effect was salutary: the questioning and definition of educational purpose, the projected contrast between study with an ennobling aim and the empiricism both of the average university course and of the average student ambition served

---

[1] See the opinion of Hajnal, op. cit., ed. cit., p. 177. Hajnal's views are sometimes expressed in exaggerated terms but it is unlikely that the Oxford situation stands alone.
[2] See *The Metalogicon of John of Salisbury*, trans. D. D. McGarry, cit., and McGarry, 'Educational Theory in the *Metalogicon* of John of Salisbury', art. cit.; for the educational ideas of Hugh of St Victor see Smalley, *The Study of the Bible in the Middle Ages*, cit., pp. 86 ff. and Paré, Brunet and Tremblay, *La renaissance du xii siècle* . . ., pp. 218–29. See also Gabriel, *The Educational Ideas of Vincent of Beauvais*, cit.

to keep a corner of Europe's intellectual life untarnished and uncompromized by the need to reduce and translate into professional terms.

Occasionally, the high purpose given to education might find a concrete expression of some significance in the universities. This can be illustrated from the English situation. The founder of St Catharine's College, Cambridge (1473), Robert Wodelarke, was one of those enlightened spirits who tried to give practical being to educational notions that were of long term import and not of immediate utility.[1] For Wodelarke, in company with other Cambridge college founders of the fifteenth century, was concerned with the basic condition of English society, with the deep-seated malaise that so disturbed contemporaries; and the collegiate movement in fifteenth-century Cambridge, insofar as it has a clear identity of motive, embodied a concerted attempt to provide an amelioration of the ills of the age.[2] Because of the narrow scale of the operation, this could amount to little more than a gesture. But if, as some came to accept, social regeneration depended on a lead from the universities, then the secular colleges could help to create that academic stimulus. And it is within this framework of thought that Robert Wodelarke's college has much of its historical attraction.

It was believed in some fifteenth-century quarters that the primary cause of contemporary social evils in England was the dearth of men of spiritual capacity within the Church.[3] In the later middle ages the ecclesiastical structure in England had become increasingly complex, with an ever-growing maze of courts and officials to implement delegated episcopal functions. By the fifteenth century, most of a bishop's diocesan work was carried out by deputies; and, more often than not, the bishop was a remote non-resident dignitary who rarely appeared in his diocese. An analysis of the fifteenth-century episcopal bench reveals the extent to which considerations of materialism prevailed in the upper echelons of the ecclesiastical hierarchy.[4] The distribution of sees appears to have been dictated by monetary values. The category of bishop who received the richer sees and who was absorbed for the most part in state affairs, accounted for the greater proportion of the fifteenth-century episcopate. A successful career in ecclesiastical administration required, above all, a degree in canon or

---

[1] See Cobban, 'Origins: Robert Wodelarke and St Catharine's' in op. cit., pp. 1 ff.
[2] Ibid., pp. 12–13.
[3] The substance of the following three paragraphs is derived from ibid., pp. 13–18.
[4] See R. L. Storey, 'Diocesan Administration in the Fifteenth Century', *St Anthony's Hall Publications*, no. 16 (1959), esp. pp. 3, 4.

civil law or both.[1] As a bombastically wealthy and multi-structured corporation, the later medieval Church absorbed a flood of personnel to serve as its judges and administrators. The universities responded to this need by turning out an army of law graduates for employment within the ecclesiastical hierarchy. The faculties of civil and canon law at Oxford and Cambridge were the largest of the superior faculties, and this would indicate the realization that a legal training held out the best prospect for a lucrative career within the Church.

It is clear that throughout fifteenth-century England there were few resident bishops to provide spiritual leadership for the secular clergy and ordinary parishioners. Only a handful of the bishops were university theologians. Theology at the English universities was pursued more by members of the religious orders than by secular clerks. The number of secular theologians who achieved high advancement within the Church in the fifteenth century was small, and seculars would not ordinarily proceed to a theological degree if they desired rapid promotion in the church establishment. There were critics, such as the Oxford chancellor, Thomas Gascoigne, who strongly attacked a system which seemed to prefer legal dexterity to religious zeal, that served to turn out priests more fitted to give a legal ruling than a spiritual lead. This concern was echoed, to some extent, in the universities by a rising body of disquiet at the pronouncedly utilitarian emphasis in the ecclesiastical arena. It is apt that criticism should stem from the source that provided staffing for the ecclesiastical bureaucracy. Although there had been alarming difficulties over the promotion of graduates in the early part of the fifteenth century, these appear to have lessened in the period following c. 1450, and few unbeneficed graduates are then to be found. A recent analysis of English parish clergy in the late fifteenth and early sixteenth centuries demonstrates that, in terms of spirituality, the Church's increasing absorption of graduate legal personnel was a somewhat Pyrrhic gain: for the greater proportion of graduate incumbents seems to have been absentee clergy.[2] The condition of the graduate secular clergy was therefore of paramount importance for those who felt that however competently the Church might manifest itself in external legal forms, it was nonetheless suffering from a spiritual atrophy; and a minority section of university opinion came to regard this spiritual

[1] Ibid., p. 22; also J. R. Lander, *Conflict and Stability in Fifteenth-Century England* (London, 1969), p. 125.
[2] See P. Heath, *English Parish Clergy on the eve of the Reformation* (London and Toronto, 1969), p. 82.

poverty as not only symptomatic of the troubles of the fifteenth century but a main cause of community malaise.

The collegiate movement in fifteenth-century Cambridge is bound up with this diagnosis insofar as it represents an effort to stimulate spiritual values in English society. This objective probably lies at the core of Robert Wodelarke's St Catharine's scheme. In association with his fellow college founders, Wodelarke appears to have believed that the spread of legal studies at the universities had to be arrested by making provision for a less utilitarian more 'spiritually uplifting' educational content. In practical collegiate terms, this could only mean a reduction in places available for law fellows and a corresponding increase in the number of theological fellowships. Such a pattern is clearly detectable at King's College, Queens' College and Jesus College, all founded at Cambridge in the fifteenth century. And St Catharine's embodied this reaction against the dominance of legal studies in the English universities in very explicit and extreme terms. Study in the college was confined solely to philosophy and theology: none of the fellows or commoners might study canon or civil law. Wode-larke's college was part of an academic splinter movement dedicated to the advancement of an educational ethos that cared nothing for lucrative rewards or social success, and which was partially institutionalized in the Cambridge foundations of the fifteenth century.[1] To a varying degree, King's, Queens' and Jesus all share in this ideal through their primary concern with a study régime of theology and philosophy and their severe curtailment of facilities for legal or medical disciplines. With St Catharine's, free from an undergraduate element, this ideal is incorporated in its purest form, no concession whatsoever being permitted in favour of law or medicine.

Robert Wodelarke's project, then, is probably best viewed as an episode in a more general movement in fifteenth-century Cambridge, characterized by a partial return to a contemplative, quasi-monastic educational ideal, having at its heart the rejection of secular utilitarian values and with a pronounced stress on an 'uplifting' concept of study.[2] This particular English example brings out well the conflict between the utilitarian and non-utilitarian principles which is fundamental to most educational systems, and which is crucial for an understanding of medieval European education. The fifteenth-century collegiate movement in Cambridge was one of those recurrent, if short-lived, endeavours to qualify the utilitarian

[1] Cobban, op. cit., p. 22.
[2] Ibid., pp. 22–3.

emphasis which usually predominated at the average medieval educational level. Whether a university can successfully or purposefully function on a purely professional diet was a problem that engaged the minds of Wode-larke and his acquaintance just as much as it has those of later generations. As St Catharine's could provide for only a handful of theologians, it must have been appreciated that even in conjunction with those colleges with similar academic concentrations the practical impact outside the university would be negligible. Wodelarke himself put no limitations upon the tenure of his college fellowships and was not particularly anxious to turn his fellows loose in the world, was not especially concerned with any minimal influence for good they might exert in a concrete ecclesiastical situation. This was not the essential purpose. The aim was rather to effect a change in the climate of educational opinion, to set an example for the way that education should be directed if the universities were to produce graduates of sufficient calibre and in sufficient quantity to raise the 'spiritual average' of the secular clergy. College founders and educationalists such as Wode-larke could not possibly assume an undertaking of these proportions. They could only hope that others would follow where they led, so that their acorn movement might swell to be a significant one in the universities, making some visible impact on the wider community.

Wodelarke's educational ideal, centring on the speculative pursuits of philosophy and theology, had insufficient substance to sustain it in a situation wherein the universities were increasingly orientated towards the professional concerns of the community. But the fact that a continuity of scholars thought deeply about the educational health of society and, either by writing or by deed, put the non-utilitarian case into the general mêlée of ideas which made up the intellectual cadre of university life, prevented the canon of utility from acquiring uncontested permanency.

The minority ideas of the progressive medieval educational theorists and educationalists were, for the most part, extensions of the self-formulated image of the academic life of the twelfth and thirteenth centuries. From the twelfth century, and crystallized especially by Abelard, came the notion of the scholar as an individual who, like a monk, has made a renunciation of an inherited social milieu and ways of thought, and has consciously opted to exercise the profession of scholar, an occupation which cannot be satisfactorily pursued unless the commitment is total.[1] The scholar clerks

---

[1] See the remarks of J. Le Goff, 'Quelle conscience l'université médiévale a-t-elle eu d'elle-même?', *Beiträge zum Berufsbewusstsein des mittelalterlichen Menschen* (Miscellanea Mediaevalia, 3, 1964), pp. 15 ff. at pp. 16–17.

of the twelfth century, as members of the wider clerical grouping, came to assert their contrasting equivalence to that of the knightly class in society.[1] The models of the perfect clerk and the perfect knight were the rival symbols of comparable areas of social advancement open to youthful aspirants endowed with the necessary energy and abilities. Poetically, this clerk-knight rivalry was enshrined in Goliardic verse where clerks and knights are frequently depicted as direct competitors in love. While the clerical and knightly estate are seen as contrasting orders in society the academic language of Abelard and his contemporaries is infused with military terminology. For Abelard, dialectic is an arsenal, arguments are arms, and disputations are combats: like a young knight, he assails his former masters in intellectual contests which have the character of tournaments.[2] This clothing of the academic life in military metaphors had the effect of presenting the intellectual calling as one of equal dignity to that of the profession of arms.

The twelfth-century committed scholar is to pursue his intellectual engagement in an essentially non-monastic environment: it is to be followed within the exciting and expanding orbit of urban life.[3] The profession of scholar was judged incompatible with manual labour and voluntary poverty: for it cannot be compromised by the ordinary tasks of mundane society. The scholar followed a vocation just as sharply delineated as that of knight or priest or monk: his work was to study and teach as objectively as the human condition allowed or as religious considerations permitted, and to do so in accordance with a strict professional ethic.[4] The calling of the professional scholar was to have a dignity derived from a high and specialist enterprise and from the exercise of his intellectual powers, particularly that of rational inquiry. These notions were not everywhere accepted in the thirteenth century: they were especially challenged by some of the mendicants (not by St Thomas Aquinas) whose commitment to an integral evangelical involvement in society was antithetical to the model of a distinct scholarly profession.[5] By the fifteenth century, however, the force of

---

[1] On this theme of clerical and knightly contrast see e.g. J. Le Goff, *Les intellectuels au moyen âge* (Paris, 1957), pp. 39–40; G. Duby, 'The Diffusion of Cultural Patterns in Feudal Society', *Past and Present*, no. 39 (1968), pp. 3 ff. at p. 10; P. Classen, 'Die Hohen Schulen und die Gesellschaft im 12. Jahrhundert', *Archiv für Kulturgeschichte*, 48 (1966), pp. 155 ff. at p. 172.

[2] Le Goff, art. cit., p. 17; Duby, art. cit., p. 10, n. 9.

[3] Ibid., p. 18.

[4] See Verger, *Les universités au moyen âge*, cit., p. 193.

[5] Loc. cit.

an independent, self-contained profession of scholars was waning: in the northern universities, at any rate, there was less emphasis on separate professional standing and a move towards involvement in political and religious areas of contemporary life.[1] With the decline in the autonomous position of the universities in the later middle ages and the growing entrenchment of university staffs in bourgeois and aristocratic society, the idea of a professional scholarity was greatly diluted, de facto if not de jure. The absentee rate of university lecturers engaged in business activities and who left their academic burdens to substitutes (often of poor quality) was probably quite high in the fifteenth century. This draining away of university talent by the lure of financial profit and social advancement was given a voguish justification by the obligations stemming from the civic participation inherent in the humanist movement. In the easier more luxurious world of humanistic culture, the traditional university values of technical exactitude, of fine analytical distinctions, and pride in independent professional scholarity were increasingly eclipsed, and alternative, less formal, centres of cultural advancement came into being outside the university framework.

With the movement of the later medieval universities towards greater involvement in aristocratic society, the former conceptual divorce between the scholar and the knight was rendered an inappropriate theoretical projection and was replaced by that of the closer identification of the two orders in society. The equivalence of learning and knighthood, no longer seen as contrasting forces but as complementary and interdependent pillars of society manifested itself in a concrete manner in the fourteenth century.[2] By 1300 the notion of an aristocracy of merit had taken root and had a special application for the lawyers in society, both those engaged in the practical administration of the law and the professors of law in the universities. As a consequence of the de facto power of lawyers in the community, as a spontaneous recognition of their authority, value and expertise, titles such as seigneur ès lois, chevalier ès lois or chevalier en lois came to be accorded to pre-eminent academic lawyers and practising jurists alike, forming a decorative parallel to the chevaliers en armes.[3] Bartolus himself, the great civilian commentator, received the accolade from Emperor

[1] Ibid., p. 196.
[2] Le Goff, Les intellectuels au moyen âge, p. 145; Verger, op. cit., pp. 185–6.
[3] R. Cazelles, La société politique et la crise de la royauté sous Philippe de Valois (Paris, 1958), pp. 292–3.

Charles IV and the right to bear the arms of Bohemia.[1] The growing idea that education ennobles, that an intellectual élite constituted a special kind of nobility in society is expounded, for example, by Petrus Rebuffus (1487–1557) in his treatise on academic privileges: '. . . quod scholares post adeptam scientiam possunt dici et intelligi nobiles scientia . . .' (in margin: 'Scholastici scientia nobilitari dicuntur').[2] Although this intellectual nobility may or ought to acquire privileges appropriate to its function in the community it could in no wise enjoy the privileges of an aristocracy of birth: '. . . quamvis dici possint nobiles scientia, tamen non gaudent privilegiis datis nobilibus genere . . .' (Rebuffus).[3] The intellectual equivalence was not with a blood aristocracy but with the military order in society.

Further testimony as to the identification of the scholarly and knightly ranks is afforded by the educational treatise written apparently by an anonymous German student at Paris University c. 1347–65.[4] Here the author asserts that in *studia* legitimately founded on apostolic or imperial privileges the masters are dubbed knights (milites fiunt) and are crowned lords of sciences (domini scientiarum coronantur) and are justly revered by lay and clerical princes, from whom they receive privileges, and by the populace at large.[5] The author then proceeds to contrast the masters who are true knights with those who, teaching in *studia* not endowed by papal or imperial privilege, lack the full dignity of knighthood: they are likened to nobles strong and praiseworthy in arms who have not yet been knighted.[6] The treatise makes further fine distinctions between the academic and chivalric grades but enough has been here indicated to suggest the extent to which the theme of the equivalence of the scholarly and knightly professions had taken hold in the fourteenth century.

In a sense, there is an essential continuity linking twelfth-century formulations of the lofty function of the scholar in society with the elaborate rôles ascribed by educational writers in succeeding centuries, if, at times, it is but feebly maintained. But while threads of continuity, preaching educational breadth and intellectual independence are sustained, the steady

[1] C. N. S. Woolf, *Bartolus of Sassoferrato: his position in the history of medieval political thought* (Cambridge, 1913) p. 3.
[2] Petrus Rebuffus, *Privilegia Universitatum, Collegiorum, Bibliopolarum, et omnium demum qui studiosis adiumento sunt* . . . (Frankfurt, 1585), p. 155.
[3] Ibid., pp. 158–9.
[4] The text and translation are given by L. Thorndike, *University Records and Life in the Middle Ages*, Records of Civilisation, no. xxxviii (New York, 1944: repr. Octagon Books, New York, 1971), pp. 409 ff. (text), 201 ff. (translation).
[5] Ibid., pp. 419, 215.
[6] Ibid., pp. 419, 215–16.

involvement of the universities in community affairs, their developing association with the fabric of organized professional life and the mundane path toiled by the average student, meant that the majority image of the universities as vocational centres to satisfy the needs of secular government, the Church, law, business and commerce is the one which prevailed.

The degree to which the universities were regarded as community extensions may be gauged from the liberal range of privileges ascribed to the academic population and based on the idea of the public good.[1] Apart from the fundamental privileges won by the universities to secure for their members a protective clerical status vis-à-vis secular jurisdictions, scholars were held to enjoy a variegated assemblage of rights and privileges pertaining to the many facets of the academic life. For the most part, these privileges were the formulations of French and Italian commentators and were inspired by Roman and canon law and by the Authentic *Habita*.[2] A number of interesting safeguards were said to operate in the sphere of accommodation. The French civilian, Guilielmus de Cuneo, for example, stated that compulsory quartering of scholars could be implemented if there was a shortage of lodgings,[3] the justification being that there was greater public utility in the profession of scholar than in the private need of a proprietor. Although the universities tried to ensure that lodging-house keepers were subject to stringent statutory controls, it is difficult to track down actual statutory cases of projected forcible billeting. Also, such was the public utility residing in books that landlords might not seize a scholar's books in lieu of rent.[4] Moreover, the jurists held that as study is more likely to flourish in a congenial environment, nuisances such as noise or bad odours were to be eliminated in the area of the university schools or in the vicinity of student lodgings: this might lead even to the removal of an offending artisan's workshop, although there was considerable legal argument over this point.[5] Likewise, it was judged to be in the public interest that scholarly privileges be extended to cover a scholar's journey to and from the *studium*, and, if he had the intention of returning, he should be allowed an absence of five years from the *studium* for whatever reason, and for longer if a just cause could be adduced.[6]

[1] See Ullmann, 'The Medieval Interpretation of Frederick I's Authentic "Habita" ' in op. cit., p. 117.
[2] See Kibre, *Scholarly Privileges in the Middle Ages*, p. 16.
[3] Ullmann, op. cit., p. 117; Kibre, op. cit., p. 13.
[4] Kibre, op. cit., pp. 14–15.
[5] Ullmann, pp. 117–18; Kibre, pp. 15–16.
[6] Ullmann, p. 121.

These, and many other privileges, were of a general theoretical nature, and their application in the medieval universities varied appreciably according to particular circumstances. But they do furnish an insight into the public utility view which the community entertained of the universities and expressed through its juristic interpreters: the generality of legal opinion appears to reveal how embryonic scholarship was regarded almost as a precious commodity, a rich piece of merchandise with a high marketable value, whose maximum protection and easement was a matter for the common good.

In general, the medieval universities fitted graduates both for specialized professional work and as useful members of the community: they formed an aristocracy of labour in medieval society. They were the opinion-makers, the indispensable props of those who directed the energies of society. Medieval graduates furnished the trained minds which influenced political argument and shaped ecclesiastical policy. In the area of ideological conflict, so basic to medieval society, there was scope for the innovatory talents of the abler products of the universities. The majority of graduates, however, served probably more as technicians of the established order than as initiators of revolutionary modes of thought and action. From the thirteenth century, the universities were the sounding boards of Europe for the public debate of the controversial political and theological issues of the age: and a collective university opinion was not lightly dismissed.

Conclusion

The formulation of the concept of academic freedom and the need to preserve it through eternal vigilance is perhaps one of the most precious features of the history of the medieval universities. The urge to dominate free intellectual associations, whether under the authoritarian heel of the ecclesiastical or the secular power, is a central issue of university development in medieval Europe. The poverty of imaginative response sometimes displayed towards the intellectual challenge of the universities, finding expression in periodic repression, is but an early foretaste of the perennial struggle for autonomous being which has been the persistent hallmark of the European university idea. The universities had their genesis in conflict, and struggle stamped every stage in their evolution and meteoric expansion. That they endured in an often hostile environment is high testimony to their fixity of purpose and unceasing quest for knowledge and comprehension.

The medieval university was essentially the indigenous product of western Europe, and it is clearly one of the most valuable and fructifying bequests of the middle ages to the modern world. The rich and kaleidoscopic pattern of university organization which spread over medieval society, ranging from extreme student republicanism to magisterial governmental forms, and with many intermediate states, has ensured that the collective European experience has known virtually every organizational permutation that can be devised. For there are only a finite number of ways in which university components can be arranged, and most of these found expression in the medieval situation. Universities in the twentieth century, whatever their deviations from traditional norms and alleged innovations, are still the lineal descendants of medieval archetypes, and they continue to perpetuate a competitive degree system and habits of ceremonial procedure, which, however disguised, are fundamentally derivatives from the medieval universities.

Nor should we regard modern universities as sophisticated evolutionary forms which have far outstripped simpler varieties of medieval animal life. The quality of training received at a medieval university, the rigorous, exacting nature of the academic courses designed to equip graduates to deal with the empirical and metaphysical problems of living and of society, gave a centre and a unified purpose to university education that is lacking in the present centrifugal academic scene where the mastery of a discipline is commonly sacrificed to a piecemeal inter-disciplinary approach leading in no particular direction. Moreover, the medieval universities were flexible entities and could adapt, if necessary, to meet the professional and business requirements of society without allowing their basic academic function to be swamped. They adapted in such a way, without laying down too much plant, that is, that they could easily jettison the voguish subject if and when the fashion had passed. The absence of inflated administrative units and all the paraphernalia and mechanical accessories considered so necessary to the functioning of the modern university can only have had a salutary effect on the intellectual life of both staff and students in the middle ages. Against this, one must reckon with the uncertainties, the hardships and the repeated interruptions with which the medieval academic had to contend. But the very fragility of the medieval university condition tended to place an urgent premium on the acquisition of education, and for those of serious intent academic labours were approached with an infectious dedication: a kind of maximum utilization of plant in a non-material sense.

The modern phenomenon of student power is but in its infancy compared to its fullsome and diversified manifestation in the medieval universities of southern Europe. An appreciation of the historical perspective of student political involvement in university government is a useful defence against indoctrination by those who would contrapose present hierarchical university régimes with the supposedly free and open democracies of the middle ages. Even where student powers were most extensive, the oligarchical rule of students by students probably led to a brand of intolerance and a narrowing of democratic channels which ill accords with romanticized or propagandist notions. While student power could be a creative moment in the struggle for university autonomy, it could also be self-defeating, and, after a lengthy period of varying entrenchment, it passed, as an atrophied force, from the university landscape. Medieval society, at any rate, had judged that experience and age maturity were sounder directors of university affairs than the mercurial qualities of youth: that masters were better conductors of their craft than student apprentices.

From their beginnings, the medieval universities functioned for utilitarian social need. It is true that in the twelfth and thirteenth centuries there was prevalent the concept of the scholarly profession as something distinct in society devoted to a specialist craft and unencumbered by mundane entanglement. In the hands of successive educational theorists these ideas were further elaborated and projected to give the scholar a finely elevated position combining study as a life-long process with the perfecting of human qualities. Occasionally, the higher purposes of education were translated into practice, as in the fifteenth-century Cambridge collegiate movement; but these ventures tended to be short-lived, and while they helped to sustain educational criteria which transcended the immediate and the mediocre, it was the principle of utility which most adequately represented the medieval university-community nexus. In the fifteenth century the palpable involvement of university staff in bourgeois and aristocratic circles removed much of the force of the image of the scholar as a separate estate in society and underlined the function of the universities as community agencies.

Much research still needs to be done in the socio-economic area of medieval university history: matters such as the maintenance and expenditure rates of different categories of university personnel, the size of private incomes, salary scales, methods of external support, the numbers frequenting universities, the degree of stratification within the academic community, the fabric of hall and collegiate life, these and other topics relating to university sociology are being vigorously pursued on the monographic scale. Especially is there scope for this kind of research on the later medieval universities which for so long were evaluated by the criteria germane to the old-established *studia* but which are now being studied as institutions in their own right, geared to the particular wants of late medieval society. Although the quest for relevance is something of an historical chimera, few can doubt that the study of the medieval universities furnishes a valuable perspective for those engaged in shaping and directing modern educational systems.

Bibliography

PRINTED SOURCES

Acta nationis Germanicae universitatis Bononiensis ex archetypis tabularii malvez-ziani, ed. E. Friedländer and C. Malagola (Berlin, 1887).

Archiv für Literatur- und Kirchengeschichte, iii–vi, ed. H. Denifle and F. Ehrle (Freiburg im Breisgau and Berlin, 1887–92).

Canterbury College Oxford, 3 vols., ed. W. A. Pantin (Oxf. Hist. Soc., new series, 1946–50).

Chartularium Studii Bononiensis: documenti per la storia dell'Università . . ., pubblicati per opera della Commissione per la Storia dell'Università di Bologna, 13 vols. (Bologna, 1909–40).

Chartularium Universitatis Parisiensis, 4 vols., ed. H. Denifle and E. Chatelain (Paris, 1889–97).

(The) Dean's Register of Oriel, 1446–1661, ed. G. C. Richards and H. E. Salter (Oxf. Hist. Soc., lxxxiv, 1926).

De Claris Archigymnasii Bononiensis Professoribus a saeculo xi usque ad saeculum xiv, ed. M. Sarti, 2 pts. (Bologna, 1769–72; 2nd ed., C. Albicini and C. Malagola, Bologna, 1888–96).

De disciplina scholarium, Patrologia Latina, ed. J. P. Migne, lxiv (Paris, 1860).

De recuperatione Terre Sancte: traité de politique générale par Pierre Dubois, ed. C. V. Langlois (Paris, 1891).

Documents relating to St Catharine's College in the University of Cambridge, ed. H. Philpott (Cambridge, 1861).

Documents relating to the University and Colleges of Cambridge, 3 vols., ed. by the Queen's Commissioners (London, 1852).

(*The*) *Early Rolls of Merton College, Oxford*, ed. J. R. L. Highfield (Oxf. Hist. Soc., new series, xviii, 1964).

Formularies which bear on the History of Oxford c. 1204-1420, ed. H. E. Salter, W. A. Pantin and H. G. Richardson, 2 vols. (Oxf. Hist. Soc., new series, iv–v, 1942).

Historia Diplomatica Friderici II, ed. J. L. A. Huillard-Bréholles, 7 vols. (Paris, 1852–61).

I più antichi statuti della facoltà teologica dell'università di Bologna, ed. F. Ehrle (Bologna, 1932).

Jiménez de Rada (Rodrigo), *Opera Praecipua* in PP. *Toletanorum quotquot extant opera*, iii (Matriti, 1793).

(*The*) *Liber Taxatorum of Poor Students at the University of Freiburg im Breisgau*, ed. J. M. Fletcher, Texts and Studies in the History of Mediaeval Education, no. xii (Notre Dame, Indiana, 1969).

(*Les*) *Livres des procurateurs de la nation germanique de l'ancienne université d'Orléans 1444-1602*, i, pt. i, ed. C. M. Ridderikhoff (1971).

Lucas Tudensis (Don Lucas de Tuy), *Chronicon Mundi* in A. Schottus, *Hispaniae Illustratae*, iv (Frankfurt, 1608).

(*The*) *Manuale Scholarium*, trans. and ed. R. F. Seybolt (Cambridge, Mass., 1921).

Medieval Archives of the University of Oxford, 2 vols., ed. H. E. Salter (Oxf. Hist. Soc., lxx, 1920–1).

Metalogicon, ed. C. C. J. Webb (Oxford, 1929).

(*The*) *Metalogicon of John of Salisbury*, trans. D. D. McGarry (Berkeley and Los Angeles, 1955).

Monumenta Historica Universitatis Praguensis, ii, ed. Dittrich and Spirk (Prague, 1834).

Morale Scolarium of John of Garland, ed. L. J. Paetow, in *Two Mediaeval Satires on the University of Paris* (Berkeley, 1927).

Oriel College Records, ed. C. L. Shadwell and H. E. Salter (Oxf. Hist. Soc., lxxxv, 1926).

Petrus Rebuffus, *Privilegia Universitatum, Collegiorum, Bibliopolarum, et omnium demum qui studiosis adiumento sunt . . .* (Frankfurt, 1585).

(*The*) *Register of Congregation 1448-1463*, ed. W. A. Pantin and W. T. Mitchell (Oxf. Hist. Soc., new series, xxii, 1972).

Register of Gregory IX, ed. L. Auvray (1896).

(*Les*) *Régistres d'Innocent IV*, i, ed. E. Berger (Paris, 1884).

Registrum Annalium Collegii Mertonensis, 1483–1521, ed. H. E. Salter (Oxf. Hist. Soc., lxxvi, 1923).

Robert de Sorbon, *De Conscientia et de tribus dietis*, ed. F. Chambon (Paris, 1903).

(*Las*) *Siete Partidas des rey don Alfonso el Sabio*, 3 vols., ed. por la real academia de la historia (Madrid, 1807).

Snappe's Formulary and other records, ed. H. E. Salter (Oxf. Hist. Soc., lxxx, 1924).

Statuta Antiqua Universitatis Oxoniensis, ed. S. Gibson (Oxford, 1931).

Statutes of the Colleges of Oxford, 3 vols., ed. by the Queen's Commissioners (Oxford and London, 1853).

Statuti delle Università e Studio Fiorentino dell'anno MCCCLXXXVII, with appendix of documents from 1320 to 1472, ed. A. Gherardi (Florence, 1881).

Statuti delle Università e dei Collegi dello Studio Bolognese, ed. C. Malagola (Bologna, 1888).

Statuti e Ordinamenti della Università di Pavia, 1361–1859, ed. L. Franchi (Pavia, 1925).

(*Les*) *Statuts et Privilèges des Universités françaises depuis leur fondation jusqu'en 1789*, 3 vols., ed. M. Fournier (Paris, 1890–2).

University Records and Life in the Middle Ages, ed. L. Thorndike, Records of Civilisation, no. xxxviii (New York, 1944; repr. Octagon Books, New York, 1971).

William FitzStephen's 'Descriptio Londoniae' in *Materials for the History of Thomas Becket*, ed. J. C. Robertson, Rolls Series, iii (London, 1877) pp. 4–5, 9.

An extensive coverage of printed sources for medieval universities is given in P. Kibre's *The Nations in the Mediaeval Universities*, pp. 167 ff; and a most valuable survey of sources and secondary works relating to each medieval university is provided by H. Coing (ed.), *Handbuch der Quellen und Literatur der neueren europäischen Privatrechtsgeschichte*, i (Munich, 1972), pp. 91–3 127.

SECONDARY WORKS

ALEXANDER, W. M. 'The four nations of Aberdeen University and their European background', *Aberdeen University Studies*, no. 108 (Aberdeen, 1934).

Atti del convegno internazionale di studi Accursiani, i, ed. G. Rossi (Milan, 1968).

ATTWATER, A. *Pembroke College, Cambridge*, ed. S. C. Roberts (Cambridge, 1931).

BALDWIN, C. S. *Medieval Rhetoric and Poetic* (New York, 1928).

BALDWIN, J. W. *Masters, Princes and Merchants: the social views of Peter the Chanter and his circle*, 2 vols. (Princeton, 1970).

BOEHM, L. 'Libertas Scholastica und Negotium Scholare: Entstehung und Sozialprestige des Akademischen Standes im Mittelalter' in *Universität und Gelehrtenstand 1400–1800* (Limburg ander Lahn, 1970), pp. 15 ff.

BOLGAR, R. R. *The Classical Heritage and its Beneficiaries from the Carolingian Age to the end of the Renaissance* (New York, 1964).

BOYCE, G. C. *The English-German Nation in the University of Paris during the Middle Ages* (Bruges, 1927).

'Erfurt Schools and Scholars in the Thirteenth Century', *Speculum*, xxiv (1949), pp. 1 ff.

BRUCKER, G. A. 'Florence and its University, 1348–1434' in *Action and Conviction in Early Modern Europe*, ed. T. K. Rabb and J. E. Seigel (Princeton, 1969).

BULAEUS, C. E. *Historia Universitatis Parisiensis*, iii (Paris, 1666).

BULLOUGH, V. L. *The Development of Medicine as a Profession* (Basel and New York, 1966).

BUTTERFIELD, H. 'Peterhouse', *V.C.H.* (Cambridge), iii, ed. J. P. C. Roach (London, 1959).

CANT, R. G. *The University of St Andrews* (Edinburgh, 1946).

The College of St Salvator, St Andrews University Publications, no. xlvii, (Edinburgh and London, 1950).

CARR, W. *University College*, College Histories Series (London, 1902).

CAZELLES, R. *La société politique et la crise de la royauté sous Philippe de Valois* (Paris, 1958).

CHARLTON, K. *Education in Renaissance England*, Studies in Social History (London and Toronto, 1965).

CHENEY, C. R. *Notaries Public in England in the Thirteenth and Fourteenth Centuries* (Oxford, 1972).

CHENEY, M. G. 'Master Geoffrey de Lucy, an early chancellor of the University of Oxford', *E.H.R.*, lxxxii (1967), pp. 750 ff.

CLARKE, M. L. *Higher Education in the Ancient World* (London, 1971).

CLASSEN, P. 'Die Hohen Schulen und die Gesellschaft im 12. Jahrhundert', *Archiv für Kulturgeschichte*, 48 (1966), pp. 155 ff.

'Die ältesten Universitätsreformen und Universitätsgründungen des Mittelalters', *Heidelberger Jahrbücher*, xii (1968), pp. 72 ff.

CLOUGH, C. H. 'Cardinal Gil Albornoz, the Spanish College in Bologna, and the Italian Renaissance', *Studia Albornotiana*, xii (1972), pp. 227 ff.

COBBAN, A. B. 'Edward II, Pope John XXII and the University of Cambridge', *B.J.R.L.*, xlvii (1964), pp. 49 ff.

The King's Hall within the University of Cambridge in the later Middle Ages, Cambridge Studies in Medieval Life and Thought, third series, vol. i (Cambridge, 1969).

'Episcopal Control in the Mediaeval Universities of Northern Europe', *Studies in Church History*, v (Leiden, 1969), pp. 1 ff.

'Medieval Student Power', *Past and Present*, no. 53 (1971), pp. 28 ff.

'Origins: Robert Wodelarke and St Catharine's' in *St Catharine's College 1473–1973*, ed. E. E. Rich (Leeds, 1973).

COING, H. (ed.). *Handbuch der Quellen und Literatur der neueren europäischen Privatrechtsgeschichte*, i (Munich, 1973).

COISSAC, J. B. *Les universités d'Ecosse depuis la fondation de l'université de St Andrews jusqu'au triomphe de la réforme 1410–1560* (Paris, 1915).

CORNER, G. W. 'The Rise of Medicine at Salerno in the Twelfth Century', *Annals of Medical History*, new series, iii (1931), pp. 1 ff.

'Salernitan Surgery in the Twelfth Century', *British Journal of Surgery*, xxv (1937–8), pp. 84 ff.

CROMBIE, A. C. *Robert Grosseteste and the Origins of Experimental Science* (Oxford, 1953).

'Grosseteste's Position in the History of Science' in *Robert Grosseteste: Scholar and Bishop*, ed. D. A. Callus (Oxford, 1955).

CURTIS, M. H. *Oxford and Cambridge in Transition 1558–1642* (Oxford, 1959).

DAVIS, H. W. C. *A History of Balliol College*, 2nd ed. R. H. C. Davis and R. Hunt (Oxford, 1963).

DELHAYE, P. 'L'organisation scolaire au xiie siècle', *Traditio*, v (1947), pp. 211 ff.

DENHOLM-YOUNG, N. 'Magdalen College', *V.C.H.* (Oxford), iii (ed. H. E. Salter and M. D. Lobel, London, 1954).

DENIFLE, H. *Die Entstehung der Universitäten des Mittelalters bis 1400* (Berlin, 1885).

DESTREZ, J. *La Pecia dans les manuscrits universitaires du xiiie et du xive siècle* (Paris, 1935).

D'IRSAY, S. 'The Life and Works of Gilles of Corbeil', *Annals of Medical History*, vii (1925), pp. 326 ff.

Histoire des universités françaises et étrangères des origines à nos jours, i (Paris, 1933).

DUBY, G. 'The Diffusion of Cultural Patterns in Feudal Society', *Past and Present*, no. 39 (1968), pp. 3 ff.

DUNLOP, A. I. *The Life and Times of James Kennedy, Bishop of St Andrews*, St Andrews University Publications, no. xlvi (Edinburgh and London, 1950).

EDWARDS, K. 'College of de Vaux Salisbury', *V.C.H.* (Wiltshire), iii (Oxford, 1956), pp. 369 ff.

English Secular Cathedrals in the Middle Ages, 2nd ed. (Manchester, 1967).

EMDEN, A. B. *An Oxford Hall in Medieval Times* (Oxford, 1927).

A Biographical Register of the University of Oxford to A.D. 1500, 3 vols. (Oxford, 1957–9).

A Biographical Register of the University of Cambridge to 1500 (Cambridge, 1963).

'Northerners and Southerners in the Organisation of the University to 1509', *Oxford Studies presented to Daniel Callus* (Oxf. Hist. Soc., new series, xvi, 1964), pp. 1 ff.

ERMINI, G. 'Concetto di "Studium Generale" ', *Archivio Giuridico*, cxxvii (1942), 3 ff.

FLETCHER, J. M. 'Wealth and Poverty in the Medieval German Universities' in *Europe in the Late Middle Ages*, ed. J. R. Hale, J. R. L. Highfield and B. Smalley (London, 1965), pp. 410 ff.

GABRIEL, A. L. 'The Practice of Charity at the University of Paris during the Middle Ages: Ave Maria College', *Traditio*, 5 (1947), pp. 335 ff.

'Robert de Sorbonne', *Revue de l'Université d'Ottawa*, 23 (1953), pp. 473 ff.

Student Life in Ave Maria College, Mediaeval Paris, Publications in mediaeval studies, xiv (Notre Dame, Indiana, 1955).

The Educational Ideas of Vincent of Beauvais, Texts and Studies in the History of Mediaeval Education, no. iv (Notre Dame, Indiana, 1956; repr. 1962).

Skara House at the Mediaeval University of Paris, Texts and Studies in the History of Mediaeval Education, no. ix (Notre Dame, Indiana, 1960).

'The College System in the Fourteenth-Century Universities' in *The Forward Movement of the Fourteenth Century*, ed. F. L. Utley (Columbus, Ohio, 1961).

'Motivation of the Founders of Mediaeval Colleges', *Beiträge zum Berufsbewusstsein des mittelalterlichen Menschen*, Miscellanea Mediaevalia, 3 (1964), pp. 61 ff.

The Mediaeval Universities of Pécs and Pozsony (Frankfurt am Main, 1969). 'The Cathedral Schools of Notre-Dame and the Beginning of the University of Paris'; 'English Masters and Students in Paris during the Twelfth Century'; 'The English-German Nation at the University of Paris from 1425–1494'; 'Preparatory Teaching in the Parisian Colleges during the Fourteenth Century': essays in *Garlandia: Studies in the History of the Mediaeval University* (Notre Dame, Indiana, 1969), pp. 39 ff., 1 ff., 167 ff., and 97 ff. respectively.

'Les Collèges parisiens et le recrutement des Canonistes', *L'Année Canonique*, 15 (1971), pp. 233 ff.

GAYA MASSOT, R. 'Provisión de Cátedras en el Estudio General de Lérida', *Analecta Sacra Tarraconensia*, xxx (1957).

GLORIEUX, P. *Les Origines du Collège de Sorbonne*, Texts and Studies in the History of Mediaeval Education, no. viii (Notre Dame, Indiana, 1959). *La faculté des arts et ses maîtres au xiiie siècle* (Paris, 1971).

GREEN, V. H. H. *Medieval Civilization in Western Europe* (London, 1971).

GRUNDMANN, H. 'Sacerdotium, Regnum, Studium', *Archiv für Kulturgeschichte*, 34 (1952), pp. 5 ff.

GWYNN, A. *Roman Education from Cicero to Quintilian* (Oxford, 1926).

HACKETT, M. B. *The Original Statutes of Cambridge University: the Text and its History* (Cambridge, 1970).

HAJNAL, I. 'A propos de l'enseignement de l'écriture dans les universités médiévales', *Scriptorium*, xi (1957), pp. 3 ff. *L'Enseignement de l'écriture aux universités médiévales*, 2nd ed., L. Mezey (Budapest, 1959).

HANFORD, J. H. 'The Progenitors of Golias', *Speculum,* i (1926), pp. 38 ff.

HANNAY, R. K. 'Early University Institutions at St Andrews and Glasgow: A Comparative Study', *Scottish Historical Review*, xi (1914), pp. 266 ff.

HARRISON, F. LL. 'The Eton Choirbook', *Annales Musicologiques*, i (1953), pp. 151 ff.

HASKINS, C. H. *The Rise of Universities* (New York, 1923). *Studies in the History of Medieval Science* (Cambridge, 1927). *Studies in Medieval Culture* (Cambridge, 1929).

HASKINS, G. L. 'The University of Oxford and the "ius ubique docendi"', *E.H.R.,* lvi (1941), pp. 281 ff.

HEATH, P. *English Parish Clergy on the eve of the Reformation* (London and Toronto, 1969).

HERKLESS, J. and R. K. HANNAY, *The College of St Leonard* (Edinburgh and London, 1905).

HILL, R. M. T. 'Oliver Sutton, Bishop of Lincoln, and the University of Oxford', *T.R.H.S.*, 4th ser., xxxi (1949), pp. 1 ff.

HODGKIN, R. H. *Six Centuries of an Oxford College* (Oxford, 1949).

'The Queen's College', *V.C.H.* (Oxford), iii, ed. H. E. Salter and M. D. Lobel (London, 1954).

HOLLAND, T. E. 'The University of Oxford in the Twelfth Century', *Collectanea II*, ed. M. Burrows (Oxf. Hist. Soc., xvi, 1890), pp. 137 ff.

HUNT, R. W. 'English Learning in the late Twelfth Century', *T.R.H.S.*, 4th ser., xix (1936), pp. 19 ff.

'Balliol College', *V.C.H.* (Oxford), iii, ed. H. E. Salter and M. D. Lobel (London, 1954).

HURD-MEAD, K. C. 'Trotula', *Isis*, xiv (1930), pp. 349 ff.

HYDE, J. K. *Padua in the Age of Dante* (Manchester, 1966).

'Early Medieval Bologna' in *Universities in Politics: Case Studies from the Late Middle Ages and Early Modern Period*, ed. J. W. Baldwin and R. A. Goldthwaite (Baltimore, 1972).

JACOB, E. F. 'Petitions for Benefices from English Universities during the Great Schism', *T.R.H.S.*, 4th ser., xxvii (1945), pp. 41 ff.

'English university clerks in the later Middle Ages: the Problem of Maintenance', *B.J.R.L.*, xxix (1946), pp. 304 ff.

'On the Promotion of English University Clerks during the later Middle Ages', *J. Eccles. Hist.*, i (1950), pp. 172 ff.

JONES, A. H. M. 'New College', *V.C.H.* (Oxford), iii, ed. H. E. Salter and M. D. Lobel (London, 1954).

KAMINSKY, H. 'The University of Prague in the Hussite Revolution: the Role of the Masters' in *Universities in Politics: Case Studies from the Late Middle Ages and Early Modern Period*, ed. J. W. Baldwin and R. A. Goldthwaite (Baltimore, 1972).

KANTOROWICZ, H. *Studies in the Glossators of the Roman Law* (Cambridge, 1938).

KANTOROWICZ, H. and B. SMALLEY, 'An English Theologian's view of Roman Law: Pepo, Irnerius, Ralph Niger', *Mediaeval and Renaissance Studies*, i (1941–3), pp. 237 ff.

KEARNEY, H. *Scholars and Gentlemen: Universities and Society in Pre-Industrial Britain 1500–1700* (London, 1970).

KIBRE, P. *The Nations in the Mediaeval Universities*, Mediaeval Academy of America (Cambridge, Mass., 1948).

'Scholarly Privileges: Their Roman Origins and Medieval Expression', *A.H.R.*, lix (1954), pp. 543 ff.

Scholarly Privileges in the Middle Ages, Mediaeval Academy of America (London, 1961).

KNOWLES, D. *The Evolution of Medieval Thought* (London, 1962).

KOEPPLER, F. 'Frederick Barbarossa and the Schools of Bologna: Some Remarks on the "Authentic Habita",' *E.H.R.*, liv (1939), pp. 577 ff.

KOLLER, H. 'Die Universitäts-Gründungen des 14. Jahrhunderts', *Salzburger Universitatsreden*, no. 10 (Salzburg, 1966).

KRISTELLER, P. O. 'The School of Salerno: its Development and its Contribution to the History of Learning', *Bulletin of the History of Medicine*, xvii (1945), pp. 138 ff.

KUTTNER, S. and E. RATHBONE, 'Anglo-Norman Canonists of the Twelfth Century', *Traditio*, vii (1949–51), pp. 279 ff.

LAISTNER, M. L. W. *Thought and Letters in Western Europe A.D. 500–900*, 2nd ed. (London, 1957).

LANDER, J. R. *Conflict and Stability in Fifteenth-Century England* (London, 1969).

LAURIE, S. S. *Lectures on the Rise and Early Constitution of Universities* (London, 1886).

LAVAL, V. *Cartulaire de l'Université d'Avignon*, 1884.

LAWN, B. *The Salernitan Questions* (Oxford, 1963).

LEACH, A. F. *A History of Winchester College* (London, 1899).

LE-BRAS, G. 'Bologne: Monarchie médiévale des droits savants', *Studi e memorie*, new ser., i.

LECOY DE LA MARCHE, A. *La chaire française au moyen âge, spécialement au xiiie siècle*, 2nd ed. (Paris, 1886).

LEFF, G. *Paris and Oxford Universities in the Thirteenth and Fourteenth Centuries* (New York, 1968).

LE GOFF, J. *Les intellectuels au moyen âge* (Paris, 1957).
'Quelle conscience l'université médiévale a-t-elle eu d'elle-même?', *Beiträge zum Berufsbewusstsein des mittelalterlichen Menschen*, Miscellanea Mediaevalia, 3 (1964), pp. 15 ff.

LESNE, E. 'Les écoles de la fin du viiie siècle à la fin du xiie' in *Histoire de la propriété ecclésiastique en France*, v (Lille, 1940).

Les universités du Languedoc au xiiie siècle, Cahiers de Fanjeaux, 5, ed. E. Privat (Toulouse, 1970).

LINEHAN, P. *The Spanish Church and the Papacy in the Thirteenth Century*, Cambridge Studies in Medieval Life and Thought, third series, vol. 4 (Cambridge, 1971).

LITTLE, A. G. and F. PELSTER, *Oxford Theology and Theologians c. 1282–1302* (Oxf. Hist. Soc., 1934).

MCCONICA, J. K. *English Humanists and Reformation Politics* (Oxford, 1965).

MCGARRY, D. D. 'Educational Theory in the *Metalogicon* of John of Salisbury', *Speculum*, xxiii (1948), pp. 659 ff.

MCMAHON, C. P. *Education in Fifteenth-Century England* (repr. from *The Johns Hopkins University Studies in Education*, no. 35, Baltimore, 1947).

MACFARLANE, L. J. 'William Elphinstone', *Aberdeen University Review*, xxxix (Spring, 1961).

MACKIE, J. D. *The University of Glasgow 1451–1951* (Glasgow, 1954).

MAGRATH, J. R. *The Queen's College*, 2 vols. (Oxford, 1921).

MALLET, C. E. *A History of the University of Oxford*, i (London, 1924).

MARROU, H. I. *Histoire de l'éducation dans l'antiquité* (Paris, 1948).

MARTI, B. M. *The Spanish College at Bologna in the Fourteenth Century* (Philadelphia, 1966).

MAXWELL LYTE, H. C. *A History of Eton College 1440–1910*, 4th ed. (London, 1911).

MICHAUD-QUANTIN, P. 'Collectivités médiévales et institutions antiques' in *Miscellanea Mediaevalia*, i, ed. P. Wilpert (Berlin, 1962), pp. 239 ff.

Universitas: expressions du mouvement communautaire dans le moyen âge latin, L'Eglise et l'Etat au Moyen Age, 13 (Paris, 1970).

MIRET I SANS, J. 'Escolars Catalans al Estudi de Bolonia en la xiiiª centuria', *Boletín de la Real Academia de Buenas Letras de Barcelona*, viii (1915–16), pp. 137 ff.

MONTI, G. M. 'L'Età Angioina' in *Storia della Università di Napoli* (Naples, 1924).

MOORE, W. G. *The Tutorial System and its Future* (Oxford, 1968).

MOR, C. G. 'Il "Miracolo" Bolognese', *Studi e memorie*, new ser., i (1956).

MORRIS, C. *The Discovery of the Individual 1050–1200*, Church History Outlines 5 (London, 1972).

MULLINGER, J. B. *The University of Cambridge*, 3 vols. (Cambridge, 1873–1911).

MURPHY, J. C. 'The Early Franciscan Studium at the University of Paris' in *Studium Generale: Studies offered to Astrik L Gabriel*, ed. L. S. Domonkos and R. J. Schneider, Texts and Studies in the History of Mediaeval Education, no. xi (Notre Dame, Indiana, 1967), pp. 159 ff.

MURPHY, J. J. 'Rhetoric in Fourteenth-Century Oxford', *Medium Aevum*, xxxiv (1965), pp. 1 ff.

NADAL, A. *Histoire de l'Université de Valence*, ed. M. Aurel (Valence, 1861).

ORME, N. *English Schools in the Middle Ages* (London, 1973).

OSWALD, A. 'University College', *V.C.H.* (Oxford), iii, ed. H. E. Salter and M. D. Lobel (London, 1954).

PAETOW, L. J. *The Arts Course at Medieval Universities*, Illinois University Studies, vol. iii, no. 7 (Urbana-Champaign, 1910).

PANTIN, W. A. 'A Medieval Treatise on Letter-Writing, with examples, from the Rylands Latin MS. 394', *B.J.R.L.*, xiii (1929), pp. 326 ff.

'College muniments: a preliminary note', *Oxoniensia*, i (1936), pp. 140 ff.

'Oriel College and St Mary Hall', *V.C.H.* (Oxford), iii, ed. H. E. Salter and M. D. Lobel (London, 1954).

'The Halls and Schools of medieval Oxford: an attempt at reconstruction', *Oxford Studies presented to Daniel Callus* (Oxf. Hist. Soc., new series, xvi, 1964), pp. 31 ff.

Oxford Life in Oxford Archives (Oxford, 1972).

PAQUET, J. 'Salaires et prébendes des professeurs de l'université de Louvain au xve siècle' in *Studia Universitatis Lovanium*, 2 (Leopoldville, 1958).

PARKER, H. 'The Seven Liberal Arts', *E.H.R.*, v (1890), pp. 417 ff.

PARÉ, G., A. BRUNET and P. TREMBLAY, *La renaissance du xiie siècle: les écoles et l'enseignement* (Paris and Ottawa, 1933).

PEACOCK, G. *Observations on the Statutes of Cambridge University* (London, 1841).

PEGUES, F. 'The Fourteenth-Century College of Aubert de Guignicourt at Soissons', *Traditio*, 15 (1959), pp. 428 ff.

POLLARD, G. 'The University and the Book Trade in Medieval Oxford', *Beiträge zum Berufsbewusstsein des mittelalterlichen Menschen* (Miscellanea Mediaevalia, 3, 1964), pp. 336 ff.

POST, G. 'Alexander III, the *Licentia docendi* and the rise of the universities' in *C. H. Haskins Anniversary Essays in Mediaeval History*, ed. C. H. Taylor and J. L. LaMonte (Boston, 1929), pp. 255 ff.

'Masters' Salaries and Student-Fees in the Mediaeval Universities', *Speculum*, vii (1932), pp. 192 ff.

'Parisian Masters as a Corporation, 1200–1246', *Speculum*, ix (1934), pp. 421 ff.

POTTER, G. R. 'Education in the Fourteenth and Fifteenth Centuries', *Cambridge Medieval History*, viii, ed. C. W. Previté-Orton and Z. N. Brooke (1936), pp. 688 ff.

POWICKE, F. M. 'Bologna, Paris, Oxford: Three *Studia Generalia*' and 'The Medieval University in Church and Society' in *Ways of Medieval Life and Thought* (London, 1949), pp. 149 ff., 198 ff.

PUGET, J. 'L'Université de Toulouse au xive et au xve siècles', *Annales du Midi*, xlii (1930).

RABY, F. J. E. *A History of Secular Latin Poetry in the Middle Ages*, ii (Oxford, 1934).

RAIT, R. 'The Place of Aberdeen in Scottish Academic History', *Aberdeen University Review*, xx (March, 1933).

RASHDALL, H. *The Universities of Europe in the Middle Ages*, 3 vols., 2nd ed., F. M. Powicke and A. B. Emden (Oxford, 1936).

RASHDALL, H. and R. S. RAIT, *New College* (London, 1901).

RICCOBONUS, A. *De Gymnasio Patavino* (Padua, 1722).

RICHARDSON, H. G. 'An Oxford Teacher of the Fifteenth Century', *B.J.R.L.*, xxiii (1939), pp. 436 ff.

'Business Training in Medieval Oxford', *A.H.R.*, xlvi (1940–1), pp. 259 ff.

'The Schools of Northampton in the Twelfth Century', *E.H.R.*, lvi (1941), pp. 595 ff.

ROACH, J. P. C. 'The University of Cambridge', *V.C.H.* (Cambridge), iii, ed. J. P. C. Roach (London, 1959).

ROSSI, G. ' "Universitas Scolarium" e Commune', *Studi e memorie*, new ser., i (1956).

ROUSE BALL, W. W. *The King's Scholars and King's Hall* (privately printed, Cambridge, 1917).

RUBENSTEIN, N. 'Political Rhetoric in the Imperial Chancery', *Medium Aevum*, xiv (1945), pp. 21 ff.

SALTER, H. E. 'An Oxford Hall in 1424', *Essays in History presented to R. L. Poole*, ed. H. W. C. Davis (Oxford, 1927), pp. 421 ff.

'The medieval University of Oxford', *History*, xiv (1929–30), pp. 57 ff.

Medieval Oxford (Oxf. Hist. Soc., c, 1936).

SALTMARSH, J. 'King's College', *V.C.H.* (Cambridge), iii, ed. J. P. C. Roach (London, 1959).

SANDERLIN, D. *The Mediaeval Statutes of the College of Autun at the University of Paris*, Texts and Studies in the History of Mediaeval Education, no. xiii (Notre Dame, Indiana, 1971).

SAN MARTÍN, J. *La Antigua Universidad de Palencia* (Madrid, 1942).

SAVIGNY, F. E. VON. *Geschichte des Römischen Rechts im Mittelalter*, 7 vols., 2nd ed. (Heidelberg, 1834–51).

SCOTLAND, J. *The History of Scottish Education*, 2 vols. (London, 1969).

SIMON, J. *Education and Society in Tudor England* (Cambridge, 1966).

SINGER, C. 'The School of Salerno and its Legends' in *From Magic to Science* (London, 1928).

A Short History of Anatomy from the Greeks to Harvey, 2nd ed. (New York, 1957).

SMAIL, W. M. *Quintilian on Education* (Oxford, 1938).

SMALLEY, B. *The Study of the Bible in the Middle Ages* (Oxford, 1952).

SMITH, A. H. *New College Oxford and its Buildings* (Oxford, 1952).

SMITH, C. E. S. *The University of Toulouse in the Middle Ages* (Milwaukee, Wisconsin, 1958).

SORBELLI, A. *Storia della Università di Bologna*, i (Bologna, 1944).

SOUTHERN, R. W. 'Medieval Humanism' and 'Humanism and the School of Chartres' in *Medieval Humanism and other Studies* (Oxford, 1970).

SQUIBB, G. D. *Founders' Kin: Privilege and Pedigree* (Oxford, 1972).

STAMP, A. E. *Michaelhouse* (privately printed, Cambridge, 1924).

STELLING-MICHAUD, *L'Université de Bologne et la pénétration des droits romain et canonique en Suisse aux xiiie et xive siècles*, Travaux d'Humanism et Renaissance, xvii (Geneva, 1955).

'L'Université de Bologne et la suisse, à l'époque de la première réception du droit romain', *Studi e memorie*, new ser., i (1956).

'L'histoire des universités au moyen âge et à la renaissance au cours des vingt-cinq dernières anneés', *XIe Congrès International des Sciences Historiques, Rapports*, i (Stockholm, 1960).

STOKES, H. P. 'The mediaeval Hostels of the University of Cambridge', *Cambridge Antiquarian Society* (Octavo Publications), xlix (1924), pp. 1 ff.

STOREY, R. L. 'Diocesan Administration in the Fifteenth Century', *St Anthony's Hall Publications*, no. 16 (1959), pp. 3 ff.

STRICKLAND GIBSON, 'Confirmations of Oxford Chancellors in Lincoln Episcopal Registers', *E.H.R.*, xxvi (1911), pp. 501 ff.

'The University of Oxford', *V.C.H.* (Oxford), iii, ed. H. E. Salter and M. D. Lobel (London, 1954).

ULLMANN, W. 'The Medieval Interpretation of Frederick I's Authentic "Habita"' in *L'Europa e il diritto Romano: Studi in memoria di Paolo Koschaker* (Milan, 1954).

'The University of Cambridge and the Great Schism', *J.T.S.*, ix (1958), pp. 53 ff.

'The Decline of the Chancellor's authority in medieval Cambridge: a rediscovered statute', *Historical Journal*, i (1958), pp. 176 ff.

Principles of Government and Politics in the Middle Ages, 1st ed. (London, 1965).

The Carolingian Renaissance and the Idea of Kingship (London, 1969).

VENN, J. *Early Collegiate Life* (Cambridge, 1913).

VERGER, J. 'The University of Paris at the End of the Hundred Years War' in *Universities in Politics: Case Studies from the Late Middle Ages and Early Modern Period*, ed. J. W. Baldwin and R. A. Goldthwaite (Baltimore, 1972).

Les universités au moyen âge (Paris, 1973).

VERGOTTINI, G. DE. 'Lo Studio di Bologna, l'Impero, il Papato', *Studi e memorie*, new ser., i (1956).

WADDELL, H. *Wandering Scholars* (London, 1954).

WAKELING, G. H. *Brasenose Monographs*, ii, pt. i (Oxf. Hist. Soc., liii, 1909).

WATT, D. E. R. 'University Clerks and Rolls of Petitions for Benefices', *Speculum,* xxxiv (1959), pp. 213 ff.

WEISHEIPL, J. A. 'Curriculum of the Faculty of Arts at Oxford in the early fourteenth century', *Mediaeval Studies,* xxvi (1964), pp. 143 ff.

WIERUSZOWSKI, H. *The Medieval University: Masters, Students, Learning* (New York, 1966).

WINSTANLEY, D. A. *Unreformed Cambridge* (Cambridge, 1935).

WOOLF, C. N. S., *Bartolus of Sassoferrato: his position in the history of medieval political thought* (Cambridge, 1913).

ZACCAGNINI, G. *La vita dei maestri e degli scolari nello Studio di Bologna nei secoli xiii e xiv* (Biblioteca dell'Archivum Romanicum, 5, Geneva, 1926).

ZANETTI, D. 'A l'Université de Pavie au xvᵉ siècle: les salaires des professeurs', *Annales: Economies, Sociétés, Civilisations,* 17 (1962), pp. 421 ff.

Index